LEARNING RESOURCES CTR/NEW ENGLAND TECH.
GEN   LA99.S73 1990

C0-AWJ-040

LA 99 .S73 1990

Stanton, Charles Michael.

Higher learning in Is

NEW ENGLAND INSTITUTE
OF TECHNOLOGY
LEARNING RESOURCES CENTER

HIGHER LEARNING IN ISLAM

HIGHER LEARNING IN ISLAM

The Classical Period, A.D. 700–1300

Charles Michael Stanton

Rowman & Littlefield Publishers, Inc.

9-91   # 20690537

ROWMAN & LITTLEFIELD PUBLISHERS, INC.

Published in the United States of America
by Rowman & Littlefield Publishers, Inc.
8705 Bollman Place, Savage, Maryland 20763

Copyright © 1990 by Rowman & Littlefield Publishers, Inc.

All rights reserved. No part of this publication may
be reproduced, stored in a retrieval system, or transmitted
in any form or by any means, electronic, mechanical,
photocopying, recording, or otherwise, without the prior
permission of the publisher.

British Cataloging in Publication Information Available

Library of Congress Cataloging-in-Publication Data
Stanton, Charles Michael.
Higher learning in Islam : the classical period,
700 to 1300 A.D. / by Charles Michael Stanton.
p.   cm.
Includes bibliographical references
1. Education, Higher—Islamic Empire.
2. Islam—Education—Islamic Empire.
I. Title.
LA99.S73   1990
378'.00917'671—dc20   89–48345 CIP

ISBN 0–8476–7645–5 (alk. paper)

5   4   3   2   1

Printed in the United States of America

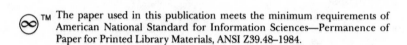 ™ The paper used in this publication meets the minimum requirements of
American National Standard for Information Sciences—Permanence of
Paper for Printed Library Materials, ANSI Z39.48–1984.

Contents

Acknowledgments

By its very nature a historical study draws on the works of a great many people. I am grateful for all the efforts of those cited throughout the text, and particularly for the translation work of my contemporary academic colleagues. The study began in earnest when I accepted the generous offer of Lewis B. Mayhew and the School of Education at Stanford University to spend a semester there as a visiting scholar. My thanks to him and to all those at Stanford who assisted me.

Many helpful people deserve my deep appreciation for their part in making the book a reality. Bernard Reams, director of the law library at Washington University, provided a room to begin the project. Debbie Barco spent long hours placing my dictation into the computer. Colleagues Jack Renard and Charles Fleener gave valuable advice after reading the initial text. Laura Goodman edited the next draft with tireless effort; her insights added much to the clarity of the final copy. Patricia Merrill, copy editor for the publisher, gave the manuscript a final polish. I am indebted to all of them and offer my gratitude and thanks.

I must mention, also, those who gave material and spiritual support during my undertaking. William Flanagan provided all the comforts of home and stimulating company during my stay in California. What I would have done without his gracious hospitality, I cannot imagine. Thomas Lay kept me sane and laughing through some trying times; his friendship provided a much needed tonic. To my family—and particularly Patti—I owe much for their understanding and patience in tolerating my long stay away from home and my frequent absences and lapses when at home. Their love and support sustained me and deserves many thanks from this grateful husband and father.

Introduction

European and American historians of higher education generally conclude that colleges and universities originated in medieval Paris and Bologna. Some authors mention earlier institutions of higher learning such as the museums of the Hellenistic world, monastery schools, and palace schools—the most noted being that of Charlemagne at Aachen. A few sentences might refer to the influence of Islamic scholars and schools on higher education in the West and suggest that a few brilliant scholars writing in Arabic did influence medieval Scholasticism and medicine. The prevalent view maintains that Islam acted as a bridge between early Greek learning and the medieval West and that it added little to the corpus of knowledge translated from Arabic into Latin and disseminated through Europe. Most histories ignore the monumental task of conservation and transmission of that body of work, much less admit to any Arabic contributions to it. Histories rarely describe the great centers of learning that arose in Islamic society and the impact of those structures on institutions of higher education as they emerged in Europe, or detail the lives of those brilliant scholars from Islamic culture whose writings became so well known in the West. Certainly their achievements stand for all time. Islamic society stimulated and nourished such scholars in a variety of ways. These men did not act in isolation, nor were they anomalies in a society that was intellectually void. Far from being exceptions, they were the culmination of a common human effort to expand and use knowledge. Through its scholars, Islamdom manifested its highest cultural achievements, and we are the beneficiaries of their unparalleled intellectual energy.

The stream of knowledge and the impetus to establish centers of higher learning in Europe ostensibly did not flow from Byzantium, the heir to Greek culture. Yet Hellenistic intellectualism did pass to the West—indeed, as a bonfire kindled primarily by Arabic-speaking scholars from the Islamic Empire. This work will focus on that bridge between Hellenistic scholarly attainments and the eleventh-century rise of universities in Europe—more precisely, or the higher learning in Islamdom during the time of Europe's Dark Ages, when educational aspirations throughout the Latin West languished at a dismally low level.

The author has two purposes: first, to raise the consciousness of professional educators and scholars to the intellectual and institutional heritage bequeathed by scholars and patrons of Islam's Classical Age, the eighth through thirteenth centuries A.D.; and second, to examine the enigma of why universities as we have come to recognize them did not germinate in the rich intellectual soil of classical Islam.

During those centuries, the most brilliant civilization then known flourished in *dar al-Islam*—the regions dominated by Islam in the Middle East, North Africa, and Spain. Yet—as inheritors of that great scientific and cultural legacy—we of Western tradition know little about it; nor do we recognize our debt to its descendants. The omissions and distortions of Western historians, coupled with regional chauvinism, largely account for our present ignorance. For centuries, students educated in the European tradition have learned little of the greatness of this Golden Age in Islamic culture. Teachers frightened their pupils with tales of the fierce Saljuq Turks and Mamlukes who engaged in battle with the forces of "good" during the lengthy invasions of Palestine by Western armies called the Crusaders.

By the thirteenth century, the Classical Age of Islamic civilization had waned under the pressure of religious fundamentalism and the encroachment of newer converts to Islam who halted the impetus for scholarly pursuits. In 1219 the torn fabric of the Islamic social order could offer only token resistance to the invading Mongol armies who slaughtered its people, laid waste its cities, burnt its libraries, and destroyed its observatories and schools. In 40 days during 1258, the troops of the Mongol Hulagu, grandson of Jenghiz Khan, massacred some 800,000 inhabitants of Baghdad, burning libraries that housed hundreds of thousands of volumes representing intellectual treasures accumulated through the centuries. The Mongols' advance was finally checked in 1260 at Ain Jalut (Goliath's Spring), near Nazareth, when Mamluke forces from Egypt destroyed their main army. After a defeat at Damascus in 1303, the Mongols retreated from the Middle East, leaving there a tattered remnant of what had been a rich cultural tapestry.

We do not recognize much of the form and structure of our colleges and universities as originating in Islamic institutions. Yet our Islamic patrimony includes much more than a storehouse of knowledge and a bridge linking ancient and modern learning—the transfer of an intellectual baton from the Greek world to the Christian West. George Sarton, in his monumental *Introduction to the History of Science,* labels those centuries from the ninth through the eleventh A.D. as "primarily Islamic," and heads them with the Arabic names of Eastern scholars— from Jabir Ibn-Hayyan, the most noted alchemist of the Middle Ages; to Umar al-Khayyam, mathematician, astronomer, and poet.[1] In formal structures, Islam pioneered the shaping of colleges, research centers, observatories, and teaching hospitals; it established great libraries and furthered the translation and dissemination of written works within its vast multicultural domains, among its own people as well as in foreign cultures.

Those Islamic institutions of higher learning, however, did not evolve into universities or even continuing colleges. Nearly all came into existence and disappeared in a comparatively short time. The al-Azhar in Cairo remains a noted exception, at least with regard to continuity in time. The impulse of Islamic scholars to search out the secrets of the natural world, once sparked, soon brought forth brilliance, and as quickly faded. Whatever the reasons for that eclipse, it presents an intriguing story with many unresolved questions. The real loss stems from the reality that, until quite recently, only a small esoteric group interested in Eastern history and religion seemed to care. The academic community—both administrators and scholars—generally has ignored its roots and branches in Islamic civilization, discounting that great contribution to the rise of universities in the medieval West and to the growth of scholarly studies in Renaissance Europe.

A general comment should be made about the sources employed in the writing of this work. Rather than fill the citations with ghosts from the past—Arabic-writing scholars and copiers whose names would not be recognized by English readers and whose Arabic manuscripts are mostly unavailable in the United States—I have chosen to cite the sources most accessible to the reader who might wish to explore a topic further. In each collection of chapter notes, the reader will find bibliographic materials that can provide background information and cognate material of special interest. My intention is to use the citations and chapter notes to inform readers rather than impress them with esoteric authors and manuscripts available only to those fluent in Arabic and in possession of a large travel budget.

The difficulties of transliteration become readily apparent when one consults a variety of sources for a volume such as this, intended primarily for a general audience. Translators have rendered the names of concepts, places, objects, and persons in a variety of spellings—all quite appropriate. But what is a writer to do when faced with several correct alternatives from which to choose? For the most part, Arabic words in this text come from the most current usage of English-writing scholars in the field; quite understandably, some may quibble with them. This writer also chose to omit the glottal scrape, on the assumption that readers unfamiliar with Arabic pronunciation would find it unutterable and hence useless. The vast majority of my readers—I suspect—will form a word picture rather than try to vocalize the Arabic word.

Let us then turn to the analysis of Islamic higher education and its contribution to the ascent of humankind—a brilliant contribution more often omitted than stated in the interpretation of the development of higher learning in Europe and later the Americas. Western interest in Islamic countries of the Middle East and North Africa really began in the eighteenth century during the colonial period during which European countries, particularly Britain and France, expanded their influence into those regions. That interest was rather lukewarm, since the general population did not really desire to learn much about the culture of Islam or its people. European intent lay primarily in uncovering remnants of ancient civilizations and promoting trade. Neither did scholars and governments undertake studies that resulted in the publication of any significant number of books.

More recently, the flow of scholars from the Middle East into Europe and America has sparked an interest in Islamic culture. The discovery of manuscripts from earlier periods continues, and their availability in English now provides an abundance of materials heretofore unknown to scholars in the United States and Britain. The interpretation of such classical Islamic works by the heirs of that culture provides a viewpoint unencumbered by a Western cultural bias.

Note

1. George Sarton, *Introduction to the History of Science,* vol. 1 (Baltimore: Wilkins and Wilkens, 1927).

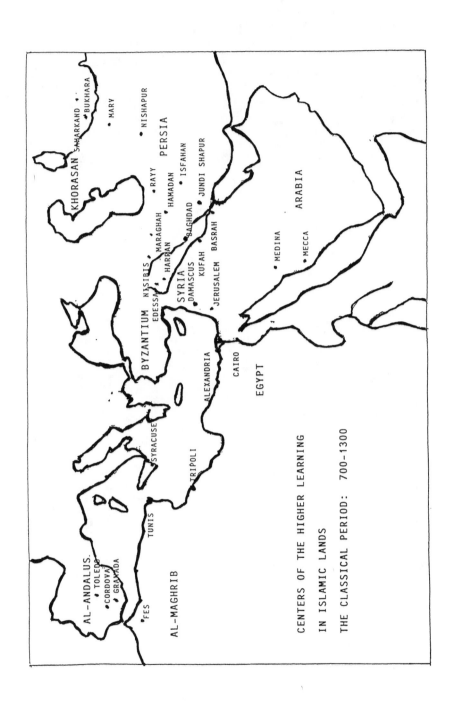

CENTERS OF THE HIGHER LEARNING

IN ISLAMIC LANDS

THE CLASSICAL PERIOD: 700-1300

1

Islam and Arabic: The Foundations of the Higher Learning

> We have revealed the Quran in the Arabic tongue that you may grasp its meaning. It is a transcript of Our eternal book, sublime and full of wisdom.
>
> The Quran 43:2–3

The Arabs—primarily a race of nomadic tribes prior to their conversion to Islam—considered the desert as the primary locus of schooling for their children. They romanticized the harsh life of wandering in poetry especially in odes that depicted the heroism of their people through brave deeds in skirmishes with rival tribes and the always precarious struggle for survival in an arid, inhospitable land. As Lyall comments,

> The Arabian ode sets forth before us a series of pictures, drawn with confident still and firsthand knowledge, of the life its maker lived, of the objects among which he moved, of his horse, his camel, the wild creatures of the wilderness, and of the landscape in the midst of which his life and theirs was set; but all, however loosely they seem to be bound together, are subordinate to one dominant idea, which is the poet's unfolding of himself, his admirations, and his hates, his prowess and the freedom of his spirit.[1]

As poetry dominated education in pre-Islamic Arabic, a single book totally directed the course of learning in the new Arabia, when the tribes of the desert and the traders of the coastal villages submitted

1

themselves to God. The foundation of any aspect of life and culture for those who received the "recitation of God's Will"—the Quran—resides in the Book and the man through whom It passed into human awareness. So, too, it is with the history of the higher learning in the Classical Age of Islam.

The Community of the Faithful, and Its Language

Mohammed, the messenger of God, was born in the Arabian town of Mecca in A.D. 571—a member of a powerful Arabian tribe and a noble clan, the Quraysh. Despite this, his immediate family had not acquired wealth and supported itself by working as merchants. Muslims honor Mohammed as the greatest messenger of God and the last of the prophets. The "Word of God" flowed through him in a number of revelations, first at Mecca and later at Medina during a time of sojourn there, after he, several family members, and a few converts were driven from their native town. In Medina the "community of the faithful"—the *ummah*—took form from which it would embrace millions through the centuries. Tradition calls Mohammed "unlettered," and initially he preserved the Quran in his memory. Later he dictated the revelations—the Word of God—to amanuenses so that they could be transmitted to future generations not from memory, but through the written word.

Although Mohammed's original Meccan converts numbered only a few relatives, once he retired to Medina his influence and power expanded rapidly, and he became the most powerful leader in that city. With Medina as a power base, his followers soon controlled the trade routes to Mecca and eventually subdued that city, where Mohammed established the seat of his religion. From there, his followers subjugated the neighboring tribes in the Arabian peninsula and began a series of conquests that, in an amazingly brief period of time, would bring a vast area under the law of Islam and the political influence of the successors of Mohammed—the caliphs.

Basically, Islam preaches a remarkably simple message—one most appealing to people subjected to very complex and legalistic religions or superstitions. This simple message coming from Mohammed espoused five basic points of confession:

1. acknowledgment of the One True God, Creator of the Universe, and recognition of Mohammed as His Apostle and Prophet on earth;

2. acceptance of basic rituals of divine worship, particularly praying in the direction of Mecca five times a day in recognition of God's sovereignty over humankind;

3. giving of alms for the support of the poor and for the sustenance of the community of the faithful;

4. fasting, particularly during the holy month of Ramadan, as a means of disciplining the body to the Will of God; and

5. undertaking a pilgrimage to the Kabah in Mecca—the earthly house of God originally constructed by Abraham—if at all possible, at least once during a lifetime.

Islam ordained no clergy and maintained that state and religion existed in unity with God. Thus it fostered the establishment of a theocracy in which the law of God became the law of the civil state and all the faithful undertook the duty of converting unbelievers to the true faith.

Mohammed valued learning; the Quran proclaims that knowledge is as powerful as the sword. Followers of Islam believe that all creation manifests the Divine Will; therefore, the study of nature would lead one to a better understanding of truth. Initially Islam placed no restrictions on the pursuit of knowledge, nor on the attempt to understand natural phenomena. Essentially the Quran contains all knowledge, but the fleshing out of the details devolved to individuals. Islamic custom interpreted the Quran in such a manner that anything not specifically forbidden was allowed. Unlike many religions of that time, early Islam did not prohibit the study of the physical universe; in fact the Quran enjoins reflection on the created world.

The rapidity of the conquests of the armies of Islam amazes us even to this day, considering the small numbers converted to the Muslim faith during Mohammed's lifetime and the lack of land transportation other than animals. Driven not only by religious zeal, but also by the desire to control trade routes and to exact tribute from subjugated peoples, the armies of Islam soon conquered the Arabian peninsula and advanced into Syria. Another factor, too, accounts for the motivating force in the conquest of so great a landmass in such a short period of time. After amassing a large and regimented army in the early conquest of the Arabian peninsula, the leaders of Islam could not disband it, and its legions swelled like a rising tide until its force dissipated at the far reaches of both Asia and Europe.

Mohammed died in Mecca in 632. Two years later, General Khalid had advanced northward and taken over the city of Damascus. In June 637 the Persian capital of Ctesiphon fell to General Sad. By 640 the area encompassed by present-day Syria, Lebanon, and Israel came into the empire; and military districts were established. It took another decade to conquer what are now Iraq, Iran, and part of Afghanistan. By 643 Islamic forces congregated at the border of India. The final surrender of the Persian Empire, which had survived for some 12 centuries, occurred in the year 652 with the assassination of the last emperor by his own people in the city of Marv. Another branch of the army advanced into present-day Egypt in 639. By 642 the city of al-Fustat—the precursor of modern Cairo—had been founded. Within the next few years, Byzantine forces attempting to retake Alexandria experienced defeat, and all of Egypt down the Nile to Aswan fell to Islamic armies.

During the reign of the first Umayyad caliph, Muawiya I (661–680), the empire expanded across North Africa to the west and to the east into Turkestan, now in the southern U.S.S.R. By 732 the followers of Mohammed had pressed beyond the Iberian peninsula over the Pyrenees and into southern France. An historic defeat of that army occurred somewhere in the vicinity of Tours in 732 when Charles Martel, the grandfather of Charlemagne, dealt the forces of Islam a defeat from which they could not recuperate; and the armies of Islam retreated southward across the Pyrenees into the Iberian peninsula, which they called al-Andalus.

One hundred years after the death of Mohammed, his followers controlled an empire larger than Rome at its greatest: It extended from the Pyrenees to the Indus River, from the Aral Sea to the first cataract of the Nile. This vast area existed under one faith, one law, one language, and loyalty to a theocratic state.

Unlike many conquerors before and after them, the Islamic armies did not lay waste the cities they subdued; nor did they destroy the institutions they found there. Churches, temples, libraries, and schools were left in place. Because the Quran forbade conversion by force, Islamic warriors encouraged people to accept the true faith but did not force them to do so at the point of a sword, as is sometimes related in Western histories. The precedent for just treatment of conquered peoples was set by Khalid, general of the army that defeated Syria and laid siege to Damascus. He sent the inhabitants the following message regarding the benefits of surrendering to him:

In the name of Allah, the compassionate, the merciful. This is what Khalid ibn al-Walid would grant to the inhabitants of Damascus if he enters therein: He promises to give them security for their lives, property and churches. Their city wall shall not be demolished neither shall any Moslem be quartered in their houses. There unto we give to them the pact of God and the protection of his prophet, the Caliphs and the believers. So long as they pay the poll tax, nothing but good shall befall them.[2]

In subsequent years, the persecution of Christians, Jews, and other nonbelievers was noted more as an exception, rather than a rule. On occasion such groups might experience harassment; but normally they received kind treatment and respect as long as they paid—in addition to a universal land tax—a poll tax levied on all non-Muslims, and did not denounce or attack the tenets of Islam.

Records indicate that many Jews and Christians held high office in provincial capitals as well as Baghdad and Damascus. Jews and Christians throughout Islamdom were considered among the most educated of people; Islamic leaders quickly realized their usefulness to the stability of the civil state, and they valued them for the knowledge that enabled them to render service to the caliph or his governors. Following the dictates of the Quran, Islamic leaders and their followers honored knowledge and learning. Indeed, they found them intriguing and useful, and encouraged their own sages to become learned in the same way as non-Muslim scholars. Because they were generally treated tolerantly, native people who were nonbelievers did not oppose the Islamic conquest since it brought stability to their lands and order to their lives. Further, they appreciated the value placed on their contributions to the community.

During the 100 years following the death of Mohammed—a time of rapid conquest—Islamdom was dominated by the Umayyad Dynasty, which established Damascus as its capital. According to custom, Mohammed did not dictate the succession of leadership over the ummah after his death; and the Quran offered no guidance. There ensued a period of infighting and internecine warfare following the Prophet's death, during which factions within the community vied for political and religious control of the empire. The first four successors to Mohammed were elected by the chiefs of the Islamic community and are recognized as the orthodox caliphate.

Not until the Umayyads took firm control of the empire did succession through bloodlines take hold. During that period of organization and restructuring of the Islamic world, higher education did not exist in any recognizable degree. The Umayyads dedicated their time and resources to establishing a secular state ruled as a monarchy; they demanded that Muslims accept them as rulers of the ummah by divine right because they were the chosen successors of Mohammed. The Umayyad caliphs also promoted a simple faith in the Quran and the acceptance of God's Will as pronounced by them in theological and civil matters.

During the Umayyad caliphate, a normalization of what it meant to be a Muslim took place.[3] The Umayyads, exercising control by force and tyranny, did not foster a dialogue through which to derive the attitude and behavior of a true believer. They attempted—rather—to maintain the faith in very simple terms, while holding the prerogative of deciding what constituted right action. More and more, their authority in such matters became suspect by religious leaders who, without benefit of ordination (since Mohammed did not establish a clergy), assumed the task of defining the faith in terms of normative, accepted behavior and adherence to basic tenets. These men assumed the task of clarifying what it meant to be a Muslim. Religious scholars in particular prospered in areas of the conquered territories where the native population accepted the faith of Islam but rejected the authority of the Umayyad caliphs. Thus arose the tradition in Islam that accepted the caliph as the successor of the Prophet but not as the infallible source of knowledge in faith and morals. In the eyes of the people, the caliph merely took on the responsibility and authority for ensuring a stable, prosperous environment in which those learned in the Quran and the customs of Mohammed and the companions—that is, those relatives and friends who knew him personally—could explicate the meaning of faith, advising adherents of their opinions based on study and meditation. In this manner, knowledgeable religious teachers in each community, who were known as the *ulama,* became the accepted repository of the tenets of the Islamic faith. Through their ability to persuade believers of the rightness of their pronouncements, they became the true religious leaders of the new faith.

In honing their skills, the ulama initiated the higher learning in Islamdom and gave it a uniquely legalistic tone. Under the Umayyad caliphs—whom they opposed—religious scholars internationalized Islam and the spread of the Arabic language, as well as providing the spiritual force to the enemies of the Umayyads—particularly the Abbasid family and their allies. In doing so, the ulama secured for themselves the role of spiritual leaders of the ummah—the community of the faithful—and wielded power based on knowledge and intellect, not force.

In the middle of the eighth century, the balance of power transferred from the Umayyads—descendants of the Arab conquerors—to the Abbasids, a family supported mainly by Muslims of Persian origins. Following the defeat of the Umayyads and their near annihilation by the Abbasids, the seat of government moved to Baghdad, a new city built by the Caliph al-Mamum on the Tigris River. With this action, the xenophobic concerns of the Umayyads became manifest, and control of Islam by Arabs began to wane. The Persians, whose intellectual background was rich in the traditions of Oriental and Greek philosophies and science, assumed the mantle of leadership. The Abbasids ruled the empire from the mid–eighth century to the mid–thirteenth century, although they lost direct civil control over many regions in the middle of the eleventh century. Most importantly, however, during that period of 400 years a Pax Islamica prevailed over the vast landholdings of Islam—a time during which those lands for the most part enjoyed freedom from external invasion and internal strife. Within this great contiguous landmass, the unification of many diverse peoples through a common religion and language gave rise to the brilliant classical civilization of Islam.

Trade routes stretched from one length of the empire to the other. Islamic navigators expanded economic enterprise throughout the Red Sea, the Persian Gulf, and the Indian Ocean—extending trade to such distant places as Cathay, Java, Ceylon, and India. In the Mediterranean, the Byzantine navy limited Islam's scope and relegated its enterprise to Spain, North Africa, and the eastern coastline. The major cities of Islam became cosmopolitan centers, offering an exciting, diverse milieu for people of many ethnic and religious groups.

Both land and sea trade routes served to transport ideas, books, and scholars as well as a great variety of goods, raw materials, and finished products. The cornucopia of goods brought into Mesopotamia by the middle of the ninth century is listed in part by a writer of that period, al-Jahiz: "from China, silks, glassware, paper, and ink, also hydraulic engineers, expert agronomists, marble workers, and eunuchs; from Samarkand, paper; from Marv, zither players, valuable zithers, carpets, and suits."[4] He goes on to mention myriad varieties of fruits, grains, and animals.

Expanded trade fostered a middle class of merchants and tradesmen whose socioeconomic status allowed them to pursue cultural activities, learning, and civic affairs. By the middle of the ninth century, available resources allowed many parts of the Islamic Empire to expand activities beyond the bare necessities. A common language and a common basic literature—primarily the Quran—bound the various ethnic groups together and exposed them to many ancient intellectual and scientific traditions. As peace continued—allowing resources within the empire to be used on ventures other than warfare—the caliphs, the nobility, and the rising merchant class looked to education as a means to enhance their lives, give them understanding over nature, and deepen their relationship with God. They now had the leisure and resources to spawn another great era of intellectual excitement and advancement similar to the one that had occurred in Athens and the other Greek city-states 1,000 years before.

Because Islamic faith accepted the Quran as the uncreated Word of God, Muslims believed Arabic to be the language of God, and those desiring to know God must learn Arabic. The Quran was not translated into other languages during the early centuries, and those converts who wished to accept and become practicing Muslims were inspired to learn Arabic fluently. In addition, non-Muslims who served the state were forced to learn Arabic, which by the end of the Umayyad Dynasty (744) became the language of government, diplomacy, and intellectualism throughout the vast Islamic Empire. The sharing of a common language throughout such a great landmass encouraged the transmission of learning from one end of the empire to the other. As Latin served the Roman Empire and Medieval Europe as a universal language of the church, diplomacy, and scholarship, so too did Arabic serve Islamdom for a period of some 400 years.

Despite pressure to learn Arabic placed on subjugated people, however, it met with much resistance from certain non-Arab ethnic groups. While the military conquests of Islamic forces took place over a relatively short period of time, the conversion of the subdued inhabitants to Islam required a longer period. The acceptance of Arabic as the common language took even longer, and still some groups clung to their native language. Jews and Christians in the Middle East, for example, adopted Arabic as their language while rejecting Islam as a religion; but Persians became devout Muslims while retaining the use of Farsi, even though Persian scholars and administrators used Arabic in their professional roles and employed it as a written language that could be read universally throughout Islamdom.[5] In the eleventh and twelfth centuries as the empire disintegrated, one of the elements that contributed to the decline of scholarship was the return of many groups to their native language and the loss of a common intellectual language in some parts of the empire.

Arabic as a structured language appeared primarily in poetry before the time of Mohammed. As a desert people, the Arabs transmitted their traditions and the glorification of their life in oral poetry, passed on from generation to generation. The beginnings of Arabic as a written language are clouded in antiquity, but by the time of Mohammed a growing body of literary works were being preserved in this medium. According to Arberry,

> The complex prosody, a rich repertoire of subtle and complicated rhythms had been completely perfected. A vocabulary of themes, images, and figures extensive but nevertheless circumscribed was firmly established. By the time that Mohammed began to preach and to reveal to his astonished townsmen the word of Allah, literary Arabic had evolved into a marvelously abundant, supple, and expressive language understood of the people.[6]

Transformation of this poetic language into prose that could convey philosophical, theological, and scientific abstractions originated with an attempt on the part of the followers of Mohammed to understand the meaning of the Quran and the requirements of faith in a world much more complex and diverse than the confines of Mecca and Medina. Because the Quran was the Word of God and contained all wisdom, it devolved to linguists initially to interpret its meaning in new circumstances. The need to construct a language that could convey the revelation of the Quran to converts emphasized the need to study the Arabic language and to initiate unique ways of explaining it to those who had not known Mohammed or his companions and who did not share Arabian culture.

Although Mohammed dictated the Quran to several secretaries, the gathering of those fragments into a single codex did not occur until two decades after the Prophet's death. In 651 the Caliph Uthman authorized the compilation of the fragments into a single version. He also ordered the destruction of several rival manuscripts of the verses held in other cities in favor of that in the possession of the widow of the previous caliph, Abu Bakr.[7]

The Quran—the Word of God—established the basic form and structure of Arabic the written language. Devout Muslims honored it as the most perfect of languages and the standard for literature and communication. As the language of God, Arabic provided the sole means through which people conversed with Him in prayer. At minimum then, a rudimentary understanding of the language of the Quran became essential in fulfilling the prescribed ritual of a good Muslim. The need for converts unfamiliar with Arabic to understand the Quran fostered the development of Arabic grammar. This initially occurred in Basrah, a Mesopotamian city that served as a bridge between the Arabian peninsula and Syria and Persia.[8] The legendary founder of Arabic grammar was al-Duali, who lived around 688. His successor, al-Khalid, completed the first dictionary around the year 786.[9]

The Quran proclaimed knowledge in the form of principles—albeit in ambiguous language—and could not answer all the questions arising during the period of conquest. The followers of Mohammed—perplexed as to how they could arrive at decisions in new circumstances and more complex times—sought a means by which to augment and clarify Quranic passages. They drew inspiration from the example and statements of Mohammed and his companions as a guide for resolving issues and as a foundation for establishing precedents not clearly defined in the Quran. Originally, anecdotes and examples transmitted orally from the lives of Mohammed and his companions formed a body of knowledge and wisdom referred to as *hadith* (tradition)—meaning the customs of the Prophet and his companions—which did not take written form until the middle of the ninth century.[10] Although of lesser importance than the Quran—because it was the Prophet speaking, rather than God—the study of hadith greatly influenced and encouraged scholarship in Islam.

In the pursuit of hadith stories, learned men traveled throughout the empire searching for the anecdotes of those early years that could enlighten future generations as to the nature of a devout life in accordance with God's Will. The transmission and study of hadith quickened religious scholarship in Islam and provided the impetus for the study of theology and law and laid the foundation for the future establishment of institutions of higher learning. During the sectarian battles of the first century of Islam before the ascendency of the Abbasid caliphate, each of the factions employed hadith to support its claims to leadership of the Islamic community, the ummah.

Eventually, in the middle of the ninth century, six books of hadith were compiled and considered authoritative. Al-Bukhari (810–870), a Persian, wrote the first of these. He is said to have selected some 7,000 traditions out of a total of 600,000 known to him and collected from learned men in the Middle East.[11] Hadith literature offered Islam a source of right behavior second only to the Quran itself and became an indispensable resource for the ulama, the religious leaders. The Quran and hadith comprised the basic course of study of Islamic learning during its early years. To understand these two religious sources, the Arabic language evolved into a complex tool for articulating ideas and abstractions to believers.

While understanding and articulating the message of the Quran and hadith provided the first impetus for the emergence of Arabic as a rich scholarly language, the second came from attempts to explain the new religion to nonbelievers. Jewish, Christian, and pagan scholars resided in many towns in the Middle East before and after the conquest, but primarily in two areas: (1) in the northern part of Mesopotamia near Syria in the cities of Harran, a pagan center of learning, and Nisibis, the center of the Nestorian Christians who had migrated from Byzantium in order to escape persecution; and (2) at Jundi Shapur, a somewhat isolated institution of higher learning established by the early Sasanian kings in the third century on the Tigris River near the present-day Iranian city of Ahwaz.

Despite their faith in Islam and its prophetic message and their commitment to it as the total source of knowledge about the universe, Muslim religious teachers and leaders—when first encountering these sources of ancient learning—recognized their own limitations in understanding many natural phenomena and their inability to debate logically with learned men who held different views. To their eternal credit, they elected to learn from them the intellectual tools and information required to defend their faith and explore their environment, rather than destroying those who differed from and challenged them.

With respect to the cosmos, Arabs shared with other Oriental tribes a belief that the stars represented divine messengers, and that by comprehending their movements one could discern the meaning of worldly events and possibly foretell future events. Thus, the caliphs—both Umayyad and Abbasid—ordered the translation into Arabic and all manuscripts on astrology and astronomy possessed by the Christians and pagans. They also appointed learned scholars from among those groups as court astrologers.

Jundi Shapur reigned as the most advanced center of higher learning in the Persian Empire, reaching its zenith in the sixth century.[12] It provided a stimulating intellectual environment and refuge for scholars from many parts of the world. Greeks, Jews, Christians, Syrians, Zoroastrians, Hindus, and Persians gathered there to exchange ideas and share manuscripts, creating an atmosphere akin to that of the

Museum of Alexandria. Jundi Shapur flourished until the end of the tenth century and served as one of the major avenues through which Oriental and Hellenistic knowledge permeated Islamic intellectual life. In addition to serving as an intellectual community for scholars of diverse backgrounds and a translation center for the dissemination of knowledge throughout the Middle East, it also included a major observatory for the study of astrology and astronomy.

The arrival of both Christian and pagan scholars in the fifth and sixth centuries endowed Jundi Shapur with its great infusion of learning from the Hellenistic world. They carried with them the medical writings of Hippocrates and Galen along with commentaries added by later physicians. With this knowledge and that derived from Oriental sources—primarily India—the physicians of Jundi Shapur established a hospital and clinic reputed to be the most advanced of its age. When the Caliph al-Mansur required a new court physician, he looked to Jundi Shapur and summoned to Baghdad the principal physician of the hospital and clinic there—a man by the name of Bakhtayashu (Happiness of Jesus), a Nestorian Christian and polymath. The caliph was so impressed with Bakhtayashu that he persuaded him to remain in Baghdad until shortly before that noted physician's death in 769. But his family remained as physicians to the court for the next six generations, during which time they constructed and staffed a hospital and clinic in Baghdad and furthered the dissemination of Arabic versions of Greek medicine compiled at Jundi Shapur. We hear little about Jundi Shapur specifically, after the move of the Bakhtayashu family to Baghdad. Evidently it survived as a center of learning for a number of centuries. Situated in a remote area at some distance from the centers of power and influence, it declined in importance during the rise of Baghdad as the intellectual center of the Islamic world. Presumably, the scholars at Jundi Shapur migrated to other cities within the empire—primarily Baghdad, but also Damascus, Rayy, Samarkand and Kufah—where they affiliated with hospitals, observatories, or gathered students around them in private study circles. Without a renewal of resources from society to support it, Jundi Shapur languished and eventually disappeared. It never became a noted center of Islamic learning, and therefore did not benefit from the patronage of the caliph, nobility, or the emerging middle class.

The towns of northern Mesopotamia provided a home not only for the Nestorian Christians who had migrated from the Byzantine Empire and whose roots lay in Neoplatonism, but also for pagan scholars from the museums of Athens and Alexandria as those two great centers of learning disintegrated. The Museum of Alexandria, which overshadowed Athens in the latter part of the Hellenistic period, prospered as the home and center of Neoplatonic thought and scientific learning for five centuries. Among its most notable residents were Euclid, Ptolemy, Eratosthenes, and Hypatia. In the early Christian period, Alexandria arose as the greatest center of learning in the Roman world under the patronage of the emperors of Constantinople. As long as the Eastern Roman emperors allowed pagans to reside and teach there, it continued as a great center of learning. With the murder of Hypatia (A.D. 415) at the hands of an angry Christian mob, however, the decline of Alexandria accelerated, with the tacit approval of the Christian community and the emperor in Constantinople. By the time of the Islamic conquest in 643, only an insignificant remnant of the vast library, observatory, and study rooms remained. The scholars from Alexandria had migrated after the time of Hypatia into the Middle East, particularly to Jundi Shapur and Harran.

In upper Mesopotamia then, we find a unique intellectual environment that brings together Nestorian and pagan scholars—both of whom espoused Neoplatonic philosophy. The interchange among them created a small but influential intellectual community on the border between the Sasanian and Byzantine empires. After the Islamic conquest, these centers of learning remained intact. As Muslim leaders learned of their existence and became intrigued by this new knowledge, they soon requested that the scholars—both Christian and pagan—translate their Greek manuscripts from Syriac into Arabic so that they could be studied by Islamic scholars.

The infusion of Hellenistic knowledge into Islamic culture would alter dramatically the formal education of Muslims and also non-Muslims residing within Islam's domain. The *awail* (foreign) sciences quickened Islamic intellectual curiosity, first in Syria and Mesopotamia and later in Transoxiana and al-Andalus. First, however, let us examine the early schooling of the Arabs and trace its evolution when exported beyond the Arabian peninsula and melded with the educational structures in the conquered lands.

Early Islamic Education

Continuing in the tradition of their Arab culture in the early Islamic era, fathers desired that their sons be taught in the desert, specifically in the skills of swimming, horsemanship, and the memorization of famous proverbs and heroic poetry. Later, writing and arithmetic appeared on the list of basic skills that constituted a proper curriculum for tradesmen and the nobility. In the desert, young men first encountered the richness of the Arabic language, primarily through poetry.

Among the conquering Arabs—no matter where they might be stationed or might emigrate—the attitude persisted that Bedouin Arabic remained the purist language for the followers of Mohammed. The Arabs took great pride in the purity of their language and—like the Greeks in an earlier age—ridiculed those who did not speak its standard form. Although the language had few written manifestations until the early Islamic period, the structure and syntax of poetry gave it a recognized grammatical format. As Arberry declares, "By the time that Mohammed began to preach and to reveal to his astonished townsmen the word of Allah, literary Arabic had evolved into a marvelously abundant, supple and expressive language understood of the people."[13]

Many parents feared their sons would adopt a corrupted Arabic, transformed by constant interaction with people who used other languages. According to Hitti, "No people in the world perhaps manifest such enthusiastic admiration for literary expression and are so moved by the word spoken or written as the Arabs."[14] The artistic expression of the Arabs—restricted as it was because of their nomadic life and lack of leisure and resources—expressed itself primarily through speech. Each tribe honored its poets, who kept alive their history, values, laws, and mores. As in most nonliterate societies, those who were readily able to memorize the oral tradition were the first teachers of the Arabs.

In the century prior to the revelations dictated by Mohammed to scribes, structured schools had appeared in the larger settlements in the Arabian peninsula, particularly at Mecca. An early Arab historian records that the first natives of Mecca to learn the art of reading and writing were taught by a Christian and that the number of literate people living in Mecca at the time of Islam's arrival was about 17.[15] Even during the early years of Islam, Christians continued the teaching of reading and writing, since those few Muslims capable of doing so were enlisted by the new religion for the copying down of the Quran as dictated by Mohammed and for its duplication so that it could be disseminated with the expanding conquests.

Although later scholars of the Arab world traced the beginnings of the elementary school—called *kuttab*—to the early period of Islam as a means for educating the young in the Quran and its message, Shalaby maintains that the first elementary schools focused on the teaching of reading and writing and quite often (as in the case of Mecca cited above) were conducted by Christians.[16] By default, instruction in the tenets of Islam occurred primarily in informal oral presentations and in the preaching that took place in the newfound structure of Islam— the mosque. Transmission of the Quran was accomplished orally, as poetry had been in all the times prior to the rise of Islam. Until copies of the Quran were more widely disseminated, it could not become the core of the curriculum in elementary education. This did not occur until after Uthman had ordered the compilation of an authentic codex in 651. Thus, for most Muslim youths in the first century, formal education—if it was available—consisted of attending a kuttab for basic instruction in reading and writing—using Arabic poetry as the text—while religious training centered about the proclamation of the Quran and its meaning in sermons at the local mosque.

Not for some time did teachers combine the basic skills of reading and writing with religious education. Evidence indicates that a separate-track elementary program existed into the fifteenth century.[17] Only when men who desired to engage in teaching had memorized the Quran did religious studies enter the kuttab. Later, with the availability of copies of the Quran, the study of religion became a major subject of elementary education. For the most part—however—from the eighth century onward, the elementary school curriculum contained reading, writing, arithmetic, and the Quran as a primary text. In such a system, the Arabic language as it appeared in the Quran became the standard language of the adherents of Islam and the most accepted form of spoken Arabic. With the greater availability of written volumes of the Quran and poetry, the study of grammar took precedence within the elementary curriculum. The Quran provided a double resource as a text—valued for its religious message, as well as for its guidance in the proper formation of syntax.

Sources tend to differ somewhat as to the location of kuttabs. Certainly they existed in private homes, where the teacher would gather pupils either in a room in the house or in an available open space outside. References also cite that teachers convened their students in the space around a mosque or public square. Although more advanced studies in the Quran and religious sciences did occur in the mosques, there is general agreement that the kuttabs—because they enrolled students of a much younger age—did not occupy space within the mosque itself. As one author emphasizes, children were much too messy and noisy to be allowed inside the mosque.[18]

Education at the elementary level also took place in palace schools and in the residences of private families; the content of the classes paralleled that of the public kuttabs. Elite and prosperous families emphasized reading, writing, religious studies, and poetry, but also horsemanship, swimming, and arithmetic. Caliph al-Rashid offered this guidance to the tutor of his son al-Amin:

> I have given you the child of my blood, the fruit of my loins and given you power over him and made him obedient to you, therefore prove worthy of this position. Teach him the Koran, history, poetry, Traditions and appreciation of eloquence. Prevent him from laughing except on proper occasions. Accustom him to respect the Shaikhs of the Hashim family, and to offer a proper place to the military commanders if they attend his Council. Do not allow any time to pass without having some useful instruction for him, but do not make him sad. Do not be too kind to him or he will take to idleness. Improve him kindly, but if that will not suffice you can treat him harshly.[19]

The existence of two forms of kuttab—one for secular learning, and one for religious instruction—also explains more clearly the manner in which teachers received compensation for their efforts. Because God had chosen the Arab people to evangelize the world, initially those who taught religion could not accept payment for carrying out a divine mission. As the ummah summoned soldiers to conquer in the name of God and to spread the new religion to foreign peoples, so it engaged holy men as teachers to instruct others in the faith and God's commandments.

Teachers who taught grammar, literature, and arithmetic in secular kuttabs did accept fees for their service—albeit modest ones. Holy men, however, who instructed in religion could not accept fees for that portion of the curriculum, but could accept payment if they also included lessons in grammar, penmanship, and arithmetic. While teachers received an exemption from some taxes, their economic status might best be described as genteel poverty. Fees for nonreligious instruction ranged widely, from 500 to 1,000 dirhams for a course of study lasting about a year (approximately US $120 to $240 in today's money).[20] The level of fees depended on the financial position of the boy's parents, and were flexible. The fee structure also reflected the achievement of the student—for, in addition to a matriculation sum, an additional amount would be requested when the student had finished learning certain assigned sections of his work (for example, a *surah* in the Quran).[21]

In both types of kuttab, teachers assumed high social status, but were expected to be humble and unpretentious in their lifestyles. Desirable traits prescribed for a teacher dictated that he "be married, not young, of good character, and no gossip."[22] Those instructors who could not survive on fees from teaching pursued other occupations or accepted work of various kinds within the community—for example, as laborers, craftsmen, or functionaries in a mosque supported out of the local treasury.

Tutors in palace schools or the homes of the wealthy received a more generous stipend, lodging, and meals—as well as other amenities. Depending on the wealth of the family, tutors might be given a horse, furniture, a concubine, and the opportunity to travel and associate with the elite of the community. Shalaby quotes the average stipend of tutors in the range of 1,000 dirhams a month (approximately US $240), although many received a great deal more than that.[23]

Methods of instruction primarily emphasized memorization and recitation of passages of the Quran and traditional poetry. Initially, students fingered their lessons in the sand. Later, clay tablets became popular; and with the arrival of paper from the Orient in the eighth century, pupils could retain their notes in manuscript form. Because of its long oral tradition, pedagogy encouraged each student to commit to memory the whole of the Quran and as much other material as possible. One cannot judge how well this was accomplished among the general population, but certainly a number of learned men did succeed in memorizing all of the Quran as well as great amounts of other material.

In subjugated lands where Arabic was not the native tongue, the establishment of the kuttab as a grammar school emerged as a primary goal and responsibility of the caliphs and local governors. In these lands, local customs in the establishment of schools prevailed, and many Islamic kuttabs took their form from existing Christian and Jewish schools. The necessity of mastering Arabic in order to accommodate to the new civil order and prosper in an Arabic-speaking world offered a powerful motivation for nonbelievers as well as converts to Islam to attend kuttabs.

The art of teaching in these schools seems not unlike the pedagogy that persists to the present day. Tritton provides the following description of the instructional process: The teacher read and recited from a manuscript. The student copied a text as dictated to him. The student then read and recited from a manuscript. The relationship between the teacher and students was primarily a caring and parental one. Teaching was approached with great humility. A basic outline that the students could understand was given to them, and was then embellished upon and added to in detail through the course of a study. The mistakes of students were corrected, but never harshly. No evidence comes forth that teachers in Islamic schools physically or verbally abused their students for either laziness or failure to learn. Classes ordinarily began at sunrise or shortly thereafter and continued until noon.[24]

During the initial centuries of Islam, the mosque emerged as the center for advanced instruction and the continuing education of adults in their religious life. Mohammed himself founded the first mosque in a village on the way to Medina during his flight from Mecca. He drew on his familiarity with Christian monasteries as both houses of worship and centers of learning in designing the mosque. Thus, he conceived of a structure that would serve as a community center for the Muslims in a town or neighborhood—as meeting hall, house of worship, and educational building. While we in the West tend to picture in our minds the great mosques of Istanbul, Damascus, and other large Middle Eastern cities, its most common form represented a rather modest building that accommodated a limited congregation. During the tenth century, it was said that 30,000 mosques existed in Baghdad alone. Each served as a neighborhood center employing perhaps only one prayer leader and one instructor, and even they might serve only part-time.

The architectural style of the mosque followed a modern dictum: functionality. The prototypic plans for a mosque incorporated a covered area to house the *qiblah* wall, a portico, and an open area protected by walls on all sides. As such, it offered space for convening the faithful both indoors and outdoors—both as a community and in small gatherings—and was also a private place for prayer. It served as a community center and manifested the essence of Islam as a synthesis of civil and religious life. The qiblah in its primitive form marked the direction of Mecca to guide the posture of prayer. In later years, the wall included a niche especially decorated to inspire meditation and commemorate the Prophet.

As places of instruction, mosques provided shelter and an invitation for any learned man to draw people around him for the purpose of reciting the Quran and discussing its message as well as other religious matters. Although unstructured, such a gathering—called a *halqa,* or study circle—often took on a formal atmosphere, some of them lasting for a number of decades. The halqa centered around a *shaikh*—a learned individual—who drew listeners to his discussions by the power of his speech and his insights. Originally this was an assumed role—the status of which was accorded to an individual by his followers. Later, with formal preparation, the leader of a study circle might be appointed to a permanent position on the staff of the mosque. The voluntary audience could choose to attend any of the discussions and could come and go at will. Unusually popular shaikhs drew a devoted following whose members became identified by the instructor's name. The instructional content in the halqa was selected to meet the needs of the participants in their search for a deeper understanding of the Quran. The study circle also served to reinforce the faith of believers and to exhort them to more religiously oriented lives. They offered a source of counsel as well, for—since everything in Islamic life centers around the message of the Quran—people brought their problems, difficulties, and questions to the shaikhs, and asked them for guidance and resolution. The leaders of the circles soon took on the function of interpreting the law proclaimed by the Quran and hadith, and formed the nucleus for the next thrust in the evolution of higher education in Islamic countries. Around many of them, schools of thought arose, projecting a specific religious viewpoint on how one should interpret revelation and apply the message of God to everyday living. From these structured institutions of the higher learning emerged in Islamic society.

Notes

1. From C. J. Lyall, *Ancient Arabian Poetry* (London: 1930), p. xviii, as quoted in A. J. Arberry, *Aspects of Islamic Civilization* (Ann Arbor: University of Michigan Press, 1983), 19.

2. Philip K. Hitti, *History of the Arabs* (London: Macmillan, 1956), 150.

3. For greater exposition of this theme, see Gerald R. Hawting, *The First Dynasty of Islam* (Carbondale and Edwardsville: Southern Illinois University Press, 1987), 1–18.

4. Robert S. Lopez and Irving W. Raymond, "Moslem Trade in the Mediterranean and the West," in Archibald Lewis, ed., *The Islamic World and the West* (New York: John Wiley and Sons, 1920), 34–38.

5. Ibid., 9–11.

6. Arberry, *Aspects,* 11.

7. Theodore Noldke, "The Koran," in *Sketches from Eastern History* (London: Adam and Charles Black, 1892), 49–50; S. Mohmassani, *The Philosophy of Jurisprudence in Islam* (Leiden: E.J. Brill, 1961), 64.

8. George Sarton, *Introduction to the History of Science,* vol. 1 (Baltimore: Wilkins and Wilkens, 1927), 523–24.

9. Hitti, *History of Arabs,* 241–43.

10. Afzal Iqbal, *The Culture of Islam* (Lahore: Institute of Islamic Culture, 1967). 191ff; Hitti, *History of Arabs,* 242–43.

11. Mohmassani, *Philosophy of Jurisprudence,* 72; Hitti, *History of Arabs,* 242.

12. For further information about this fascinating institution, see Sarton, *History of Science,* 435; Mehdi Nakosteen, *History of Islamic Origins of Western Education* (Boulder: University of Colorado Press, 1964), 13–35; F. E. Peters, *Aristotle and the Arabs* (New York: New York University Press, 1968), 33–55.

13. Arberry, *Aspects,* 11.

14. Hitti, *History of Arabs,* 90.

15. Ahmad Shalaby, *History of Muslim Education* (Beirut: Dar al-Kashshaf, 1954), 16.

16. Ibid., 16–17.

17. Ibid.

18. Ibid., 21.

19. Shalaby, *History of Muslim Education,* 25.

20. A. S. Tritton, *Muslim Education in the Middle Ages* (London: Luzac, 1957), 25. The unavailability of information on purchasing power and the effects of inflation make it nearly impossible to translate monetary amounts from one age and culture to another. Using estimates from Durant, Hitti, and Suyuti (see the Bibliography), the value of a dirham in U.S. dollars in the mid–twentieth century would come to about 24 cents.

21. Shalaby, *History of Muslim Education,* 135.

22. Tritton, *Muslim Education in Middle Ages,* 16.

23. Shalaby, *History of Muslim Education,* 136.

24. Tritton, *Muslim Education in Middle Ages,* 39.

2

Formal Institutions of Higher Education

A band from each community should stay behind to instruct themselves in religion and admonish their men when they return, so that they may take heed.

The Quran 9:1–3

In many cultures throughout history, the distinction between elementary and higher education remains blurred. Generally, studies that went beyond the basics of reading and writing were considered of a higher order, pursued by only a handful of students. Our perspective on what constitutes higher education, however, is distorted by immediate experience. What passed for higher academic endeavors in another age may now appear as elementary or preparatory to more sophisticated realms of knowledge in the present framework of schooling. Yet, in Islam the distinction between lower and higher education seems eminently clear because of the function of the mosque as community center, concerned with the religious education of adults within its congregation. Almost from the beginning of the faith, men knowledgeable in the Quran presided informally over discussion groups, reciting surahs and explaining their meaning. With the organization of the theocratic state, learned men were appointed specifically to teach religious studies and to preside over the study circles (halqas). In the formation of such circles within mosques, the history of formal institutions of higher learning in Islamic lands commences.

The Rise of Jurisprudence

All elements were now in place for the genesis of jurisprudence—the formal study and exposition of religious and civil law throughout Islamdom—which remains the core of higher education in Islam even to the present day: the need for interpretation of the Quran and hadith, the emergence of study circles to guide the faithful in religious matters, and the establishment of the mosque as a community center. The Quran as the Word of God proclaimed principles for submitting oneself to His Will, but it did not provide specific instructions for right behavior. Only about 200 of the 6,000 verses dealt specifically with human behavior in a way that could be considered legally binding; and many of these concerned marriage, women, and inheritance. Despite a lack of specificity, the Quran remains the basis of all Islamic law. During his lifetime, the Prophet Mohammed continually admonished his followers in matters regarding just behavior. Additionally, as leader of the religious community he adjudicated many disputes. The companions of Mohammed, as leaders in both the Arabian peninsula and in the conquered lands, drew on this reservoir of Quranic interpretation as manifested in Mohammed's actions and sayings to legislate and render judgments in personal as well as civic matters.

Thus, in addition to the Quran, Islam drew on the exemplary conduct of Mohammed and his companions as a guide to right behavior. This was given the name *sunnah,* and it refers to the interpretation of revelation by the action of the Prophet and those who knew him intimately. *Sunnah* itself means accepted custom and initially was coextensive with hadith. After the death of Mohammed and the compilation of the hadith stories in an authoritative codex (eighth century), the concept of sunnah was expanded to mean the accepted custom of the community, which went beyond hadith and included interpretations of revelation not specifically mentioned in the Quran but accepted by the ummah. This expanded concept of sunnah accorded Islam a means of resolving dilemmas and issues not encountered at the time of Mohammed. Sunnah gave vitality and flexibility to the practice of Islam for generations to come.

Because the Quran defined the basic tenets of Islam so straightforwardly, theology did not emerge as a major intellectual thrust in Islam. Since the Quran lacked clear guidance on many matters—however—and since Islam proclaimed the unity of civil and religious law, the beginnings of intellectualism and debate among Muslims focused on the interpretation of God's Will as it related to daily living. Basic beliefs were accepted by the faithful without dissent, but the area of practical living spawned much debate. Those living near the geographic source of Islam—the Arabian peninsula—found it easier to consult tradition for guidance in religious and civil matters than did the occupants of conquered lands—particularly in Mesopotamia, Persia, and Syria—where Islamic and Arab laws conflicted with customary law and norms of behavior. In response to the need for a more meaningful approach to religion and the difficulty of imposing a totally foreign order of laws on conquered peoples, men learned in the Quran and hadith instituted the study of law as a religious science. Removed from the strong force of tradition and the simple life of the Arabian peninsula, these sages tended to rely heavily on the consensus of the community when they could not find clear direction from the Quran and hadith. In reality, this meant the opinion of the learned faithful— that is, those men recognized for their knowledge of the Quran and hadith and their wisdom in rendering advice and judgments. A major center for this approach to jurisprudence arose in Kufah, a trading town located on the Euphrates south of Baghdad—an influential city for Syrians and Persians.

Within this expanded view of sunnah two major techniques arose: analogy and consensus. Analogy compared a present issue or point of disagreement about behavior to a previous situation of similar circumstances on which a clear direction for action could be deduced from the Quran or hadith. The analogy could draw on either a similar or opposite relationship between the two situations. Those who defended the use of analogy cited Quranic verses, sunnah, and the practice of the companions as a precedent for their pronouncements. The binding nature of consensus or opinion as a means of resolving disputes on the application of the law to ordinary life arose from an interpretation of this Quranic verse: "My community will never agree upon an error." Who comprised the "community" became a matter of debate among various Islamic groups. For some, it meant consensus among those recognized as experts in the law of a particular time and place; for another group, it meant agreement of four orthodox caliphs.

With the acceptance of analogy and consensus as authoritative in interpreting Quranic revelation, the process of consulting required intellectual and deductive skills. A necessary next step became clear: a means to educate specialists who could perform these particular hypothetical deductive exercises. Thus, higher education in its more concrete form appeared in Islamic communities. In order to interpret the Quran and hadith, jurisconsults—as the experts were called—

found it necessary to study grammar and philology so that they could understand the meaning of language and the intent of both sources of the law. This also required memorization of that part of the Quran that gave insight to the proper rules of behavior. A more prodigious scholarly undertaking, however, was the memorization of literally thousands of individual hadith stories.

During the century following Mohammed's death, sectarian differences arose among the various factions of Islam. Since hadith provided a rich resource used to justify the position of the various groups, a number of questionable or false hadith stories became popular within certain sects. In the ninth century, those who compiled the authoritative collections of hadith had to identify those flawed anecdotes in the oral tradition and not perpetuate them in written form.

Each hadith story has two sections. The first part—the "chain" of transmitters—traces the communication of the story back to the time of Mohammed through its various spokesmen to the individual who actually observed or heard the Prophet formulate a specific opinion in prescribed circumstances, thus establishing the authenticity of the hadith story. The second part—the "body"—proclaims the decision and the context in which it occurred.

The method of analogy required special preparation, since that process included not only knowledge of the Quran and hadith, but also the intellectual skills of logic and reasoning. The jurisconsult had to demonstrate creativity and invention in selecting that verse or that story most analogous to the situation presented to him for a judgment. The method of analogy could be complex and subject to broad interpretation or error. Thus, some groups did not accept it to the degree that they did other sources of the law. This occurred particularly in certain geographic areas that tended to emphasize the Quran and hadith as the most important means of defining the law—relegating analogy to a method of last resort.

Historians can only approximate the number of different schools of law—called *madhahib*—that emerged during the first two centuries of the Islamic era, but it is estimated at more than 500.[1] Of those many schools, only four persevered for several centuries, becoming well known in Islamic society. Three of those appeared prior to the permeating influence of Greek philosophy on Islamic culture: the schools of Abu Hanafi, Malik, and al-Shafii. All three are considered orthodox in their interpretation of Islamic law, yet they did differ among themselves in the degree to which they allowed and relied on the third and fourth roots of the law—namely, analogy and consensus. All accepted without question the primacy of the first two roots: the Quran and hadith. In an earlier period, their relationships were marked by rivalry and some intolerance, but this gave way later to tolerance and a desire to understand opposing views. Often the proponents of each school existed side by side in the same community, and eventually even occupied different sections of the same mosque.

The Hanafite school was founded by Abu Hanafi in Kufah during the eighth century. Abu Hanafi was very much a disciple of the "People of Opinion"—as the religious community of Kufah was labeled, because of its acceptance of analogy and consensus in arriving at decisions. This occurred primarily because of its location in lower Mesopotamia and its interaction with Persian cultural and social institutions. Kufah's distance from Medina and Mecca also accounts for its assigning tradition a less important role than did those who resided in the land of Mohammed. The source of tradition was lessened in this outpost of the empire; and many of the jurisconsults—including Abu Hanafi, were Persian by descent, and not Arab. His approach to the law and those of his successors can be summed up in several phrases attributed to him:

This knowledge of ours is opinion; it is the best we have been able to achieve. He who is able to arrive at different conclusions is entitled to his opinion as we are entitled to our own. . . . If I do not find my answers in the book of God or in the traditions of the prophet, I would seek the views of the prophet's companions from whose opinion I would not deviate to the opinions of others. But when it comes to Ibrahim, al Shabi, Imam Sirin, al Hasan, Ata, and Said Ibn Jubayr, well, they are people who had resorted to independent interpretation and I would do likewise.[2]

In addition to his scholarly life and role as a jurisconsult, Abu Hanafi earned a living as a textile merchant. Perhaps that fact also explains why so much of his approach to the law depended on rules of reasoning and logic and on the circumstances under which transactions took place. He was a man of the world—much involved in practical matters—and thus sought a method of arriving at legal opinion consonant with the lifestyle of both a man of affairs as well as one for whom the message of God was made manifest directly in the Quran or interpretively through Mohammed and hadith.

The second major *madhhab* to have survived into the twelfth century was that of Malik, which arose in Medina during the eighth century. Malik gave his name to the Medina school of jurisprudence, which emphasized the traditions of the people of Medina as well as one aspect of law unique to his school—that of public interest. Medina—having been the home of the Prophet for a number of years—was steeped in the example of his life and the opinions he made while living there. Malik's approach seemed bound by those traditions and the consensus of the Islamic community at Medina more than other schools of law. He did, however, use analogy when those other sources failed him. He authored a volume on traditions entitled *Al-Muwatta,* the first legal textbook in Islam and an important reference in the study of Islamic jurisprudence. Two versions of that manuscript still exist, having come down to us from those early centuries. Arab soldiers and conquerors transmitted the Maliki school into Egypt, over North Africa, and into Spain, where it dominated legal thinking during the classical age of Moorish Islam.

Al-Shafii synthesized many principles of the schools of law of the eighth century, offering a more balanced orientation among the four sources of the law. Al-Shafii—a more cosmopolitan man than either Abu Hanafi or Malik—traveled widely throughout the Middle East and Egypt and drew on regional approaches to the law to synthesize his own system. He disdained "the geographical approach to Islamic law which had predated him and attempted to strike a compromise between the dictates of the divine will and the use of human reason in law."[3]

During his earlier years, al-Shafii studied under Malik in Medina and then traveled to other provinces where he sat with jurisconsults of differing views. A man of great intellect and eloquence, he used his talents to integrate the school of opinion with the school of tradition. As a result, he promoted the acceptance of all four sources of the law: the Quran, hadith, consensus of opinion, and analogy. From the Hanafite school, he rejected the method of preferences; and from the Maliki school, the method of public interest. Al-Shafii was the first to write about the origins of jurisprudence and the sources of law in a comprehensive and systematic way. According to Mohmassani,

> This essay discusses the text of the Koran and the Sunnah, the aggregated verses of the Koran, the obligatory religious observances, defects of the traditions, the prerequisites for accepting a tradition if recounted by only one narrator, consensus of opinion of jurists, independent interpretation, preference, and analogy.[4]

Al-Shafii continued his scholarly work, writing another treatise on the law titled *Al-Um* that comprised seven volumes written in dialectical form. Shafiite law took hardy root in Egypt, becoming the official approach to the law during the Ayyubid Dynasty; and it still dominates in Islamic communities in Palestine, Jordan, parts of Syria, and Lebanon as well as the Far East.

The fourth and last of the orthodox Sunni madhahib that evolved during this age and have continued to the present takes its name from its founder, Ibn Hanbal. Although it now draws the least number of adherents within Sunni Islam, it enjoyed a period of popularity in the Middle East during the period of reaction to the moral liberal religious views promoted by the Mutazilites and its suppression by the Caliph al-Mutawakkil and his successors during the ninth century. Ibn Hanbal, a native of Baghdad, was born in 780 and died in 855. He studied under al-Shafii but traveled widely in his quest for hadith stories—a source of the law to which he was particularly devoted. Ibn Hanbal exemplified the reaction of traditional legal consults to rationalism and a reliance on analogy in coming to legal decisions. His system discounted opinion and emphasized the primary sources of the Quran and traditions. But even here, he set more discriminating criteria than his colleagues, in that he would accept hadith stories only if they could be traced to Mohammed directly or to his immediate family.

Ibn Hanbal was acclaimed for his steadfastness with regard to orthodox belief during the ascendency of the more liberal and rationalistic Mutazilite theology. For this, he suffered punishment and imprisonment. He persisted in his orthodox beliefs, however, and survived the inquisition of the Mutazilim only to gain greater acceptance during the traditionalist reaction after 847. Despite the accord bestowed on him in the traditionalist upsurge, the Hanbali school prospered for only a short while. It spread slowly beyond Iraq, gaining some adherence in Egypt by the twelfth century.

Until quite recent times, the Hanbali school had drawn few adherents as compared to the other three Sunni schools. It experienced a major revival during the eighteenth century under the leadership of al-Wahhab, whose reform movement centered in the northern Arabian peninsula. As a result of this revival, Ibn Hanbal's approach to jurisprudence spread throughout the Arabian peninsula and became that form of the law accepted by the Saud family—which rules modern Arabia—and thus presently constitutes the legal system of the kingdom of Saudi Arabia.[5]

Each of these four legal scholars influenced students and disciples, who spread the study of jurisprudence throughout Islamdom. Higher education took root in Islam around the scholarly adherence to these classical schools of law. The general term for the leader of a halqa was *shaikh;* but one who instructed in the law was called a *mudarris,* to note the area of his specialization. In mosques throughout the vast Islamic Empire, instructors would gather their students to discuss the sources of the law and to render a legal opinion—called *fatwa.* Prior to studying with a shaikh, young men had to be prepared in grammar, arithmetic, the Quran, and logic—the rudiments of elementary education. The students who sat in the mosque around an instructor were indeed entering into the realm of a higher education in Islamic society.

Some mention should be made here of the organization of law, jurisprudence, and law schools within Shiite Islam—the minority sect that rejected the succession of the caliphate to Abu Bakr, Omar, and Uthman and championed instead the ascendency of Mohammed's cousin and son-in-law, Ali. Despite the political nature of this split between the two main groups of Islam, some minor differences arose in the development of jurisprudence. The Shiites, for the most part, accepted basically three roots of the law: the Quran, hadith, and consensus of opinion. Due to their belief that leadership within the Muslim community could be exercised only by the direct descendants of Mohammed, they accepted hadith stories as authoritative only if they could be traced directly to the Prophet himself or to his immediate family.

They interpreted consensus of opinion to mean the specific pronouncements by the infallible *imam* and not just the agreement of learned lawyers and jurisconsults at any particular time. In general terms, the title *imam* refers to the man within an Islamic community who leads a prayer service. As such the Prophet Mohammed was given the title "Imam." To followers of Shiite Islam, only those true descendants of the Prophet who were designated as leaders of the faith community deserved to be called imam. In this regard, the Shiite movement is separated into several divisions: those who accept the authenticity of 12 imams from the time of Ali; and those who accept a fewer number of legitimate imams who can speak in an authoritative way on religious matters.

In general, the Shiite schools resemble most closely the school of al-Shafii, diverging only in a few details, such as temporary marriage and matters of inheritance. Perhaps a more important difference stems from the Shiite belief that imams rule by divine right and their pronouncements are to be accepted as the Will of God. Shiite Moslems tended to dominate in Persia—now Iran—and to some extent in parts of Iraq and Lebanon. It is their adherence to the role of the imam that accounts in large part for the establishment in Iran (after the expulsion of the Shah in 1979) of an Islamic republic under the leader of the Imam Ayatollah Khomeini. Shiites through the years have tended to reject the separation of civil and religious rule and adhere strongly to the traditional view of Islam as a theocracy.

Schools for the Religious Sciences

The halqa most commonly associated with the mosques were of two kinds: those that pursued the religious sciences at an advanced level, and those that specialized in the study of jurisprudence according to one of the four major schools of law (that is, a madhhab). In classical Islam, two types of mosques served the population. The first type was the congregational mosque—the *jami*—established by the state through the aegis of the caliph or governor as a meeting place for great numbers of people to hear the Friday sermon *(khutba),* and through which affairs of civic and religious importance were announced to the people. Congregational mosques were generally large and ornately decorated structures funded from the public treasury. The caliph officially designated them as places to provide a link between the government and the population. In a place such as Baghdad, there would be only five or six congregational mosques that served this purpose. Contrary to normal Islamic practice, Cairo supported a great number of congregational mosques. According to the tradition of the Prophet, each city should have only one jami; more than that required justification and approval of a legal decision (fatwa).

The other type of mosque (the *masjid*), a local or exclusive mosque—was much smaller in structure and served the special needs of a small group of the faithful, either by proximity or adherence to a specific school of law (madhhab). Such a mosque received support from its constituency, or through patronage, or endowment. The masjid abounded in Islamic cities; Baghdad numbered several hundred of such structures in the eleventh century. The study circles attached to a congregational mosque were headed by a shaikh appointed by the caliph to instruct in designated areas of the religious sciences or jurisprudence. Leaders of the community and courtiers attempted to influence the caliph in his choice of leaders for the halqa in many of the mosques; and in provincial cities, the caliph's designate would make the decision as to who would occupy the instructional chairs in the congregational mosque. A halqa would gather in a designated area of the mosque, in a corner or near a pillar at a prescribed time, usually early morning. As stated earlier, the name applied to the circle was often that of the leader. Because he could not preside over more than one circle in any given mosque, there was no possibility of confusion. In some instances, the circle assumed the name of the subjects offered. Under certain circumstances, shaikhs could be appointed to preside over a circle in another mosque as well—thus increasing their teaching duties and reaching a larger group of students, as well as adding to their earnings.

The shaikh ordinarily received his appointment to preside in a specific mosque for life—barring some unfortunate incident in which he might be called into question for heretical teaching or immoral behavior, and expelled. Leaders quite often tried to secure succession of the chair for their own progeny or favorite students, in which case they would petition before their death that a specified individual would be named to succeed them. Records exist verifying that certain circles did pass from father to son over a number of generations.[6] A shaikh of special renown might move from mosque to mosque during the period of his professional career, always trying to secure a position in a more prestigious institution.

The various circles in any given mosque would offer a variety of subject matter so that the total curricular offering available within the structure of the mosque would include such subjects as hadith, exegesis, law, legal theory, grammar, and Arabic literature and grammar. Subjects considered outside the pale of religious fundamentals were excluded from instruction provided by the halqa leaders of the mosque. These included all the books of Greek philosophy and science as well as many other secular studies from the Orient. The size of the study circles depended to some extent on the popularity and renown of the shaikh who presided over it as well as the subject matter offered. Ordinarily, attendance ranged from 10 to 20 young men.[7] Generally speaking, the religious sciences drew more students than the study of law, which was considered a specialized curriculum offering somewhat less mobility in Islamic society.

If the circle drew a large attendance, or the mosque had poor acoustics, or the shaikh spoke softly, an assistant *(muid)* would repeat his phrases to those students on the outer fringes of the gathering. In addition to reading aloud from books and commenting on the content of the lessons, the leader quite often engaged students in argumentation as well. A mudarris—an instructor of law—would entertain questions on legal matters from visitors as well as students. Legal debates were held, with both the professor and his students challenged to hone their skills at the scholastic debate that exemplified the teaching of law in its advanced stages.

The congregational mosque as an open or inclusive building welcomed declared students as well as casual students and visitors to join the study circles meeting within its precincts. People of any age might become interested in a subject and listen to the lectures and discussions whenever they wished, without formally joining the coterie of the shaikh. Learning depended primarily on the student himself and the diligence with which he pursued his studies and read outside sources so as to understand better the lectures and comments of the shaikh.

Students paid no fees to attend the circles offered under the auspices of the congregational mosque and had no restrictions placed on them with regard to where they lived or worked. They could come and go as they pleased and partake of any subject they desired. No age limitations barred men from seeking education at the mosque; but those of a younger age would have had to be properly prepared in Arabic grammar, literature, and a rudimentary knowledge of the Quran and hadith in order to understand the more advanced lectures offered.

Both instructors and students enjoyed academic freedom to explore any subject matter so long as it did not impinge on heresy. Discussions, debates, and new insights were encouraged within the basic framework of the Islamic faith. Students could move freely from circle to circle, mosque to mosque, and even city to city. The peripatetic scholar emerged as a model much emulated in Islamic society. Such mobility greatly facilitated the transmission of books and knowledge from one region to another within the borders of Islamdom.

In addition to the congregational mosque (jami), the limited or neighborhood mosque (masjid) also provided a formal home for higher studies in religion and law. *Masjid* can also be translated as mosque-college; the institution appeared as early as the eighth century and consistently dominated the educational scene during the Classical Age. Although most closely associated with legal education—where it provided homes for each of the four Sunni schools of law—a few masjids did specialize in transmission of the religious sciences. Like the jami, the masjid was a place of worship and included among its limited staff an imam and muezzin (prayer caller), in addition to the shaikh and his assistants. The positions of shaikh and imam could be combined in the same person—and often were, as a matter of economy. More accurately, an instructor of law was called a *mudarris,* and that title most commonly designated the leader of the mosque-college. By tradition the masjid employed only one mudarris, who set the curriculum and the tone of instruction. The institution became a manifestation of the man himself, and students identified with him and his approach to learning. He exercised much control over his students and tended to treat them in a fatherly manner. Attendance at the mosque-college was by invitation of the mudarris after an application had been made. Limited enrollment ensured a personalized form of education, and one in which conflict with the master was not tolerated.

Appointment of the leader of the masjid occurred in several ways. Theoretically, the caliph or his designate had the power to appoint all positions connected with a mosque. As a practical matter, this did not happen in the case of the smaller neighborhood mosques. Local officials and respected religious leaders performed this function with the approval of the qadi, the local magistrate. If the masjid was founded and supported by a specific sect to meet its needs, the members of that sect engaged a mudarris who represented their religious views. In the case of a mosque-college supported through an endowment, the terms of the endowment—called a waqf—generally stated the manner in which the leader should be appointed. The donor of the endowment ordinarily stated the qualifications of the mudarris with regard to what madhhab he must follow. The benefactor might even have a specific individual in mind in setting up the masjid. In both instances, the qadi would review the appointment and consult with local religious leaders to assure himself that the designated person was appropriate for the position.

On the occasion of his appointment to an endowed chair, the recipient delivered an inaugural lecture open to the public. This was a noted event in the calendar of the institution; and even the caliph and other members of the court might attend, if the shaikh were particularly well known. By this public presentation, the scholar aspired to present himself very well, displaying his erudition and knowledge of the subject area in which he was to teach.

Although most scholars and holders of endowed chairs did not acquire wealth, they did receive enough recompense to enable them to dedicate their lives to the pursuit and teaching of their special academic interests. Although the dilemma of whether or not a scholar could receive fees from students for teaching the religious sciences persisted throughout the Classical Age, there seems no doubt that he could derive financial support from an endowment or through patronage enough to meet his needs. Stipends earned by the faculty of the mosque-colleges varied greatly depending on the resources available to it through private contributions and income from endowment. In general, chronicles of the time maintain that the profession of teaching provided a middle-income existence for its members.[8] To be sure, the famous and most popular professors received more than generous remuneration for their efforts—some becoming quite wealthy. There seems little evidence, however, that men pursued the profession to attain material goods. Education was considered a ministry within Islam, and those who entered it did so out of dedication and a genuine interest in the life of the mind.

The leader of a mosque-college or a *madrassah* (discussed later in the chapter) received something in the range of 15 to 60 dirhams per month. Those of lesser positions within those structures also received less money. It must be remembered, however, that a scholar could hold chairs in several institutions at the same time, thus doubling or tripling his monthly income. For those teaching legal studies or foreign sciences, a system of fees was allowed. Ordinarily, the amount was agreed on between the student and his mentor, and the sum paid in advance. A fee of one dirham a day was considered fairly common, and some individual scholars did acquire wealth from their instructional performance—as much as 1,000 dirhams a month. But these cases seem to be unusual. Monetary gain was not the major consideration of individuals who dedicated so much of their lives to pursuing knowledge. The status and honor accorded to learned men seems a much more reasonable explanation for the great effort undertaken by scholars during the classical period of Islam.

In addition to the remuneration that the leader of the masjid received, he might also occupy housing within the structure of the masjid or in an attached residence. A shaikh could hold appointment to chairs in more than one mosque, thus increasing his earnings accordingly. The holders of the subordinate positions within the mosque structure might also benefit from room and board offered through the institution. In addition, they could augment their earnings by taking other employment within the community.

Those other positions of a halqa housed in the masjid—in addition to the shaikh—included an imam to lead the prayers of the congregation and to preach at the Friday sermon. The Friday sermon—in this circumstance, called a *waz*—could be delivered in any mosque, as distinguished from the khutba, the Friday sermon that could be proclaimed only in a congregational mosque as designated by the civil authority. In certain instances, the mudarris took on the religious functions of the imam in addition to his duties as instructor and administrator of the mosque-college. Where finances permitted, the masjid expanded its staff by employing associate instructors, repeaters, and tutors. The associate instructor *(naib)* substituted for the mudarris if the latter were occupied with other matters connected with the administration of the mosque-college. The repeater *(muid)* was trusted with repeating the lectures to students who could not hear them or were absent from the session and also gave private help to students having difficulty with their studies. The tutor *(mufid)* assisted younger or less advanced students, but was not yet judged capable of repeating the lecture.

With the development of personal schools of law, a proliferation of masjids occurred through which particular groups chose to pass on their particular viewpoint to younger adherents. The number of such personalized schools of law began to diminish during the tenth and eleventh centuries, until only the four primary schools of law—discussed in some detail earlier in the chapter—remained. Numerous masjids dedicated to these four schools of law were founded throughout Islamdom. As mentioned previously, geography had some bearing on the acceptance of one madhhab over the others. For example, in al-Andalus, the Maliki school of law was the most prominent; while in Baghdad, all four schools were represented by mosque-colleges, with the Shafiite and the Hanafite schools being the most common. The most usual source of funding for the establishment of these masjids derived from a system of endowment—waqf—a traditional means in Islam to support institutions that served the common good.

The Law of Waqf

Through the law of waqf, an individual could establish an endowment, the assets of which would support an institution of his choosing.[9] Devout Muslims would undertake this as an act of charity, expiation, or thanksgiving. Donating material wealth for the common good fell under a major tenet of the Islamic creed—that of giving alms for the support of the poor and for the sustenance of the faith. Education clearly fell within the latter category, and those who supported educational institutions in a material way were greatly honored. It was common, even in the early centuries of Islam, for wealthy individuals to endow mosques to meet the needs of the community or—in some instances—to promote a specific sectarian approach to the faith. In the case of the four sustaining orthodox schools of law, individuals wishing to promulgate their particular view endowed mosque-colleges whose primary function was instruction in that particular madhhab. In this manner, donors circumscribed the functions of the institution and assured that their particular denominational approach to religious studies or law would continue.

On another level—perhaps a more human one—waqf could be used by individuals to shelter their wealth from the acquisitive nature of a powerful ruler or taxation. Once granted to an institution in the form of waqf, those assets lay beyond the power of outside forces. Although he could not directly enjoy the income from the endowment, he could administer the earnings from it. Further, he could perpetuate the name of his family by attaching it to the institution supported from the waqf.

Like many legal constructs, the law of waqf was complicated and subject to interpretation through legal decisions over the centuries. An individual desiring to endow a charitable institution drafted a legal instrument that was formally notarized. This document described the property that was to form the assets of the endowment and the manner in which money derived from investment, rents, or sale of the property should be used. In addition, the benefactor also named the trustee or trustees to administer the endowment—who were quite often himself and his heirs. If the endowed institutions were a mosque-college, the donor could specify the criteria for appointments to the teaching staff and the basic approach to the curriculum. Control over the endowment, as allowed by the law of waqf, distinguished the Islamic approach to the process from that customary in Medieval Europe. In the Western world, the donor forfeited all his authority over the assets once he transmitted them to the specified institution, with allowances only for a general designation of the purpose for which the endowment was established.

Islamic law allowed the donor greater liberty in defining the structure and adminstration of the mosque-college. The benefactor also had to provide a means to replace a trustee, if through death, incapacitation, or removal the original appointee could not carry out his duties. When provisions had not been made and a trustee was judged incompetent and challenged in the judicial system, the qadi would decide who should replace him as trustee. Also, in matters of conflict that might arise out of the endowment or when difficulties occurred within the structure supported by the endowment, the qadi was empowered to review and decide the issue. Thus, the trustee could not decide to liquidate the endowment. This again devolved to the qadi. In certain circumstances, the donor might select a group of individuals to act as joint trustees over the endowment, and thus avoid reliance on a single trustee for decisions.

Because a masjid had the status of a mosque—despite its primary function as a college and the source of its support from private means—decisions regarding its religious involvement remained with civil and religious authorities. Thus, the qadi or the caliph himself had to approve appointments to the position of shaikh and imam. If charges of immorality or heresy were brought against a staff member, these officials would sit in judgment on the matter and had the power to remove personnel if the evidence warranted such action.

Because the income from a waqf might vary from year to year due to economic fluctuations, the priority of allocations was established within the contract. First priority accrued to those staff members whose presence was essential to the mission of the institution. In the case of the mosque-college, the mudarris or shaikh, the imam, and the muezzin had first claim on income. Second priority accrued to those in the lesser posts of repeater and tutor. Third priority went for stipends to support students and provide services for them. When surplus income accrued during a particular year, it could not increase the principal of the trust. If the donor had provided for its dispersal— perhaps to the poor or to purchase books—the trustees followed his dictates. If he had not made a provision of this kind or the trustees could not act on his wishes, the imam of a mosque-college could dispose of the surplus for some religious purpose, including a pilgrimage to Mecca for himself.

Particular care was taken in drawing the document because, once signed, it could not be altered. Even though the benefactor might designate himself as trustee of the endowment and thus retain control over the assets as well as influence over the choice of personnel, he could not remove assets or income from the endowment. Nor could he modify the mission of the institution. If, for example, he had designated the approach of instruction to be that of Ibn Hanbal, he could not at a later date install a Shafiite mudarris.

With the legal concept of waqf in place and its general acceptance by wealthy patrons who endowed mosque-colleges throughout Islamdom, the elements coalesced for an important transition of higher learning in Islamic culture that would create more formal, structured institutions of higher learning. In the tenth century, Badr ibn Hasanawaih al-Kurdi (d. 1015), a wealthy nobleman, accepted the governorship over several provinces that had been ruled by his father. His reputation as a philanthropist was legendary—particularly his patronage of educational institutions.[10] He supported scholars as well as pilgrims on their way to Mecca and established a number of mosque-colleges. In doing so, he added a new element to the college: residential living. Badr established 3,000 mosque-colleges to which an inn was attached—a *masjid-khan*.[11] The term *khan* may be translated as an inn or caravanserai—a lodging place for travelers—but in this combination, it referred to a residence hall for law students who had come from distant villages. Abu Ali al-Fariqi, a student who had come to Baghdad to study Shafiite law, describes it thusly: "I took up residence in an inn adjacent to the mosque college of abu Ishaq in the quarter of Bab al-Maratib wherein resided the fellows of the Sheikh and the scholars studying under his direction."[12]

The practice of providing living arrangements that brought together students and instructors in the same building continued throughout the history of higher education in both East and West, and promoted an atmosphere in which learning could be emphasized and reinforced through the living situation and the great advantage of total emergence in a scholarly life. Badr used the terms of waqf to create these institutions and to make certain stipulations guaranteeing that monies from the endowment should support living arrangements for students. Since masjid-khans fell under the rubric of mosques, the line of succession of the leader came under the prerogative of the caliph or his deputy.

The Madrassah

The next step in the evolution of institutions of higher learning in Islamic society occurred under the patronage of the Vizier Nizam al-Mulk around the year 1064. Called a *madrassah,* this new structure was modelled after the masjid-khan and took a form easily recognizable as a "college" in the way we use that term today. By this time the Seljuk Turks had usurped the civil authority from the Abbasid caliphate in the Middle East. Originating in Central Asia, they migrated west, converting populations to Islam en route. Before invading Baghdad, the Seljuk leaders agreed not to displace the caliph as the religious sovereign of Islam, but to create a political administration under the authority of one of their own who would take the title of sultan. Nizam al-Mulk was a powerful vizier, or prime minister of the sultan; and in securing his power within the realm, al-Mulk endowed hundreds of law schools of the Shafiite madhhab.

The Islamic doctrinal movement behind the Shafiite school of law—known as Asharism—attempted to synthesize elements of both the liberal and conservative approach to Quranic law and to incorporate both reason and faith as a balanced means of interpreting the law.[13] As a new movement in Islam, it rejected the extremes of other factions and took a middle road on religious questions. As such, Asharism was opposed by those of extreme views on both sides. Nizam al-Mulk, by endowing institutions through the law of waqf, introduced Asharite views and championed Shafiite colleges throughout his realm. Although religiously oriented, the madrassah was not an official mosque. Thus, by endowing such independent institutions, Nizam al-Mulk assured that he would retain control over the curriculum and appointments and provide for a succession not under the control of the caliph—a clever political move, with great impact on higher education. By not attaching the residence hall to an official mosque, he freed the institution from direct religious control, albeit still within the mainstream of the faith-oriented Islamic society. The madrassah indeed evinced the unique nature of a private institution of higher education.

The distinction between the masjid and the madrassah lay in the priorities for dispersal of income from the endowment, as provided by the law of waqf. In the case of the madrassah, the shaikh—not the imam—was considered more essential. Thus the madrassah provided first for the instructor, and then filled the other positions as funds allowed.

The madrassah also incorporated a library within its structure. While libraries had long existed in the palaces and homes of the nobility and the wealthy, they rarely formed an integral part of a mosque-college.[14] In making manuscripts available to students, the madrassah borrowed a practice from study circles of the rationalistic movement that had gained intellectual insights from Hellenistic culture and initially flourished under Abbasid rule. The availability of a variety of works beyond that comprising the text for instruction greatly enhanced the learning experience of students by exposing them to several points of view as well as to writings beyond that of immediate concern in the lectures.

In establishing the madrassah, the Vizier Nizam al-Mulk provided an endowment to support a mudarris, an imam, and also students who received a stipend as well as room and board. The accrual of these benefits to students constituted another distinction between the madrassah and the mosque-college because it meant that the former became a more attractive institution for less well-to-do students. In this we have the origin of residential colleges for impecunious scholars—which later also took root in the medieval West at Paris, Oxford, and Cambridge.

Other patrons followed the lead of Nizam al-Mulk. By the eleventh century, the basic pattern for establishing institutions of higher education separated from the mosque—with its implied control by religious authorities—but still dedicated to a certain theological viewpoint took hold and continues to the present day in Islamic countries. Such institutions took the shape of the mosque-college in size, curriculum, and instruction, except that their independence from direct religious control and their financial support of students distinguished them from the traditional masjid founded several centuries earlier.

With one notable exception, the endowment of madrassahs continued throughout the Classical Age of Islamic civilization. In the Islamic provinces of al-Andalus on the Iberian peninsula, the madrassah did not become common.[15] Because those regions adopted the more conservative and traditional Maliki interpretation of the law, the rules governing waqf did not allow a benefactor to influence the appointment of the shaikh or his successors, or appoint himself as trustee. The inevitable consequence of this loss of control over the assets of the endowment greatly reduced the incentive of wealthy patrons in these provinces to endow formal centers of higher learning similar to those in other Islamic regions. The stimulation of institutions of the higher learning devolved to ruling families—the caliph in most instances, who became the chief patron of centers of learning in Granada, Seville, and Cordova. Though jurisprudence remained the core of the curriculum in these centers, the focus lay on the school of Maliki law rather than any of its rival *madhahib,* and the instructors and curriculum fell under the perusal and dictates of the caliph and his advisers. Since ruling families provided the resources for institutions of higher learning in al-Andalus, schools flourished or declined with the interest of a particular patron.

Moorish Spain influenced Western Europe more than did the Middle East; and this form of support for higher education migrated to Sicily and thence to the Italian peninsula during the twelfth century, where it provided a model for the establishment of schools for the study of Roman and canon law—which became the most important faculty of the medieval university in southern Europe.

It should be noted that, despite the advantages to patrons desiring to extend their own views of religion and the law through the endowment of a madrassah, the mosque-colleges still remained the dominant formal structure of higher learning during the eleventh and twelfth centuries. Although Goldziher maintains that the founding and prolif-eration of the madrassah marked a victory for a moderate and more liberally oriented Islam, Makdisi argues that indeed the more conserva-tive and traditional Hanbali colleges of law prospered in the eleventh and twelfth centuries.[16] Only slowly did the compromise view of the law espoused by the Shafiite school prevail and Asharism flow into the intellectual and legal mainstream of Islam. The stature and persuasive powers of al-Ghazzali, the eleventh-century scholar, theologian, and mystic, facilitated the acceptance of Asharism not only in his writing and preaching, but also in his role as muddarris of the flagship madras-sah founded in Baghdad by Nizam al-Mulk—the Nizamiya.

Along with the masjid, the madrassah still exists in Islamic countries and has a continuing impact on educational, social, and political affairs. In recent years, much has been made of the mosque-schools and madrassahs of Iran—particularly those that form the religious structure in support of the Ayatollah Khomeni. Western viewers of television have become well aware of the importance of the Friday sermon as a political and religious event that inspires loyalty to the government and forms public opinion.

The Nizamiya—taking its name from Nizam al-Mulk—stands as the preeminent madrassah of the eleventh century. Situated at the heart of the empire, it became one of the most noted centers of higher learning during that century and created a blueprint for the foundation of other similar structures throughout Islamdom. Further, because records from it are available, scholars know more about the Nizamiya and its workings than of any other madrassah. The document establishing its endowment endures, though only as an incomplete copy. Neverthe-less, the format of the waqf that founded and sustained Nizamiya becomes apparent:

1. The Nizamiya constitutes an endowment for the benefit of mem-bers of the Shafiite school who are Shafiite in both law and legal theory.

2. The possessions with which the Nizamiya is endowed are also for the benefit of those who are Shafiite in both law and legal theory.

3. Key members of the staff must be Shafiite in both law and legal theory: the professor; the preacher; and the librarian.

4. The Nizamiya must also have a teacher of Quranic science to teach the Quran.

5. It must also have a grammarian to teach the Arabic language.

6. Each member of the staff receives a definite portion of the endowment revenue.[17]

The Nizamiya, as well as all the other madrassahs founded by Nizam al-Mulk, remained under his control during his lifetime; and he appointed the professors of law in them. Among those he chose to lead the Nizamiya was the famous scholar and theologian, al-Ghazzali (about whom we will learn much more in Chapter 3).

From its founding in 1067 until 1234, the Nizamiya remained the premier institution of higher learning in Baghdad. At that time, the Caliph al-Mustansir established a multistructured institution of higher learning that bore his name. Within the confines of the Mustansiriya were included four colleges of law, each representing one of the four Sunni madhahib. Each school maintained separate instruction and housing for its 62 students as well as its staff. All of them, along with the staff, received stipends from the generous endowment provided by the caliph. Descriptions of the buildings indicate them to be sumptuous, highly ornate, and well appointed.[18] With the founding of the Mustansiriya, yet another major transition in the evolution of higher education occurred: The small institution with a single shaikh gave way in some cities to larger, more complex institutions of higher learning. Madrassahs supported by large endowments tended now to incorporate more than one madhhab within their structures.

Despite some distinctions between the mosque-college and the madrassah in administration and the use of its resources, the curriculum and the methods of instruction remained standard. The madrassah remained the college of law par excellence and employed the teaching methodology and course of study that had evolved in those mosque-colleges dedicated to the study of law. Methods of instruction did not differ greatly from those used universally in schools of that period. This involved the copying of notes from a lecturer, recitations, writing of position papers, and participation in debates.

By the twelfth century, Islamic countries maintained a sophisticated and pervasive system of higher education, although it lay heavily under the influence of prevailing religious fundamentalism. Jundi Shapur still existed, but in what form we do not know. According to Nakosteen, physicians and scientists still resided there.[19] In that city and in others throughout Islamdom, hospitals and observatories functioned, offering a haven for scientists and physicians who could not find instructional positions in the religiously oriented structures of the mosque-colleges and the madrassahs. Towering intellects lived during this time and wrote profusely on many topics, greatly enhancing our understanding of the universe and the relationships between religious, political, and social life. With the exception of al-Ghazzali, they pursued their intellectual life in informal structures rather than in the mosque-colleges or madrassahs. Their lives and contributions will be discussed at some length in conjunction with the rise of spontaneous centers of higher learning—the parallel system of higher education in Islamdom. The flowering of Islamic institutions of the higher learning—it should be noted—occurred prior to the quickening of intellectual life at Paris and Bologna in the Christian West. Not until the twelfth century would universities as we have come to recognize them occur in Italy and France and spread to other European countries.

Curriculum

During the Classical Age of Islam, control over the curriculum in formal institutions of higher learning lay primarily with the ulama—the body of men learned and accepted as the authority on religious and legal matters.[20] Their own beliefs took root in religious conservatism and a fundamental faith in revelation as the core of all knowledge. Following the rejection of Greek-inspired philosophic movements—particularly after the time of al-Ghazzali—the curriculum in mosque-colleges and madrassahs patterned itself after the study circles of the jami (the congregational mosques).

In preparation for the study of religious sciences and jurisprudence, students engaged in the study of Arabic grammar, which included the study of both syntax and composition as well as an introduction to prose and poetry. Such propaedeutic studies could be attained through private tutors or by attending the study circle of a grammarian. Islamic educators accepted the Greek notion that the ability to think logically and clearly had a direct correlation to one's ability to speak and write properly. Accordingly, tutors placed great emphasis on exercises that fostered facility with the language.

The study and progression of grammar had received a great impetus from the introduction of Hellenistic learning into Islamic culture.

Although the ulama accepted the supposition that grammar relied on Greek logic as a methodology, they also feared that too great an emphasis on grammar could lead to fascination with other Greek intellectual sciences. Thus they always sought to subordinate the study of grammar to the Islamic religious sciences and to limit the influence of grammarians over young men. Their attitude toward grammarians is exemplified in the statement made by the biographer of Abu 'l-Hasan, a noted grammarian (d. 1107), in which the latter is declared as being "trustworthy and religious, and rare it is that a grammarian is religious."[21] Thus it happened that *adab*—belles lettres—forfeited its place in the study of grammar as presented in mosques and madrassahs and survived only in private study circles located in residences or libraries.[22] Adab would comprise an important element in the curriculum of informal structures of higher learning and greatly influence the cultural life of Islamic society.

The religious sciences dominated the curriculum in formal structures of higher education, and the Quran comprised its core. Those subjects required to understand and expound on the meaning of the Quran emerged as the focus of instruction—namely, hadith literature followed by exegesis. The major challenge in acquiring knowledge and skills in the study of hadith was in memorizing literally hundreds of stories and acquiring the insight to select from among them the appropriate one to respond to a legal inquiry. Exegesis—the method of interpreting the meaning and context of religious literature—relied heavily on the expertise of the shaikh and his ability to teach methods of interpreting and clarifying the language of the Quran. The art of preaching also formed an important part of instruction in the religious sciences, for the ability to deliver a persuasive sermon and a scholarly lecture lay at the heart of a learned man's role in the religious and educational life of the community. The skill of public speaking incorporated all aspects of the educational experience. As in the Greek system of rhetoric, the religious sciences subsumed many other subject areas under their title. Logic and grammar underlay the study of hadith and exegesis. In addition, hadith and exegesis depended on a knowledge of history and geography, and a general awareness of government and the social order. The religious sciences could not be taught in isolation, and the more expert instructors in any of the fields incorporated a vast amount of knowledge in their interpretation of the Quran and hadith literature.

Devout Muslims accepted without question or reservation the basic tenets of their faith as laid down by the Quran, and also believed that all necessary knowledge appeared in that Holy Book. Thus, theology and philosophy—the means by which scholars study the nature of God and humankind—did not evolve as part of the curriculum in formal structures of higher education. Many brilliant Islamic scholars debated issues and authored many volumes in both fields, but they did so privately or in the security of informal learning circles; and few of their writings entered the curriculums of mosques or madrassahs. To be sure, diligent students did become acquainted with such works and cautiously incorporated them into their own views. The autonomy of scholars in Islamic regions during the classical period allowed both theology and philosophy to flourish outside the formal system of higher education—attesting to the intellectual freedom permitted learned men in Islamic society.

Jurisprudence took its place within the system as a specialized study of one of the schools of law, in which knowledge of the religious sciences constituted a prerequisite.[23] In mosque-colleges and madrassahs, the law course was set forth by the shaikh in a great syllabus called a taliqa. This opus was compiled by each instructor from copies of the lecture notes made during his own experiences as a student, his own reading, and his own conclusions about the subject matter. It detailed the material of the course of study and might take as much as four years to present in lectures. Students copied the taliqa from dictation; and in some instances, they might merely copy the mentor's with very little change. Others—more industrious perhaps—might add glosses from class discussions or from their own research so that their taliqa would reflect much of their own interpretation of the course material presented by the shaikh.

The taliqa took the form of a written disputation: That is, it posed questions followed by both the affirmative and negative responses on the issue, as well as the proper resolutions with some rationalization for the conclusion. In this regard, it resembled closely the form of intellectual inquiry known in European medieval universities as the scholastic method, based on dialectic. A student strived to include in his taliqa the major disputed questions of the day along with the responses of noted scholars to them. The more sophisticated and complete the approach to the point at issue, the more valuable the manuscript became to the student, especially if he intended it as a teaching device or as a basis for legal council to clients.

The materials contained in the taliqa also provided the background information needed for oral disputation—another form of instruction in the law colleges. The oral disputation took the model of a formalized debate, dependent on the rules of logic and rhetoric, in which an individual defended a thesis—in this case, a particular stance or decision in jurisprudence—against challengers who would try to discredit his logic and argumentation. According to Makdisi, a spirit of competition prevailed among legal scholars, each vying for the title of a premier debater.[24] As in medieval European universities, scholars challenged each other to formal debates; those successful in defeating their opponents earned much honor within the intellectual community. The driving goal for many scholars was to achieve recognition as the foremost practitioner of disputation in the city or region. Failing to establish such a reputation for himself might prompt a scholar to try his talents in another place where his efforts might receive greater recognition.

The taliqa was not confined to the study of law; other subject areas employed it as well. Grammarians, in particular, adopted the format for their course of instruction. The method of questions and answers exemplified by the taliqa augmented instruction in the religious sciences also. As such, they tended to focus on those current issues and interpretations of the Quran and hadith that prompted opposing or varying opinions. Preparation of a syllabus and mastery of disputation became associated primarily with higher learning—rather than with secondary education, where study skills and memorized data prepared the student for more advanced work.

The scope of the curriculum in Islamic institutions of higher learning by the tenth century is well known from a variety of sources.[25] Among these are the *Fihrist (Index of the Sciences)* by ibn al-Nadim in 988. A second source comes from the works of the Brethren of Sincerity (also known as the Brethren of Purity)—a Sufi fraternity dedicated to enhancing education in the Islamic world—which presented its comprehensive educational program in a series of theses. Their encyclopedic approach to learning, which originated in Basrah in the second half of the tenth century, appeared in compilations throughout much of the Islamic Empire in both the tenth and eleventh centuries. Friedrich Dieterici gives the following summation of materials and subject matter contained in the encyclopedia of instruction advanced by the Brethren:

> Mundane studies: Reading and writing, lexicography and grammar, calculation and computation, prosody and poetic art, the science of omens and portents, the science of magic, amulets, alchemy and legerdemain, trades and crafts, buying and selling, commerce, agriculture and cattle farming, and biography and narrative.

Religious studies: Knowledge of the Scriptures (i.e., the Quran), exegesis of the Scriptures, the science of tradition, jurisprudence, and the commemoration of God, admonition, the ascetic life, mysticism (Sufism), and the ecstatic or beatific vision.

Philosophical studies: Mathematics, logic, numbers, geometry, astronomy, music, arithmetical and geometrical relations; natural science and anthropology; matter, form, space, time and motion; cosmogony; production, destruction, and the elements; meterology, mineralogy; the essence of nature and its manifestations; botany; zoology; anatomy and anthropology; sense-perceptions; embryology; man as the microcosm; the development of the soul (psychical evolution); body and soul; the true nature of psychical and physical pain and pleasure; diversity of languages (philology); psychology—understanding, the world soul, etc.; and theology—esoteric doctrine of Islam, the ordering of the spirit world; the occult sciences.[26]

Note the inclusion of the foreign sciences—those of Hellenistic origin—in this listing. Such areas of study did not constitute a part of the education offered by a mosque, masjid or madrassah; and though al-Farabi—a noted Peripatetic philosopher and educator of the tenth century—enumerates them as part of his curriculum, he treats them as preparatory only to advanced studies in religion and jurisprudence. Therefore, one must conclude that such subjects were offered at a rudimentary level, and were likely similar to what would not constitute the curriculum at the secondary level. Study of the foreign sciences beyond such a preparatory level took place in private study circles.

Student Life

Those men who pursued higher studies in formal structures of education did so out of a desire for the intellectual life. The course of study was rigorous and not entered into lightly. The life of the scholar—while not entirely impecunious—did not accrue great wealth for its followers. Opportunities for advancement in the form of an appointment to the post of jurisconsult did exist for those who persisted, and opportunities to serve as advisers or tutors in the houses of the rich and famous were also a possibility. But for many an intelligent student, recognition as a scholar and the social status that came with it sufficed to justify his efforts.

While individuals could attend the study circles at the jami at no cost, belonging to the halqa of a shaikh in private quarters might require payment of some kind. The more noted the shaikh, the higher the fees, usually. If he had the means, the shaikh often took it upon himself to offer assistance to his brightest students, who then became his favored disciples. The fee structure varied greatly depending on the financial circumstances of the student or his family. A fee of one dirham (equivalent to US $.24 today) a day was quite common. Those fortunate enough to be accepted in a madrassah might qualify for a stipend from the endowment, as well as room and board. Students at a masjid usually did not receive such largesse, and it fell to them or their families to provide support during the years of study. Often, students augmented their income by taking on work in the community in a variety of capacities—skilled and unskilled. Brighter students assisted the shaikh as repeaters and tutors and received some compensation to continue their studies. While not a common practice, students were permitted to marry, if they could afford it.

The madrassah provided a special educational atmosphere; it combined the academic and social lives of those who resided within its confines—bringing together faculty and students in a community of scholars. Such an organization greatly enhanced the assimilation of the student into academic life and the intellectual world. The shaikh and other members of the staff could have greater impact on students in such a close-knit community. Further, the life of the apprentice scholars could be more easily monitored and guided along the ways of responsibility and piety.

The number of years devoted by students in pursuit of specialized learning varied greatly according to individual goals. The law course ordinarily took four years, but students could take as long as they or the shaikh deemed necessary to achieve the desired knowledge and skills. The diligent scholar might devote his entire lifetime to studies with various learned men. The autobiographies of several scholars relate that they spent in excess of 20 years pursuing their studies with several mentors.[27] A clear distinction between student and instructor did not always exist for those serious about the intellectual life. Islamic society greatly honored the pursuit of knowledge and did not exert pressure on individuals to complete a set curriculum and then pursue a career.

The schedule for the average day in a mosque-college or a madrassah became fairly standardized—commencing and concluding with prayers. These could be in conjunction with the early morning and evening prayers required of all Muslims or could be special events. The early morning hours were occupied with recitations from the Quran followed by a short period of meditation. Next, the shaikh led the formal lessons—usually a lecture from his syllabus—in which he presented new material to the students or reviewed difficult issues discussed on a previous occasion. Then followed a period devoted to disputation, during which students could become actively involved in the educational experience and match their wits and skills in debate with both their peers and the shaikh. This part of the day—ordinarily presided over by the shaikh—ended about noon with another formal prayer.

In the afternoon, the repeaters and tutors would review material and drill those having difficulty with various concepts. This would continue on an informal basis throughout the afternoon and into the evening hours. Since memorization comprised such an elevated role in the curriculum, students devoted many hours in the afternoon and evening to that particular exercise.

The shaikh could schedule formal lectures every day of the week, but ordinarily he allowed students three days for individual study and personal activities—quite often Tuesday, Friday, and Saturday. Friday, the Muslim sabbath, often featured special disputations among the instructional staff and the students, along with academic sermons. Formal group meetings recessed during the entire month of Ramadan—a period of penance, prayer, and fasting.

Students belonged to classification levels that denoted progress toward completion of the course, the kind of stipend awarded (if any), specialized area of study, and degree of participation in class activities.[28] Three categories of progression existed: beginner, intermediate, and terminal. Participation referred to the difference between a working student (that is, one who received a stipend to perform some particular in-house function) and an auditor (a student who merely attended lectures).

Another distinction made between students reflected the acceptance of the individual as a disciple by the shaikh. He invited those chosen for such status to sit near him in the circle. He took extra care to instruct these students in his taliqa, in anticipation that as his chosen disciples they would carry his work and reputation to other regions or to replace him in the circle as leader. Few students within a study circle would be accorded such an honor. A shaikh would bestow that status only on the most promising of his students and, by so doing, admitted them to the inner company of his followers. The term applied to such status is *suhba*—meaning fellowship—and it entitled the student to a more intimate association with his mentor. Henceforth, he would receive the special attention of the leader, who would tutor him and encourage his intellectual growth. In return, the student would demonstrate loyalty to his mentor and champion his interpretation of the subject matter. Through selection of students for the special designation as suhba, the leader could anticipate a continuation and proliferation of his views. From among those students selected for suhba, a few might be awarded an appointment as repeater or tutor in the later stages of their course of study and would receive concomitant remuneration.

When a student felt confident that he was prepared in a particular subject area, he submitted himself for an oral examination. Should his performance meet the shaikh's standards, he would receive from his mentor the *ijaza*—a letter certifying his proficiency to teach a certain subject. If he were a student of law, the ijaza also attested to his capability of delivering fatwas—legal opinions. He who possessed an ijaza in jurisprudence could leave the circle of the master and try to establish himself professionally in another similar institution, or try to develop a professional career in the civil service acting as a jurisconsult or within the diplomatic corps. If the *ijaza* were in another of the religious sciences, the recipient could pursue a career as adviser or tutor in the bureaucracy or in private houses in addition to seeking an appointment to the staff of a mosque. At some time in the future—having achieved stature as a scholar of some repute—he might be offered the professorship in a masjid or a madrassah.

The autobiographical notes of 'Abd al-Latif, a reknown shaikh of the thirteenth century, illuminate the expectations of mentors for their students. His words offer a fitting summary to this chapter on formal institutions of higher education in Islam, in that they portray the attributes fostered by such structures. While somewhat idealized, al-Latif's counsel embraces the goals of structured higher education as manifested in personal and intellectual development. He begins with an admonition to examine one's conscience (know thyself):

> Every night, as you go to bed, you must call yourself to account, and look to see what good deed you have accomplished during your day, thanking God for it; and what evil deed you have committed, that you may ask His forgiveness, resolving not to repeat it. Then concentrate on what good deeds you can perform the next day, asking Him to help you do them.

He continues with a caution to view study as a shared venture, involving a more experienced scholar:

I commend you not to learn your sciences from books unaided, even though you may trust your ability to understand. Resort to professors for each science you seek to acquire; and should your professor be limited in his knowledge take all that he can offer, until you find another more accomplished that he. You must venerate and respect him; and if not, then do so by word of mouth, singing his praises.

Next he offers hints for developing good study habits, based on sound learning theory:

When you read a book, make every effort to learn it by heart and master its meaning. Imagine the book to have disappeared and that you can dispense with it, unaffected by its loss. Once you apply yourself eagerly to studying a book, trying to understand it, take care not to work on another, spending on it time which should be reserved for the one alone. Also, take care not to work on two subjects all at once, rather devote yourself steadily to the one subject for a year or two, or whatever period is necessary. Then when you have achieved your purpose with it, pass on to the next. Nor should you suppose that when you have acquired a science you can rest easy; on the contrary, you will have to keep it up so that it will grow and not diminish. The way to do this is to keep it in fresh rehearsal, calling it often to mind; and if you are a beginner, by reading aloud, and studying, and holding discussions with your peers. If an accomplished scholar, then by teaching and writing books. When you undertake to teach a science or to engage in a disputation on it, do not mix it with another; for every science is sufficient unto itself, able to manage without others. Your having recourse to one science for another is indicative of your inability to exhaust its contents, as one who would make use of one language for another when he knows it (imperfectly), or is ignorant of some part of it.

One should read histories, study biographies and the experiences of nations. By doing this, it will be as though, in his short span, he lived contemporaneously with peoples of the past, was on intimate terms with them, and knew the good and the bad among them.

Finally, he exhorts young scholars to "model your conduct on that of the early Muslims" and to lead a life of humility and simplicity, knowing "that learning leaves a trail and a scent proclaiming its passenger; a ray of light and brightness shining on him, pointing him out . . . like the torchbearer walking in the deep black of night."[29]

Notes

1. A. Mez, *Islam,* trans. S. Khuda Bukhsh and D. S. Margoliouth (London: Luzac, 1937), 212.

2. S. Mohmassani, *The Philosophy of Jurisprudence in Islam* (Leiden: E.J. Brill, 1961), 5–6.

3. Noel J. Coulson, *A History of Islamic Law* (Edinburgh: Edinburgh University Press, 1964), 70.

4. Mohmassani, *Philosophy of Jurisprudence,* ch. 4:5.

5. See ch. 5 in ibid.

6. George Makdisi, *The Rise of Colleges* (Edinburgh: Edinburgh University Press, 1981), 170.

7. Ibid., 184.

8. Shalaby, *History of Muslim Education* (Beirut: Dar al-Kashshaf, 1954), 136ff; Makdisi, *The Rise,* 163–64.

9. For a thorough treatment of the law of waqf, see Makdisi, *The Rise,* ch. 3:35–74.

10. See George Makdisi, "On the Origin and Development of the College in Islam and the West," in Khalil I. Semaan, ed., *Islam and the Medieval West,* (Albany: SUNY Press, 1980), 32–33.

11. Ibid., 35.

12. Ibid., 34.

13. George Makdisi, "Muslim Institutions of Learning in Eleventh-century Baghdad," *Bulletin of the School of Oriental and African Studies* 24 (1961):1–3, 50–52.

14. George Makdisi, "Law and Traditionalism in the Institutions of Learning of Medieval Islam," in *Theology and Law in Islam,* ed. G. E. von Grunebaum (Wiesbaden: Harrassowitz, 1971), 83.

15. See George Makdisi, "An Islamic Element in the Early Spanish University," in A. T. Welch and Pierre Cachia, eds., *Islam: Past Influence and Present Challenge* (Albany: SUNY Press, 1979), 116–37.

16. Makdisi, "Muslim Institutions of Learning," 3.

17. Ibid., 37 (paraphrased here).

18. A. S. Tritton, *Muslim Education in the Middle Ages* (London: Luzac, 1957), 104.

19. Mehdi Nakosteen, *History of Islamic Origins of Western Education* (Boulder: University of Colorado Press, 1964), 34–35.

20. Az-Zarnuji, *Instruction of the Student: The Method of Learning,* trans. G. E. von Grunebaum and Theodora M. Abel (New York: Kings Crown Press, 1947), 13–17.

21. Makdisi, *The Rise,* 215.

22. Ibid., 306.

23. Ibid., 111–12.

24. Ibid., 130.

25. Nakosteen, *Islamic Origins,* 53.

26. Fredrich Dieterici, *Seventeen Monographs in Moslem Philosophy in the 9th and 10th Centuries* (Berlin: 1858–1895), quoted in ibid., 53.

27. Makdisi, *The Rise,* 96–98.

28. Ibid., 171ff.

29. Ibid., 88–91.

3

Hellenistic Influence on the Higher Learning

The Greeks have been defeated in a neighboring land. But in a few years they shall themselves gain victory; such being the will of God before and after.

The Quran 30:1–3

If higher learning in Islam were relegated only to formal structures such as the mosque, mosque-college, and madrassah, the historical account would end with the founding of the Mustansiriya in Baghdad—that complex culmination of masjid and halqa, incorporating all the elements of authorized higher learning under one roof. But the higher learning in Islam involved a great deal more than just the study of the religious sciences and jurisprudence. Spontaneous institutions created a curriculum that embraced the accumulated knowledge in science and philosophy advanced by the neighbors of Islam—the Hellenistic world and the Orient. Such areas of study took root in the rich intellectual soil of Islam, but not within the formal structures of higher education discussed in the previous chapter. They flourished informally in private circles and in the lives of polymaths who devoted their considerable talents—in Greek fashion—to exploring and advancing all knowledge available to them. This chapter will discuss those spontaneous and informal components of the higher learning throughout Islamic lands during the Classical Age.

53

The Greek Legacy

Of all the booty and tribute gained through the Islamic Conquest, nothing proved a richer or more lasting treasure than the knowledge and wisdom of the Greek world that fell into the hands of the Arab conquerors. Though the Alexandrian Museum had dominated philosophy and science in the waning years of the Hellenistic era, by the time it came into the sphere of Islam it could offer nothing but a few shards of what had been the center of a thriving intellectual community, buttressed by a magnificent library and astronomical observatory. During the fifth and sixth centuries prior to the Islamic conquest of North Africa, the migration of scholars from Alexandria, Athens, and Byzantium into the protected areas of the Sasanian Empire transported the legacy of Hellenistic scholarship to the region of northern Mesopotamia between the Tigris and Euphrates rivers—the frontier between Persia and Byzantium—and also to Jundi Shapur near the Persian Gulf. The intellectual endeavors of numerous original and interpretive works in medicine, science, and philisophy—the accumulated knowledge of the Greek world—flowed into Islam.

The major impetus for the growth of these centers of Hellenistic culture in such remote areas derives in part from the presence of Nestorian Christians. The migration of these followers of Nestorius— the patriarch of Constantinople during the fifth century who was exiled by the Emporor Leo after being condemned for heresy by the Council of Ephesus—followed continual persecution of their sect for proclaiming humanistic views on the nature of Jesus Christ and the role of Mary in the reincarnation. Specifically, the Nestorians emphasized the humanity of Jesus and attributed his divine powers to the Holy Spirit that flowed through him to address humankind. Thus, they rejected those titles of the Virgin Mary that referred to her as the "Mother of God"; nor did they attribute her with any special powers deserving of devotion. To escape persecution they fled to the Sasanian frontier—at first Edessa and later Nisibis—where they founded monasteries and schools to promote Neoplatonism in its Christianized form.

In 529 the Emporor Justinian—in a move prompted by religious zeal and economics—closed the Museum of Athens, the heir of the Athenian philosophical school that traced its roots to Plato's Academy. He thus terminated an institution that had survived for nearly 1,000 years. Justinian confiscated the endowment (part of which came from Plato himself)—depriving the faculty of its salaries—and decreed that pagans could no longer teach there. Pagan philosophers and rhetors migrated to Byzantium and then to upper Mesopotamia and Jundi Shapur, where they joined Nestorian Christians and pagan scholars in an open intellectual climate that honored the study of philosophy and science unimpeded by doctrinal restraints.[1] Another infusion of Greek literature and science into this region occurred when Neoplatonists under persecution by the Christian Byzantine forces that conquered Alexandria moved their school from Alexandria to Antioch and later to Harran, a neighboring town of Nisibis. The common language of learned men in Sasanian regions was Syriac. The followers of Neoplatonism and Greek sciences—whether Christian or pagan, Greek or Byzantine—commenced that great task of converting their manuscripts from Greek to Syriac to further the communication and dissemination of ideas and volumes among scholars of whatever native tongue.

Philosophy

The Greek philosophy encountered by Islam in its Syriac guise was an amalgam of Platonic and Aristotelian thought interpreted and transformed by Hellenistic philosophers through centuries.[2] The most dominant form of Neoplatonism introduced to the Muslims originated in third-century Athens, where the noted Hellenistic philosophers Plotinus (205?–270?) and Proclus (410?–485?) resided at the famous museum located there. Scholars transported the corpus of their works and the spirit that guided it to the Alexandria Museum, where it flourished until the sixth century. Adopted by Christians, Neoplatonism spread throughout Byzantium, particularly by the Nestorians. The tenets of Neoplatonism, as elaborated by Plotinus, defined the following concepts:

1. a godhead uniting all the universe;

2. a cosmic mind that binds all reality into a whole and is the source of creation;

3. the human soul, made out of divine nature and part of cosmic mind;

4. material matter, as flesh and evil;

5. spheres of existence between the godhead and the world; and

6. emanations along whose invisible paths souls have descended from the godhead and might return again to it.

Neoplatonism perceived reason as that part of the intellect through which one could learn of nature and the universe and might ascend intellectually and spiritually through the spheres to unite with the godhead. Reason, as proclaimed by Plotinus, incorporated more than logic and deduction and also included intuition and speculation as faculties of the mind to enlighten reason.

Proclus subscribed to a mathematical interpretation of philosophy in his definition of Neoplatonism.[3] Such an approach valued numerology and the need to perceive the universe in harmony and unity as reflected in symbolic numbers. He also proclaimed that fasting and purification could facilitate understanding of supernatural beings and hasten the soul's journey to intuiting and communing with the cosmic mind and the eternal godhead.

Nestorian scholars transformed the works of Plotinus and Proclus into a metaphysical base for Christianity so as to reflect the Trinity, and advocated the use of reason and grace to interpret revelation by which means one could comprehend the meaning of Scripture. They also adopted the humanistic approach of the Greeks in their desire to use knowledge and its general content to serve human needs and make life on earth more bearable. They accepted the notion that no conflict could exist between knowledge of the material world and the dictates of faith, and that reason guided by grace could not lead one to err or to be in conflict with the Will of God.

Islam also inherited Aristotelian thought as interpreted and restated by the philosophers of some six centuries. Plotinus's interpretation dominated the form of Aristotelian thought that entered the intellectual stream of Islam.[4] His synthesis of Aristotle was paraphrased by Porphyry of Tyre (ca. 300) in his "Isagoge," an introduction to Aristotle's *Organon* that couched Aristotle's views in Neoplatonist terms. With the passage of time, the "Isagoge" became an integral part of the *Organon;* in fact, the works were translated into Syriac and later into Arabic as a single opus. Later scholars did not distinguish between the contributions of Aristotle and Plotinus. In the sixth century, Boethius translated the "Isagoge" into Latin, in which form it became an important source for the later development of medieval philosophy. Porphyry continued the process of absorbing Aristotelian thought into Neoplatonism by writing commentaries on Aristotle's works and incorporating them into a Neoplatonic curriculum that was taught in the philosophical schools of the late Hellenistic age. No record comes to us that early Islamic scholars were aware of the works of the pre-

Socratics or the Stoics, nor is there any mention of either Aristotle's *Dialogues* or *Politics*.

Alexander of Aphrodisias (ca. A.D. 200), drawing on the Neoplatonic works of his predecessors, interpreted Aristotle in theological terms.[5] He defined the active and passive intellect, reaffirming the theory of emanations—originally stated by Plotinus—through which humans could learn of the Divine Presence. This was a Christian view readily accepted by Muslim scholars because it described the process by which one could employ meditation and prayer to achieve understanding of the created universe and God. Alexander recast Aristotelian philosophy, illuminating the issues of determinism and free will— concepts that many early Islamic scholars would embrace and develop in several schools of thought. Disagreements over the interpretation of free will and determinism would eventually divide Muslim scholars and become a cause for persecution.

Early Islamic scholars apparently did not distinguish between Aristotle and Plato.[6] They accepted the Greek philosophic works as an integrated whole from the epitomes and paraphrases of the Greek manuscripts available to them, first in Syriac and then in Arabic. Their historical knowledge of Greek philosophy seems not to have gone beyond the Alexandria Museum and the roots of Plotinus in third-century Athens. Muslims had no interest in the historic personages of Aristotle and Plato, nor in the evolution of these original works into the much later paraphrases that they encountered. What they drew from Greek philosophy served their purpose by reconciling a revealed faith with the natural order of the world. They exhibited little curiosity about Plato and Aristotle and their original works or conflicting statements within them. Indeed, later Islamic scholars went so far as to attempt to reconcile Aristotelian and Platonic views to prove that no disagreement separated them.

Muslim scholars embraced with ease the major tenets of Greek thought in its syncretized form. The Christian Neoplatonists provided them a natural theology—a theory of the divine as revealed in the nature of reality and as accessible to human reason. The Quran stated that, because the universe is a whole whose parts cannot be separated, nature and the Will of God must be the same. Muslims propounded the notion that grace—which includes reason—comes as a gift of God, and that reason can provide the means to explore the natural world and ultimately demonstrate the unity of all creation. In the Neoplatonist concept of emanations, Islamic scholars recognized the power of God descending from the highest point of the celestial region to lesser beings. They accepted the Christian view that through reason, piety, and a righteous life the truth of God's creation would be made known. Muslims felt comfortable with the Neoplatonist world view that conjoined God, creation, and knowledge into a unity that could be studied in its separate parts through reason.

The study of mathematics, science, and philosophy would illuminate nature and could not lead to conflict with revealed truth, as presented in the Quran. Islamic scholars were drawn to the systematic method of scholarship used by the Greeks. Greek philosophy provided them with such useful tools as dialectic, syllogism, and deductive logic to resolve issues in theoretical areas of knowledge—specifically, philosophy—and the religious sciences, the core of life in the Muslim world. Muslims accepted the Neoplatonist view that reason could be employed without denying the use of intuition and speculation as part of the process of seeking truth.

Medicine

When Islam first encountered Greek medicine in the Nestoriam and Neoplatonic centers of learning in upper Mesopotamia, by the time of the Islamic conquest of the Sasanian Empire, the city of Jundi Shapur stood as the center of both the study and the practice of medicine. It had the greatest influence on the advancement of medicine in Islamic regions in later centuries. The Oriental and Egyptian foundations of medicine—primarily based on magic and folk remedies—paled in the presence of the knowledge and healing skills possessed by scholars from Alexandria, Athens, and Persia during the fifth and sixth centuries. Greek medicine as an organized body of theory and practice originated with Hippocrates (460–377? B.C.), who separated medicine from superstition and religion and offered a natural explanation for the causes of ill health.[7] Though rife with fallacies on the cause of diseases, Hellenistic medicine nonetheless made use of the rationalistic approach to treatment through observation and experience and did offer numerous effective remedies. Aristotle made two contributions to the study and practice of medicine: (1) by advocating logic and reasoning to diagnose diseases from symptoms; and (2) by contributing to the study of anatomy.[8] Aristotle's descriptions of natural processes became authoritative in both Hellenistic medicine and among Islamic physicians, who adopted his views as their own.

Greek medicine suffered from an intellectual bias that honored a theoretical approach over a practical one. The Greeks of Aristotle's and Plato's time considered working with one's hands demeaning and believed that it could actually erode the intellectual power of the soul. The use of hands in labor was fit only for slaves, serfs, craftsmen, and laborers. Thus, physicians—treating symptoms with only a rudimentary examination of the body and almost total reliance on oral reporting from the patient—would send patients to a barber for surgery, setting of fractured bones, and bleeding. Medicine in the Hellenistic world followed the theoretical method of the early Greeks and eschewed practices drawn from clinical experiences.

Greek medicine evolved in its Neoplatonist form from parallels drawn between the microcosmos and the macrocosmos: That is, the four elements of the universe—earth, air, fire, and water—were said to have their human manifestation in blood, phlegm, yellow bile, and black bile. Physicians attributed the disruption of normal bodily functions to an imbalance in these four basic elements and sought to treat disease by returning them to a harmonious state. Thus, they relied heavily on bleeding, purgatives, and diet to produce a remedy. Pythagorean mathematics, with its esoteric view of numbers, led to the designation of critical days for the treatment of disease—thereby contributing to a continuing practice of medicine grounded in mysticism, rather than science.

The Arabs received Greek medicine through the writings of Galen, a Peripatetic physician and writer who lived during the latter half of the second century A.D. Galen compiled and interpreted Greek medicine from the time of Hippocrates to his own day. He accepted the theoretical approach and furthered the humoral views of Hippocrates and the penchant for numerology.[9] To this Galen added his own theory of spirit *(pneuma)* as penetrating all of human anatomy. It was this addition to the study of medicine that later gave rise to psychosomatic illness as conceptualized by Islamic physicians. Galen prepared a large encyclopedia of medicine characterized by system, organization, and theory. He wrote a great many treatises on various aspects of medicine: 9 in anatomy, 17 in physiology, 6 in pathology, 16 on the blood system, 14 on therapeutics, and 30 on pharmacy.

The Greek bias against physicians using their hands in surgery, compounded with the Christian aversion to desecrating the human body through autopsy, halted the investigation of human physiology and anatomy through its most direct means. Galen based his work in anatomy on dissection of animals (primarily pigs and goats) and the perceptions of previous commentators, and not on his direct experience with the structure and inner processes of the human body. As

Aristotle dominated both the philosophic and scientific thinking for many centuries beyond his time, so Galen's encyclopedia on medicine dominated that profession until the sixteenth century. Islamic physicians in particular accepted his word as authoritative; and although they advanced treatment in a variety of ways, they never challenged his basic tenets and theories.

Mathematics

Every civilization about which we have an historical record has devised a system of counting and notation of quantity through the use of symbols. The Greek system incorporated a complicated use of letters, rendering basic arithmetic computations most difficult. More sophisticated mathematical functions did not exist because of the clumsiness of using letters instead of digits to denote quantity.[10] Roman numerals added little to the ease of computation; and in common practice, numbers were written out rather than represented symbolically.

Greek mathematics was not so much a science that dealt with the exact value of a number, but valued numbers as signifying a relationship to all other numbers. In the study of geometry and astronomy, the Greeks adopted the sexagesimal system originally conceived by Egyptian and Babylonian astronomers in very early times. Both groups based their system of a base of 60 on astronomical observations.[11] The source for this lay in the approximate number of days during a solar year: 360 plus a few more. The Egyptians and Babylonians both divided the year into 12 months of 30 days each, with a few festival days at the end to make up the proper allotment of time for the completion of the solar year. Early geometricians deduced that the three angles of an isosceles triangle were comprised of 60 equal subdivisions; they extended this information to all triangles and to the circle. Thus they hit on a method for solving problems in geometric and astronomical computations by using a base of 60 degrees without ever assigning an exact measurement to the distances involved. Because the Greeks did not establish a standard measure of length, they sought to deal with mathematical quantities in relational form. In this the sexagesimal system worked well enough.

The origin of our present "Arabic" numbering system lies in obscurity. In general, scholars agree that its roots lay in a Sanskrit numbering system of nine symbols. A treatise on that system appears in manuscripts in both Hindi and in Arabic at about the same time, during the last quarter of the ninth century.[12] Historians do not know exactly when this particular system of numeric symbolization came into common use in India and entered the Persian Empire. Undoubtedly, the transference was expedited through trade routes that linked the Middle East to India in the sixth and seventh centuries. During that time, such numbers came into common use at Jundi Shapur and from there spread throughout the Islamic world.

The attainments of Greek mathematics and science entered Islam in much the same way as philosophical thought—primarily, in several great epitomes that were the major textbooks in both areas during the dominance of Alexandria as the center of the Hellenistic intellectual world. During the early rise of Alexandria around 300 B.C., Euclid—noted more as a teacher than a scholar—presided over a school famous for the study of geometry. Euclid compiled the Greek tradition in geometry into the *Elements,* a logically organized textbook of Greek knowledge in geometry summarizing the works of Pythagoras, Hippocrates, Thales, as well as later and forgotten geometricians. Despite his lack of originality, Euclid's name comes down through history almost synonymous with geometry, and his compilation became the required textbook in the study of the field well into the twentieth century. While geometry had its roots in Egyptian studies, the Greeks perfected it as a study of space—the measurement of the dimensions of length, width, height, and their relationship to each other and to the angles between lines.

Science

During the apex of Alexandrian scholarship, Ptolemy (second century A.D.) wrote major works on science and astronomy that ultimately entered the Islamic world as the *Almagest.* Ptolemy owes his place in history for his mathematical arrangement of the stars, a geographical outline, and his four books on astronomy. He rejected the theory of Aristarchus that proposed a heliocentric universe, and advocated a theory that both honored common sense and remained consistent with religious faith. Despite the fact that Ptolemy's geocentric model of the universe perpetuated one of the greatest scientific errors of all time, it nevertheless offered a mathematical system for measurement of the movement of heavenly bodies that had great predictive powers. Considering the crude instruments available to astronomers at the time, Ptolemy's system provided an amazingly accurate and useful tool in plotting the orbits of planets and the location of constellations at any given time. To accomplish this he calculated a table of chords—again a relational system of dealing with dimensions—which proved a valuable tool in the study of planetary movement. His writings dominated the field of astronomy until the European Renaissance, when the geocentric model gave way to the Copernican heliocentric model of the universe. Interestingly, Christopher Columbus based his estimation on the circumference of the world on Ptolemy's work and thus miscalculated greatly the distance between Europe and Asia when he sailed west.[13]

Ptolemy was much more helpful in his contributions to geography, by introducing a grid arrangement for locating places on a map. His mathematical approach focused primarily on geometric relationships. Drawing on the Babylonian's sexagesimal system, Pyolemy divided the world sphere into 360 degrees, with each degree further subdivided into 60 minutes and each of these into 60 seconds. The basic idea of his system of longitude and latitude is still in use today. He drew maps noted for their accuracy, grounding them on his own travels and observations as well as the accounts of others to which he was privy at the Alexandrian Museum.

Hero—another Alexandrian polymath who is, however, less known than Ptolemy—compiled works on mathematics and physics that were incorporated into the general knowledge base of the Alexandrian school; and from that source, his works migrated with Neoplatonists to Mesopotamia. He wrote of levers, the pulley, hydraulics, and steam power. In this he drew heavily from the works of Archimedes—the greatest of the Hellenistic physicists—whose treatises on geometry were also known in Alexandria.

Literature

Having their own rich tradition of poetry with formal conventions on the presentation of materials in written form, either the Islamic scholars were not introduced to the literary works of Greek authors such as Homer and Sophocles, or they dismissed them as having little of value to offer a society whose religious beliefs strongly condemned polytheism and anthropomorphic gods and goddesses. None of the later Roman authors—including Virgil and Cicero—are noted in the writings of Islamic polymaths of this Classical Age. Unlike their Christian counterparts, Islamic teachers did not offer the moral and ethical lessons from these noted works by placing them into a compatible religious context. While sharing a common root in the Bible, Islam and Christianity split on the relevance of literature from the Greek and Roman world. The followers of Mohammed disallowed that corpus from their tradition, while the followers of Christ adopted it and in later years would enshrine it as the fountainhead of Western Civilization.

The Initial Period of Translation

The main current of Greek thought that entered the Islamic world did not come through original Greek manuscripts, nor even the compilations, paraphrases, or epitomes of the Hellenistic era. The vitality of Greek scientists and philosophers had ended with the decline of the Museum in Alexandria. Rather, the route of entry lay in the Syriac writers who preserved Hellenistic culture in translation, while adding minimal insight to it. These were scribes and practitioners of the ancient learning but not creators or inventors of new ideas. The first span of the bridge, then, between Hellenistic knowledge and Islamic culture consisted of the translation of Greek manuscripts into Syriac, the intellectual language of the Middle East—understood by Persian, Greek, Jewish, and Christian scholars who were seeking religious freedom and intellectual stimulation in Persian lands in the two centuries prior to the Arab occupation of the Sasanian Empire. The first major interface between Arab and Greek culture occurred with the capture of Damascus and its initial reestablishment as the provincial capital of Syria and later the imperial city of Islam under the Umayyad caliphs.

During the seventh century the Umayyads drew on the Nestorian community of Syriac scholars in nearby Nisibis for physicians. Arab medicine had relied heavily on herbs, bleeding, and spiritual consolation as the means for curing disease. The reputation of Christian physicians for successful treatment of the ill and as possessors of the Western art of healing had reached the caliphal court. More importantly, the Nestorians practiced a more natural rather than a magical approach to the process of treatment and cure that was consonant with the Quran and Islamic teaching. The Quran states that for every disease there is a cure. Christian physicians continued in this capacity as court physicians through the entire Umayyad period and as such served as advisers to the caliph, thus influencing his ideas in areas other than medicine. As learned men, the Christian physicians not only practiced Greek medicine, but were polymaths as well—engaging in the study of philosophy, mathematics, and science. Intrigued by this great body of knowledge unknown to them, curious members of the court as early as 683 requested the Nestorian Christians to translate their Syriac manuscripts into Arabic, and thus began the initial translation process. It commenced with manuscripts on medicine, viewed by the Arab conquerors at this time as the most useful information for them.

The ancients held a particular fascination for the movement of the stars and planets in the heavens above them. Oriental religions looked to the stars as a means of deciphering the supernatural and as the bearers of messages from various deities. Islamic doctrine claimed that the stars indeed were moved by the Will of God, and thus could be used to interpret the Divine Will. Thus, curiosity about astrology also stimulated the process of translation under the Umayyad caliphs. Khalid, the second son of Yazid the third Umayyad caliph (680–683), became curious about the astronomical knowledge of the Nestorian community, primarily through his acquaintance with physicians at the court. He commissioned Stephen of Alexandria, a Neoplatonist scholar, to translate various Greek and Syriac works on astronomy/astrology into Arabic. Khalid's interests soon extended to alchemy—the method by which baser metals could be turned into more precious ones—and asked that these texts also be translated.

Despite exposure to Hellenistic philosophy and theology, the Umayyads were less interested in furthering the study of philosophy and theology than in establishing a civil state. They advocated a simple faith that empowered them to rule by divine right, and seemed reluctant to promote a system of religious law that would lessen their power to define the ways in which Islamic congregations could live out the message of the Quran. Nor were they concerned with the sophisticated interpretation of the Quran and sunnah; in fact, they saw in that activity a possible threat to their authority. They could anticipate an erosion of their jurisdiction if Islam evolved a theology and religious law based on interpretation of the original message of revelation.[14].

The proximity of scholars of the Greek tradition to emerging sages in Islam fostered an interchange of ideas between the two cultures. Like cracks in a dam, at first it appeared as a trickle, and later as a flood. The more serious among Islamic scholars perceived a great need to transform their faith into a living guide for the faithful. The absorption of peoples of many other cultures and language made it incumbent on Muslims to generate a rational explanation of the Islamic creed. In their encounters with pagan and Christian philosophers, Muslim sages were ill equipped to explain their religion according to the rubrics of Greek rationalism. To meet the challenge of defending their faith, they resolved to learn the methods of dialectic, logic, and rhetoric. In Greek philosophy they perceived both a means and an example of how to conceptualize a faith system and to present those arguments in a logical manner to converts.

The quantity of translations, which had been a minor undertaking under the Umayyads, reached major proportions during the reign of the early Abbasid caliphs. The Abbasids claimed the caliphate not only on their relationship to Mohammed, but also on their promise to establish a theocratic state more consonant with Quranic dictates and the message of hadith. As Goldziher states of the new regime, "religion is now not simply a matter of interest to the state, but its central business."[15] The Abbasids—descendants of Arabian families—had intermarried with Persian families. They proclaimed that, in the future, taxation would be more just and that non-Arab Muslims would not be treated as a clientele with lower class status. Further, they encouraged the structuring of a legal cannon as an evolving—not static—system to guide the faithful in making decisions about moral, ethical, and civil dilemmas. Under the Abbasids, peace reigned throughout most of Islamdom for some 400 years, bringing with it prosperity through trade and stable government. The Abbasid caliphs—as befit their status—supported culture and intellectualism, built magnificent palaces, established the court in Baghdad, and promoted education and learning.

Under the patronage of these early Abbasid caliphs—especially al-Mansur, al-Rashid, and al-Mamun—the high period of translation flourished between 750 and 850. Not only were the volumes of the Nestorians and the Neoplatonist pagans of Mesopotamia available in great abundance; but through conquest of the borderlands of Byzantine, additional manuscripts comprised part of the treasure brought back to Baghdad. Absorbed by a desire to learn more of the knowledge of the Greek world, the caliphs—when not able to acquire manuscripts by conquest—even purchased them from their enemies, particularly from the Byzantine court of Constantinople.

Under al-Mamun, the translation process reached its zenith. A highly educated man already familiar with some Greek treatises, al-Mamun adopted the teachings of a group of Islamic intellectuals called Mutazilites, who maintained that faith and reason could not be contradictory. He hoped to strengthen their ideas by increasing the availability of Arabic translations of Greek and Syriac manuscripts—particularly those that dealt with philosophy.

The Christians who had translated Greek manuscripts into Syriac treated the philosophical and religious texts as sacred works; thus they would not alter a word in the translation process.[16] Each Greek word was transmitted literally. Where a comparable Syriac word did not exist, translators merely wrote down the Greek word. These early translations—while difficult to interpret and awkward to read—remained true to the original Greek and even now provide an important key in comparing later translations of Greek classics to those of a much earlier period.[17]

The early attempts of translating these into Arabic occurred similarly. In literal translation, Arabic synonyms replaced the Syriac words. When the translator could not think of an Arabic counterpart or one simply did not exist, he penned in the original Syriac or Greek word. Arabic at this time was just beginning to invent the sophisticated vocabulary required to accommodate abstractions. Thus, translators and scholars struggled to enrich their language with new words to portray the concepts that appeared in Syriac manuscripts. Arabic-speaking scholars found these initial translations quite awkward grammatically and difficult to understand. The arabian philosopher al-Kindi gave his own interpretations to Neoplatonist thought as it entered the Islamic world.

More polished Arabic versions of these earlier translations appeared during the caliphate of al-Mamun; they were the products of a special translation center established at his court.[18] The most noted translator residing there was the Nestorian physician Hunain (809–873), fluent in Greek as well as Syriac. So dedicated to the process of translation was al-Mamun, that he paid Hunain an equal weight of gold for each page rendered into Arabic.[19] Under Hunain, the literal word-for-word translation process developed into a contextual approach that was more easily read and understood.

The usual procedure for translation occurred in two stages. Hunain set the Greek manuscripts into Syriac, and his son and other associates then undertook the task of transcribing them from Syriac into Arabic. Because they elected not to bring over Greek words without clarifying the meaning, the translators thus created a language to convey philosophic and scientific abstractions that brought Arabic to a more intellectual and sophisticated level. By setting these Greek works into an Arabic context, the translators recast Greek thought into a Semitic form much more palatable to Islamic scholars.

The number of Greek treatises rendered into Arabic during this period was prodigious. By the latter part of the ninth century, nearly all the known works of the Hellenistic museums had become accessible to Islamic scholars. To Hunain we attribute the translation of almost all of Galen (some 20,000 pages); of Aristotle, he transcribed the *Categories, Physics, Magna Moralia,* and *Hermeneutics;* of Plato, *The Republic, Timaeus,* and the *Laws;* of Hippocrates, his *Aphorisms;* of Dioscorides, the *Materia Medica;* of Ptolemy, the four books on astronomy; and also the Old Testament.

Hunain's son Ishaq was particularly enamored with Aristotle and translated the *Metaphysics, On the Soul, On the Generation and Corruption of Animals,* and the Aristotelian commentaries of Alexander of Aphrodisias. By the middle of the ninth century, most of Greek science, medicine, and astronomy appeared in Arabic. Al-Hajjag (786–833), a scholar of the pagan Neoplatonic school at Harran, translated Ptolemy's *Mathematike Syntaxis*—which acquired the name *Al-megiste* (the Great Work) and comes to us through time as *Almagest*—and Euclid's *Elements.* Also available in Arabic were Apollonius's *Conics,* Hero's *Mechanics,* and Phylos's *Pneumatics.* By the beginning of the tenth century, translations of Archimedes and a new translation of Euclid were also on hand.

The placement of this magnificent undertaking in historical context with regard to events in Western Europe is captured in a quote by Hitti:

> All this took place while Europe was almost totally ignorant of Greek thought and science. For while al-Rashid and al-Mamun were delving into Greek and Persian philosophy, their contempories in the West, Charlemagne and his lords, were reportedly dabbling in the art of writing their names.[20]

From this early period of translation forward, higher learning in Islam had the potential of developing a diverse curriculum, embracing all areas of knowledge known in the Hellenistic world as well as those unique to its Oriental culture. As noted in Chapter 2, this did occur; but instead of offering such breadth in a single institution, Islamic society formed a two-track system: one focusing on the religious sciences and located in formal schools; and the other emphasizing the so-called foreign sciences of Greek philosophy and science, which flourished in informal structures.

Together, these two elements constituted the basic liberal education for students in such far-flung places as al-Andalus and Khorasan. This rich heritage of the Greek intellectual corpus—infused with Oriental studies in science, astronomy, and literature—provided a sturdy base for the launching of original studies in all areas of knowledge. In that endeavor, too, Arabic-speaking scholars succeeded magnificently. Eventually, they passed on to the Western world all they had inherited from various earlier civilizations, but with the addition of their own genius. This transmission feature is a major concern in studying the higher learning in Islam during the Classical Age.

Islamic Perspectives on Knowledge and Learning

At the core of any study of higher learning—or indeed of any educational enterprise—lies a philosophical attitude toward knowledge and the process of its acquisition. On the surface, the terms "curriculum" and "instruction" take precedence in the discussion of schooling; but at a deeper level, epistemology truly holds the key to the learning process in a specific cultural milieu. How a person knows an object and what objects are worth knowing remain the essential questions in an examination of education. These are questions of value; and in Islamic society of the Classical Age, the answers to such inquiry resides in the creed of Islam itself.

As in most theocratic societies, higher education and the pursuit of knowledge in classical Islam depended on and was circumscribed by prevailing religious beliefs—in this case, the Islamic view of the universe and reality.[21] Learned men in Islam pursued not so much a philosophy of education to guide both the schools of higher learning and the quest for knowledge, but strove for a theosophy as a basic framework to govern all aspects of life within the ummah, the community of believers. Muslims of the Classical Age believed in the unity of all nature and felt it repugnant to divide knowledge into segments such as religion, philosophy, mathemetics, and science. Their system of theosophy, which unfolded from the Quranic revelation, combined all of these together in a world view that guided them in all their cultural and intellectual activities.

Relying only on the Quran as a basic source and on hadith as a means of interpreting the Divine Will, many natural and social phenomena remained ambiguous and obscure to Islamic scholars. Fortuitously, when those men encountered Greek philosophy and science, they discovered a perspective on learning and knowledge compatible with their faith. Neoplatonism in its Christianized form provided an explanation of the universe consonant with the revealed truths ambiguously set forth in the Quran. The Arabs were astute adaptors of the ideas from other cultures that they judged to be an enhancement to their own knowledge. Scholars in Islam welcomed Greek learning because, while God had given his final revelation to Mohammed in the Quran, He had communicated both methods and insights in the search for truth to other peoples in earlier times. The methodologies and information of Greek philosophy and science offered to Islamic scholars previously unknown intellectual tools to unlock the secrets of the universe. Although they first undertook the use of logic and dialectic as a means of debating with learned men of other faiths, they quickly perceived the benefit of these tools in explaining the created world. Neoplatonism also reinforced the basic Islamic religious view that the higher order of the cosmos (that is, the Divine Presence) could be understood only through intellection, contemplation, and intuition— all gifts of God that were contained in each soul and that had descended from universal intelligence to humankind.

The unity of God and the universe stood as the primary and basic principle governing Islamic intellectual life. God created the universe in perfect harmony, and all the interrelated parts reflected the oneness of God's nature. One Islamic model of cosmology viewed the universe as structured in five hierarchical tiers.[22] At the highest order was the Divine Essence itself; below that came four layers: universal intellect; angelic substance; psychic or "subtle" manifestations; and finally, the terrestrial world. Each of the lower tiers was governed by the guiding principle above it. The terrestrial world was a physical manifestation of universal intellect continuously re-created by God. The terrestrial world, then, manifested the symbols of universal reality that could be recognized in their materialistic presence through the five human senses. Beyond the materialistic features of any object in the world lay a deeper essence knowable only through faculties of the soul such as intuition and reasoning. Intellection—the process by which the human soul seeks divine wisdom—could be activated primarily through contemplation. Knowledge gained through intellection becomes a conscious reality in the individual through intuition—the process by which God's emanations to the terrestrial world can be known by a human mind.

Within this schema, reason (when exercised properly) cannot yield untruth—that is, knowledge that might be in conflict with divine truth. As a gift of God, reason enables humans to understand the cosmos more fully and can be used to unlock the secrets of God's creation, but only in limited fashion. Beyond a basic level, human reasoning cannot illuminate truth. To attain a more lofty level of wisdom, reason must give way to intellection—the faculty requisite to ascend to universal mind. Because of its dependence on human experience, reasoning is flawed in its quest for knowledge, particularly when used by the immature or the impure. At an even deeper level, reason and scientific inquiry have the potential to mislead individuals into materialism—the belief that earthly objects embody value in their own right, rather than simply providing a means to pursue higher truth. To orthodox believers, such an attitude was tainted with heresy. In the hands of the truly righteous, however, knowledge of earthly objects facilitates understanding of the universe and God's workings. Indeed, it serves to illuminate the truly marvelous nature of God's creation.

From this perspective, nature can be viewed as a text (much like the Quran) that conveys truth but must be interpreted through the use of the mental faculties such as reasoning, contemplation, and intuition (all of which are enlightened by the revelation in the Quran). One readily discerns in this epistemology a hierarchy of knowledge. The most valuable knowledge resides in abstractions—ideas that really emanate from the upper layers of the cosmos—rather than in concepts that relate only to the physical properties of objects on earth. Scientific methods such as experience, observation, and experimentation yield knowledge of the symbols of the universe; and this mundane knowledge must be subservient always to wisdom, which is knowledge of the universal truth contained in the upper layers of the cosmos and known through higher intellectual faculties such as contemplation and intuition. The Islamic view here parallels that of the Greek Neoplatonists in that a hierarchy of truth extends from the physical and utilitarian at the lowest level of creation to the abstract and ideal at the highest level.

The faith of Islam affirms the basic goodness of all things created by God and the concept that physical objects appear in the terrestrial realm to provide a facilitative environment for humankind. The things of this world, then, exist for the benefit and enjoyment of all, as long as one realizes the priorities of truth and does not fall into idolatry—the worship of earthly things. Mundane knowledge should be valued not for itself, but as an instrument in knowing God's Presence in creation.

Because Islam so strongly emphasizes the unity of all things in nature, it also views knowledge of the natural world as harmonious, interconnected, and part of the greater oneness of the Divine Intelligence. As a result, the early Islamic scholar—called *hakim*—pursued all aspects of knowledge, and ordinarily did not concentrate on any particular subject matter. To do so would be analogous to exercising only the arms of the body, forgetting the legs and other muscles vital for life. In this, a hakim (a wise man) took the Greek polymath—who was learned in all areas of knowledge—as his model. Indeed, Islamic scholars conceived of intellectual specialization as a kind of abnormality, much as a malformed body. True to the Islamic theosophy that governed all aspects of their culture, hakims linked mathematics, philosophy, science, medicine, and jurisprudence together and always attempted to interrelate the theories and the information of each thread into a completed fabric of universal knowledge. During the Abbasid caliphate, Islamdom produced many models of the polymath for us to learn from and admire. They were truly Renaissance men whose breadth of knowledge still amazes us. The concept of emanations flowing from the Divine Essence down to the world—a view shared by both Islam and the Neoplatonists—eventually placed a powerful restriction on the function of science in the Islamic world. Because terrestrial objects were re-created constantly through the descent of emanations from the Divine Intelligence, scientific inquiry was not perceived as searching for causation in natural phenomena. Events in the world occurred because God willed them—not because of any properties of the involved objects. Fire is hot because God wills it to be so. Water freezes or becomes steam because God wills it—not because of any unique properties within the substance itself that allows it to change form. Phenomena observed to occur consistently merely reflect the habits of God; it would be presumptuous to assume that they would always happen in the same way.

The function of science is to describe natural phenomena—primarily through observation—not to discover why such activities occur. Thus the hakim tried to cooperate with God's design rather than to presume that he could comprehend and, perhaps, control an integral process of the natural order. The physician could not produce a cure by himself, but—rather—sought to cooperate with God's habit of healing, by introducing into the treatment an intervention perceived through experience that God had allowed to improve the physical well-being of a patient. The nuance here has a fine distinction not readily understood or appreciated by the modern scientific mind; but as a pervasive principle regarding inquiry into the nature of the universe, it did place dramatic parameters around the acceptable pursuit of scientific inquiry by Islamic scholars.

This Islamic perspective can be recognized in the categorization of seekers of truth and knowledge written by the famous Persian astronomer, mathematician, and poet, Umar al-Khayyam. He consigns to the lowest level those theologians whom he judges as being content with disputation and "satisfying proofs" as providing sufficient means for discovering truth. Above them he places the philosophers and learned men of science who use rational arguments in seeking understanding of the universe. He sees these individuals, however, as becoming entangled ultimately in logical methodologies that cannot lead to the essential nature of truth. He assigns to a higher plane those who seek knowledge from a "learned and credible informant"—that is, through interpretations of the Quran and sunnah. Such men are aware of the flaws in the use of disputation and reason in seeking truth and hope to discover ultimate knowledge of God and creation in the thoughts of sincere, righteous men. At the highest level he places the Sufis—those who purge their inner being and purify it through spiritual exercises. From them the veil of ignorance is lifted, and they experience the Divine Wisdom in a truly spiritual way.[23]

In this hierarchy of knowing, we see reflected the Islamic view of the pursuit of truth as ascending from material to supernatural objects. The view of knowledge defined above represents mainstream Islamic theosophy as it relates to the pursuit of knowledge during the Classical Age. While some notable scholars dissented from this basic view—particularly during the caliphate of al-Mamun, when Greek rationalism achieved popularity in some study circles—most did not. Those individual sages who did champion reason as equal to or higher than intellection had little impact on formal institutions of higher learning. Al-Ghazzali, the great intellectual and spiritual writer of the eleventh century, effectively defended traditional pietistic views; and from his time on, the perspective elaborated by al-Khayyam dominated Islamic scholarship and instruction.

The Centrality of Philosophy in the Higher Learning

With theosophy as a background, we can examine the advancement of knowledge in Islamdom more clearly during the Classical Age—the period of intellectual flowering in the Arabic language. For purposes of clarity and convenience, the categories discussed will appear under the subdivisions of knowledge familiar to the Western academic mind. One must understand, however, that true to the Islamic ideal of the unity of knowledge, progress in each discipline occurred simultaneously, with many a hakim (wise man or sage) making creative advances in most—if not all—areas of knowledge. While we label these divisions of knowledge according to specialized disciplines, Arabic nomenclature reflected a more global approach, categorizing knowledge into two major groupings: the religious sciences based on the Quran and its interpretation; and the foreign sciences grounded in Greek philosophy and science. The interrelatedness of all sciences and the hierarchical structure of knowledge imposed by Islamic theosophy occupied the intellectual energy of many Muslim scholars during the era. This was exemplified in the many epitomes authored during the ninth through eleventh centuries, and the preoccupation of scholars with the ordering of various sciences according to their related hierarchical value in the universe. Such approaches established priorities for the emerging curricula of institutions of higher learning, resulting in acceptance of the religious sciences as the proper course of formal studies in mosque schools and consignment of the foreign sciences such as Greek philosophy, medicine, mathematics, and the natural sciences to informal and private structures.

An appropriate beginning to this section recommends a closer look at the manner in which Islamic scholars adopted philosophy in its syncretized Neoplatonic and Aristotelian form and applied it to Islamic intellectual life. Of all the sciences absorbed from the Hellenistic intellectual tradition, philosophy proved the most divisive as well as catalytic during Islam's intellectual awakening. Greek logic and dialectic contributed an ambiguous weapon when wielded in the debate between reason and faith, particularly when a main tenet of Islam stated that no disjuncture could exist among the various spheres of the universe. For Islam, natural phenomena as observed by humans reflected the Divine Will and could not conflict with the Quran and sunnah. Basically, Islam already was endowed through revelation with a creed, an ethic, and an essential knowledge. The need for rational thought to illuminate human experience drew divergent opinion from scholars. Almost immediately upon the acceptance of rationalism by followers of Greek philosophy, its use exposed inconsistencies between revealed truth and individual observation of natural and social phenomena. This apparent inconsistency sparked a dialogue that questioned the validity of relying on such intellectual processes to attain truth.

Attempts to reconcile the religious doctrine of Islam with Greek thought dominated intellectual life during the Abbasid caliphate and affected all areas of knowledge. The controversy began after the introduction of Greek scientific and philosophical works during the mid–eighth century and became recognizable as a movement within Islamic intellectual circles through a group of scholars originating near Hira (a village between Basrah and Kufah in lower Mesopotamia) who became known as the Kadarites, from the Arabic *kadar*—meaning "divine power."[24]

Scholars in contact with Nestorian Christians at Hira were among the first Muslims stimulated to sharpen their own ability to debate the Islamic cause persuasively. The issue that attracted them to Greek philosophy was the concept of predestination—a major tenet of Islam, but one that an emerging group of learned men could not accept without some reservation. Drawing on Greek rationalistic methods, the scholars of Hira attempted to reconcile reason and faith.

The Kadarites drew the core of their doctrine from the Nestorian Christians, who espoused free will and individual responsibility for personal behavior.[25] They accepted limited free will with regard to behavioral choices and limited predestination to events outside human control such as natural phenomena. In this they questioned the un-bounded determinism and fatalism that lay at the heart of a Muslim's faith. The influence of the Kadarites expanded beyond Hira and even impressed some of the Umayyad caliphs, who accepted the new doctrine as their own. Both Muawiyah II (r. 683) and Yazid III (r. 744) converted to the Kadarite view.[26] Neither held power long enough, however, to impose their religious views on the main body of believers. Yazid, along with most of his family, was assasinated in the Abbasid rebellion.

Another more influential and enduring school of thought emerged at about the same time in Basrah. The Mutazilites, also under the influence of Nestorianism, accepted free will in much the same way as the Kadarites.[27] The Mutazalites became a larger sect within Islam and soon were influential throughout lower Mesopotamia—particularly in the new capital, Baghdad. They maintained that individuals could control their behavior and that the means of knowing how to act lay in a speculative approach to theology. Following Greek rationalism, they applied dialectic and logic in the pursuit of religious truth, and placed great emphasis on the use of dialectic to support faith instead of relying totally on traditional views of revelation. They also rejected literal interpretations of the anthropomorphic descriptions of God in the Quran—preferring to view them as symbolic and metaphorical statements only. Their most noted departure from traditional views, however, lay in their acceptance of the createdness of the Quran. They questioned the traditional assumption that the Quran was the uncreated and eternal Word of God. The Mutazilites adopted the Aristotelian dictum that nothing could be created from nothingness, and therefore concluded that God had created the Quran and transmitted it to the world.

The Mutazilites renounced any tenets of belief that limited the role of God in the area of divine justice. For them, it was a fundamental imperative that God had to reveal Himself to humankind. They accepted God in this role as the Judge who would mete out justice to each person. This implied that humankind possessed free will and could choose to act rightly or wrongly in any specific situation—an article of faith in conflict with the basic predeterminism of traditional Islam.

This acceptance of reason as a means of discerning right behavior required that individuals be educated to draw on human experience as well as rational processes. The Mutazilites borrowed Greek philosophical tools—dialectics and logic—in their method for deriving opinions and grasping truth. This promoted the study of exegesis and hermeneutics as means of understanding revelation and applying it in present circumstances. While accepting Mohammed as the final and authoritative messenger of God, the Mutazilites believed that God had revealed His creation to others throughout history. They particularly honored Greek science and philosophy as a means chosen by God to illuminate the reality of the cosmos.

The Caliph al-Mamun (r. 813–833) converted to Mutazilite teachings and wielded his royal power to establish a translation center and the Bait al-Hikmah (House of Wisdom)—the first private institution of higher learning founded by Muslims. The Bait al-Hikmah became the locus for the study and propagation of Mutazilite theology and philosophy, and attracted scholars from great distances to read Arabic translations of Greek manuscripts and to debate with others in all areas of science—religious, philosophical, mathematical, and natural. Scholars employed by the caliph strove to harmonize the tangible knowledge of the world with the intangible knowledge of the spheres of the universe beyond the terrestrial realm. During this exciting and stimulating period nurtured by the Bait al-Hikmah, learned men expanded the Arabic vocabulary to express more sophisticated scientific and philosophical concepts.

Three caliphs accepted the Mutazilite creed; and from 813 to 848 it became the authorized theology of Islam. However, since the Mutazilites did not tolerate traditional beliefs, they attempted to eradicate them through a series of persecutions. To uncover heretics, agents of the caliph posed this question: Do you believe that the Quran is created or uncreated? An answer of "uncreated" betrayed the individual as a heretic in the eyes of the Mutazilites and often brought punishment on the responder. In 848, the Caliph al-Mutawakkil reversed this course and persecuted the Mutazilites, banning their books and driving them from court and positions of power. In doing so, however, he also stemmed the rise of rationalism as a means of pursuing knowledge and truth for a great part of Islamdom. From his time forward, a more traditional creed would dominate Islamic society, with serious consequences for higher education and the advancement of knowledge in the sciences.

The Mutazilites did leave an impressive legacy—however—which endured after the persecutions and affected the intellectual awakening of Islam. This manifested itself in three major intellectual schools: *kalam, falsafah,* and "Asharism." Each emerged as a consequence of the tension among different philosophic views with regard to the use of rationalism in matters of faith.

Kalam defined a system of dialectics used in theological disputes— much as disputation became the methodology of Scholasticism in Western Europe. Kalam provided a means by which differing views on religious beliefs were resolved by stating propositions that would support or reject opposing views and analyzing them in a formal manner. Those who used Kalam—the *Mutakallim*—had little interest in the Greek philosophy for its own sake.[28] The Mutakallim did not adopt Greek ontological assumptions about the creation of the world or causation in physical phenomena. They remained firm in traditional beliefs in that regard. Followers of Kalam did not cite Greek philosophers as authorities in matters of ontology, but rather drew from Greek texts the methodology that was most useful for their purposes in defending the Islamic point of view and primarily in formulating legal opinions firmly couched in Islamic doctrine.[29] As in Western Scholasticism, Kalam was circumscribed by assumptions about faith that could not be challenged. Thus, Kalam could not be used to pursue knowledge of the supernatural spheres of the cosmos—that is, the Divine Will, the intelligibles, and angels. But it could facilitate understanding of the meaning of revelation and produce a more precise explanation of right action. In contrast, the quest for true knowledge occurred only when an individual purged himself of worldliness and opened his soul to discern God's Word, which would come through intuition and imagination.

Even with these restrictions, traditionalists viewed Kalam with great suspicion. According to Goldziher, *"Kalam* is a science which does not result in the reward of God even if one reaches truth through it, and on the other hand one may easily become a heretic if one falls into error through it."[30] This expressed the view of many traditionalists, who proclaimed—further—that reason was not necessary for grasping religious truth since such knowledge was already revealed in the Quran and hadith. Kalam as a method of investigation survived criticism and outright persecution, becoming firmly implanted in the law colleges as a means for deducing a legal decision (fatwa). It still persists as the major intellectual tool of jurisprudence in Islamic society and—as such—entered the curriculum of institutions of higher learning in both the mosque-colleges and the madrassahs.

The Mutazilites spawned another major intellectual heir: the Islamic school of Peripatetic philosophy named *falsafah*. While adopting dialectical methods from the Greeks, these philosophers *(faylasifah;* singular: *faylasuf)* differed in several important ways from the Mutakallim. The Faylasifah accepted Greek ontological assumptions, particularly those of Aristotelian origin, as long as they did not directly conflict with major tenets of Islam.[31] The Faylasifah adhered to a belief that no disagreement could exist between Islamic revelation and Greek philosophical thought. They expended much of their intellectual energy attempting to harmonize the two systems and to present an apologia for their Greek philosophical stance on religious issues. Unlike the Mutakallim, they scrutinized the Greek texts, interpreted them, and commented on them—always maintaining that their philosophical assumptions did not conflict with their Islamic faith. Falsafah placed greater reliance on syllogism and observation than did Kalam, with its emphasis on dialectics. The Faylasifah dealt with causality and, in large part, adopted a form of atomism somewhat similar to that of the Greek Neoplatonists.

Unlike Kalam, the philosophical method adopted speculation as a means of deriving new knowledge—not relegating it to the position of merely illuminating that already understood from the Quran and sunnah. Because the Faylasifah espoused the unity of all knowledge, they greatly valued information and methodology from the Greeks and devotedly pursued all the sciences of which they were aware—confident that they could not fall into error and, indeed, believing that they pursued God's work in trying to understand natural phenomena more fully.

The core of Peripatetic philosophy as practiced by Faylasifah came from the "Isagoge" and *Organon*, which they accepted as a single volume. Later, they absorbed all the Neoplatonist and Aristotelian texts available to them in Arabic. After the persecution of the Mutazilites by the caliphs in the latter part of the ninth century and the destruction of the Bait al-Hikmah (the House of Wisdom), instruction in Greek philosophy and sciences continued privately with older scholars passing on their knowledge and skills to younger men. The foreign sciences remained strangers to the mainstream institutions of higher learning—the mosques. Because of their faith in the unity of all knowledge, the Faylasifah did not pursue the Greek sciences exclusively, but embraced the religious sciences as well. They were true polymaths and explored philosophy and medicine (which they linked very closely together) as well as mathematics and the natural sciences. Because this instructional role was not formalized in Islamic society, those who pursued it generally earned their living in some other occupation or profession, such as physician, jurisconsult, or civil servant.

The high point of intellectual awakening in Islam manifests itself primarily in the achievements of the Faylasifah. Their writings constitute the rich cultural heritage that sparked the kindling of Western thought in the Middle Ages. Never very numerous, they at times suffered persecution and adversity, yet at more favorable times were accorded much respect. Caliphs and nobles valued them highly for their expertise and wisdom. In most instances, however, such honor and patronage stemmed from their practical knowledge of medicine, law, and diplomacy—rather than their intellectual and scientific accomplishments.

With the acceptance of more traditional views and a return to a more pietistic form of Islam in the eleventh century, Falsafah died out in Islam.[32] Certainly, the rule of the Seljuk sultans accelerated this. Like so many converts to a new religion, the sultans preferred and supported traditional and literal views of faith, rather than the more intellectual and liberal orientation offered by the philosophers. The sultans felt their strength would come through a traditional faith unchallenged by rationalism. Thus, they sought to secure conformity through the establishment of schools that espoused a simple faith.

The third intellectual derivative evolving from the Mutazilite movement arose as a mediating school of thought between Falsafah and traditional faith with its reliance on the Quran and hadith as the sole avenue to true knowledge. It took the name "Asharism," after al-Ashari of Baghdad (873–935)—an imam who had studied under the

Mutazilites and was identified as one of them.[33] At a later date al-Ashari rejected what he considered to be the extreme uses of rationalism in matters of faith; he longed for a return to the traditional, simple position on both causation and ontology. What is presently recognized as Asharism was more a product of his disciples and may not in fact represent fully the religious views of its assumed founder.

The Asharites absorbed into their movement a number of Mutazilite teachings. They took a middle road on free will and predestination and viewed the anthropomorphic texts of the Quran as true, but maintained that such descriptions could not be equated to human anatomy. They embraced Kalam as a valid methodology in clarifying religious belief, but not for establishing causality in natural phenomena. Indeed, Asharism employed the dialectical method to challenge Mutazilite views as well as the Aristotelian grounding of Falsafah. Followers of Asharism adopted a conceptual atomism of creation from the Mutazilites and believed that the natural workings of the universe reflect God's habit, but they also espoused that nothing occurs without God's willing it so. Thus, they espoused the momentary re-creation of the entire universe. Because of this, Asharite scholars felt little compulsion to investigate the natural sciences to any extent that might hint at a possible explanation of the causes of natural phenomena or human behavior.

As mentioned in Chapter 2, the Asharite view was championed by the Nizam al-Mulk, vizier under the Seljuk sultans during the middle of the eleventh century. To establish Asharism as the orthodox creed, the vizier founded a large number of madrassahs throughout the Middle East to propagate the Asharite position. These institutions greatly accelerated the establishment of Asharism as the basis of Sunni Islam, which comes down to the present as the most populous sect of the Muslim religion. Through the acceptance of Asharism, dialectic became an integral component in the study of the religious sciences, but the foreign sciences were disallowed as a proper part of the curriculum in Sunni institutions.

The interplay of these schools of thought—all descending from the Kadarite and Mutazilite movements—provides an excellent means of depicting the intellectual awakening of Islam. The next section will introduce the most noted hakims of this era—a fascinating group of polymaths by any standard and whose legacy of brilliant writings constitute, perhaps, the greatest gift of Islam to higher education in Europe and the Americas.

While the sages introduced in the following pages are known in the

West primarily for their works in philosophy, it must be remembered that—true to the tradition of the polymath in Hellenistic cultural and Islamic society—they contributed to all the known areas of knowledge. For them, the interrelatedness of all things created was a matter of faith as well as philosophy, and they would not think of pursuing one area of knowledge to the neglect of another. To do so would create a malformed human intellect. Certainly, some had greater talents than others and concentrated their efforts more heavily in their areas of strength, but as a group they chose to investigate all things and to practice the professions of law and medicine as well. Without specific patronage, scholars of this era could not expect to earn a living from their teaching alone. If they did have a patron—a wealthy merchant, nobleman, or perhaps the caliph himself—they were expected to perform certain civic duties, such as a legal advising, healing, and tutoring. In some instances they served as diplomats, adjudicating disputes between various provincial governors. This section will outline primarily their major contributions in philosophy; their achievements in other areas will appear in the appropriate sections to come.

The earliest hakim to gain recognition beyond Islamdom is al-Kindi (801–73), the "Philosopher of the Arabs"—so honored because he was of pure Arab blood. His father served for some time as the governor of Kufah, but al-Kindi was born in nearby Basrah and studied in both cities. Because these cities were situated near ancient sites of learning—including Jundi Shapur—they were acknowledged as the intellectual centers of southern Mesopotamia. This area came under the strong influence of Nestorianism—whose advocates were not only tolerated by their Islamic overlords, but recognized by them as the best teachers of their day.

As a young man, al-Kindi moved to Baghdad; there his brilliance impressed the Caliph al-Mamun, who offered him a position in the court as part of a group of scholars and translators in residence at the Bait al-Hikmah. He would serve the court in this capacity not only under al-Mamun, but also al-Mutasim. Although al-Kindi knew some Greek, he relied primarily on the work of Hunain—that prolific translator of Neoplatonic commentaries of Greek philosophic and scientific works.

Al-Kindi founded Falsafah in Islam. His introduction to Greek works came through the Neoplatonic epitomes of both the Athenian and Alexandrian schools; however, he leaned more toward the Athenian school, which emphasized Platonism over Aristotelian thought. The *Fihrist* of ibn al-Nadim, the major bibliographer of this period, lists

some 240 manuscripts written by al-Kindi.[34] Few of these arrived in
the European world until quite recently, when the discovery of some
40 treatises in Istanbul suddenly came to light. Evidently, al-Kindi
expressed himself in all areas of knowledge, but gained particular note
for his essays and commentaries in philosophy. He fell into disfavor
during the caliphate of al-Mutawakkil, who persecuted the Mutazilite
sect. Al-Kindi—if not a Mutazilite himself—certainly adopted many of
their views and strongly supported their rationalistic approach to the
acquisition of knowledge. Dismissed from court, he died in relative
obscurity—having lived the last part of his life without the beloved
volumes of his personal library, which was destroyed in the persecutions.

Although certainly not the first Arab scholar to come under the
influence of the foreign sciences, al-Kindi did articulate the position of
Falsafah in a treatise on metaphysics:

> We should not be ashamed to acknowledge truth and to assimilate it from
> whatever source it comes to us, even if it is brought to us by former
> generations and foreign peoples. For him who seeks the truth, there is
> nothing of higher value than truth itself; it never cheapens or evades him
> who reaches for it, but ennobles and honors him.[35]

In commenting on the Greek philosophers and in the articulation of
his own positions, al-Kindi invented an Arabic vocabulary to express
concepts in philosophy and science. He himself states, "My principle
is first to record in complete quotation all that the ancients have said
on the subject; secondly, to complete what the ancients have not fully
expressed, and this according to the usage of our Arabic language, the
customs of our age, and our own ability."[36] In addition to expanding
the vocabulary by which later Faylasifah expressed their philosophic
views, al-Kindi is attributed with beginning the process of reconciling
faith and reason in Islam—a task that would occupy philosophers in
the Middle East and Moorish Spain for the next several centuries.

He spoke of two forms of knowledge: divine and human—the highest
form of the latter being philosophy. Although al-Kindi allowed that
divine knowledge was superior to human knowledge, he argued that
no conflict between the two could exist because they each reflected
different parts of one and the same universe. He took a faith-oriented
approach to ontology, rejecting the Aristotelian position that the universe was eternal. He espoused the traditional Islamic belief that the
Prophet "has divine knowledge through intuition, which is superior to
human reasoning and knowledge."[37]

Persuaded by Neoplatonist theories, al-Kindi had no difficulty in maintaining the primacy of divine knowledge over that derived from rational methods. Thus, he saw no inconsistency in believing in a universe created out of nothing and in the resurrection of the body, even though they could not be demonstrated through philosophical means. Though he placed the sciences on a lower level than philosophy in his herarchical structure, al-Kindi pursued Greek medicine, science, and mathemetics and introduced these into his general treatises on knowledge.

Al-Kindi's legacy to those who succeeded him included three main concepts: First, he presented a model of the philosopher-scientist still in communion with the basic tenets of Islamic religious faith; second, he valued and advanced the use of knowledge acquired from foreigners and blended it into the intellectual stream of Islam; and third, he formalized the methodology of Greek philosophy into Islamic intellectualism with his discussions on the use of syllogism, dialectic, and other rational approaches to the acquisition of knowledge.

The tradition of philosophy passed from al-Kindi to al-Farabi (870–950), a Turk from the province of Khorasan (which lies in present-day Turkmen S.S.R.). Born in the city of Farab on the banks of the Oxus River, al-Farabi grew up in the prosperous family of a general. He studied in both Harran and Baghdad, where he delighted in the study of logic. In Baghdad he became a disciple of Ibn-Yunus, a Nestorian Christian achowledged as the master of logic.[38] Al-Farabi assumed the mantle of his mentor when the latter died. While at Harran he completed his formal education, pursuing studies in all the philosophies, sciences, and religious sciences then known. He returned to Baghdad to continue the work of al-Kindi as the acknowledged head of the Baghdad circle of Peripatetic philosophy. For some 20 years, he taught and wrote in Baghdad, authoring some 70 known manuscripts. From Baghdad he moved to Aleppo as teacher and consultant to the provincial court and died there in 950.

Al-Farabi's texts exemplify the manner in which Islamic intellectuals drew from both Aristotle and Plato according to their needs, and how the views of the particular Greek philosophers fit into their own conception of metaphysics. Al-Farabi had a greater advantage than al-Kindi because the translations of Greek classical works available to him had been skillfully crafted by Hunain's son Ishaq and his friend Bishr Matta—both more talented than previous translators, and both more concerned with contextual translations of Aristotelian philosophy.

More than any other philosopher-scientist, al-Farabi attempted to establish an Islamic natural theology with Kalam—that is, scholastic methodology—at its core.[39] Al-Farabi's studies led him to conclude that the method of the philosophers provided the only valid interpretation of Islam; and he stated that rational faculties were humankind's greatest talent and that knowledge gained from them was superior to prophecy, since he considered the latter to be an innate faculty of the soul and not the result of supernatural powers. He proclaimed that the soul as the principle of life, reached its perfection in reason and disciplined thinking. He placed imagination as intermediate between perception and reason, and felt that it could be activated on its own—not reliant on the senses, nor acted on by superhuman powers. It was the harmonious relationship between the active intellect and imagination that created prophetic powers. He espoused that imagination was subordinate to reason, and prophecy was subordinate to philosophy.

Al-Farabi delighted in Aristotelian logic, ethics, and metaphysics—on which he wrote an exemplary commentary that provided a foundation for his successors (particularly Ibn-Sina). Al-Farabi wrote the definitive Arabic work on logic, and in so doing developed a vocabulary that continues to the present day. Concerned by the instability he saw in the social order during his later years, he attempted to instruct rulers on the nature of the ideal state and the philosopher-king. He drew heavily on Platonist texts in this regard, using as his authority the *Republic* and the *Laws*. As such, al-Farabi was the founder of political philosophy in Islam, referring to Plato as the "Imam of the Philosophers." According to Nasr, al-Farabi "sought to identify the figure of the philosopher-king of Plato with the prophet and lawgiver of the Abrahamic tradition and described the perfect state in which a single revealed law would reign supreme over the world."[40] The titles of several of his treatises in this area exemplify his desire to bring order and justice to Islamic society. These include "Treatise on the Opinions of the Citizens," "On the Ideal State," "On Attaining Happiness," and "On the Government of the City State."

Al-Farabi made a great effort to rationalize the positions of Plato and Aristotle. Like many of his colleagues, he considered the writings of both to be divinely inspired, and thus never in contradiction to each other. One of al-Farabi's most noted manuscripts, *The Divine Plato and Aristotle,* demonstrated this point by recording a "debate" between the two giants of Greek intellectual history.

Al-Farabi gained special fame with his interest in music. In addition to being an excellent performer, he wrote numerous works on musical theory. *The Grand Book of Music*—the most noted—was considered the definitive work on the subject in both the medieval East and West.[41] In his musical theories, he drew heavily from Pythagorean principles, which stressed harmony and numerical symbolism. Despite his absorption with Greek philosophers, al-Farabi remained loyal to his religious background and faith. He lived the life of a Sufi, eschewing pretension and worldly wealth; he led a simple ascetic life and always tried to teach his disciples and students in a natural setting, such as along the riverbanks. He wrote a book on wisdom which, even though it was a basic treatment of metaphysics with Greek philosophic roots, also defined the steps in the process of gnosis—that is, the method by which individuals through ascetic living and spiritual purgation could ascend the various spheres of the universe and reach communion with God. The book was accepted as authoritative by the Illuminationist school and became a part of its curriculum in religious sciences; it is still taught in religious schools to this day. Unlike others more transcendent in their religious views, al-Farabi—because of his interest in the Platonic ideal state—focused his religious interests on social and political aspects of Islam. He also spoke of God in the Aristotelian vocabulary of "First Cause" and not as al-Kindi had done, as "the One and the True."

Al-Farabi was recognized as the greatest logician of his day by scholars and students across the empire. In his attempt to introduce the foreign sciences into Islamic intellectual life, he was among the first to compose an integrated curriculum of all the sciences—both foreign and religious—that depicted the hierarchical structure of the universe and affirmed the distinction between human and divine knowledge.[42] In his *Enumeration of the Sciences,* al-Farabi listed the foreign sciences either as propaedeutic studies or as a lesser category of physics. As previously noted, these studies were not part of the formal curriculum in higher education. His curriculum, however, did have an impact on the philosophers who—in their private study and circles— followed it and then offered variations. His commentaries on both Platonic and Aristotelian works became the standard corpus on Greek philosophy during his day and provided the groundwork for those who came later—particularly, Ibn-Sina and Ibn-Rushd.

One of the towering intellectual figures of all time—Ibn-Sina (980–1037)—was known in medieval Europe as Avicenna. Although awarded the title "Prince of Physicians" by later generations, he was more than a medical practitioner, for his writings focused on healing both the body and the soul. He was born near Bukhara (in present-day Uzbek

S.S.R., not far from the town of Farab). His father was a wealthy man, and Ibn-Sina grew up in a house that honored learning and where a circle of scholars gathered to discuss intellectual issues. A brilliant student, he acknowledged that, by the age of 18, he had mastered all of the known sciences and philosophies and then proceeded to construct his own positions in all areas of knowledge.[43] He was a favorite of the provincial ruler and became a member of the court, where he served as both physician and diplomat. His most productive years were spent at Isfahan, Rayy, and Hamadan (all in present-day Iran). A man of boundless energy, he wrote some 250 treatises in all matters of philosophy and science. He is most known in the West for two great works: *Kitab al-Shifa (The Book of Healing),* the longest encyclopedia of knowledge ever authored by a single person; and *Qanun fi al-Tibb (The Canon on Medicine). Kitab al-Shifa* manifests the high point of Islamic Peripatetic philosophy, covering all of Aristotle's division of philosophy—natural, moral, mental, and metaphysics. Ibn-Sina, especially noted for his work in cosmology, envisioned a universe based on Greek philosophy but consonant with Islamic revelation. His second great tome, *Qanun fi al-Tibb,* contains more than 1 million words and stands even today as the epitome of Islamic science. In its Latin version, it became the main textbook for medical education into the Renaissance.

Ibn-Sina's knowledge of Greek philosophy came entirely from Arabic manuscripts; he did not read Greek nor have access to the earlier translations from the Hellenistic world, and relied on commentaries of such philosophers as al-Kindi and al-Farabi. Ibn-Sina is the paragon of the Islamic hakim. His catholic interests compelled him to pursue all aspects of knowledge. His genius was such that he could combine the philosophical tenets of the Peripatetic school and the presentation of his religious views into gnostic treatises—the source of many Illuminationist texts that would endure into the following centuries. Ibn-Sina differed from his predecessors in his views on the role of prophecy. Unlike al-Farabi, he saw it as higher than reason and philosophic methods, and not linked to imagination but—rather—attached to active intellect.[44] In his cosmology, Ibn-Sina depicted the descent of God's creation through ten spheres of intelligences before reaching man and the terrestrial world.[45] The intelligences at each level related to the Islamic belief in supernatural beings that could be called angels and that existed at the various levels between God and man, and through whom man receives enlightenment and comes to know objects of the intangible spheres of the universe. The tenth intelligence comprised the interface with man's active intelligence and allowed him to attain true knowledge and become a prophet—that is, a carrier of God's message.

Ibn-Sina's ontology drew on Aristotelian principles for the most part, but went beyond them to rationalize the Greek views with Islamic revelation and faith. He accepted the Aristotelian concepts of essence and existence as essential parts of an object, but he went further and introduced as parts of the elements of being the impossible, the possible, and the necessary—a triad later adopted by Thomas Aquinas in his approach to ontological distinctions in objects. These concepts used by both Ibn-Sina and Aquinas provided the basis for their proof of the existence of God as the "necessary being" who—as stated by Nasr—"could not be since his essence and being are the same; being is his essence and his essence, being."[46] The entire hierarchical structure of the universe—argued Ibn-Sina—depended on the balance of these elements being contained in each object. In the terrestrial level of the cosmos, humans enjoyed the most favorable combination, allowing them to know God—albeit in a limited way—and to control much of their behavior—a gift of free will—both through rational and intellectual processes.

Ibn-Sina's theories on learning relied heavily on Aristotelian premises and were widely accepted by philosophers in both Europe and Islamdom. They entered Medieval Europe and greatly influenced the rise of Scholasticism. The process of knowing—according to Ibn-Sina—begins with the five external senses, which reach their fullness in humankind and distinguish it from other animals. In addition to these senses, humans embody two faculties by the presence of the human soul—these being practical and theoretical intellect. The practical intellect governs bodily movements, while the theoretical intellect governs the higher orders of reasoning and thought processes within the soul. Ibn-Sina categorized this faculty into four distinct processes: (1) the potential to acquire knowledge, which he referred to as the "material intellect"; (2) the ability to use acquired knowledge, or the "habit intellect"; (3) the ability to generate intellectual activity, the "activating intellect"; and (4) the ability to internalize knowledge of the intelligible world, the "adoptive intellect." All were considered by him to be present in the basic nature of humankind. On a higher order altogether lies the active intellect—a special faculty of the soul attainable through union with the intelligence, which allows knowledge to enter the soul through illumination (as in the case of prophets). In Islamic terms, the tenth intelligence in the case of Mohammed would be identified with the Archangel Gabriel. In Ibn-Sina's schema, only a few individuals ever attain the ability to use the active intellect and thus acquire illumination. This exalted state cannot be achieved through the use of the reasoning process, but rather through the practice of asceticism. Such a view challenged Ibn-Sina to explore and write on the process of gnosis, in addition to his many philosophical and scientific works.

Ibn-Sina had a powerful impact on both the East and the West. Islamic philosophers after him could not ignore or reject his teachings outright. His works mark the standard by which others compared their own positions. His nonphilosophic works remain as standard texts in the curriculum of many Islamic schools to the present time. His philosophic works were consigned to obscurity with the return of a traditional Islamic view based on Asharism, which in the eleventh century became the guiding principle of higher education as manifested in the mosque schools and other formal institutions of higher learning.

As Ibn-Sina's influence waned in the East, however, it grew in Medieval Europe through the translations of his works that entered Europe primarily through Moorish Spain, but also through Sicily. His commentaries on Aristotle—while at first rejected at the University of Paris—soon became a standard text in the medieval study of philosophy, and remained so for a number of centuries. Ibn-Sina had a dramatic impact on Scholasticism, and particularly on Thomas Aquinas. While his works on cosmology and gnostic writing never entered the Western world, his manuscripts on rationality, scholastic methodology, and science went through numerous publications until the Renaissance—particularly affecting the thinking of Albertus Magnus, Roger Bacon, Thomas Aquinas, Robert Grosseteste, and Duns Scotus.

The scholar who more than anyone else ended the debate between faith and reason in Islam and whose views became the standard treatment on the subject was al-Ghazzali (1058–1111)[47] Not known particularly as a scientist or a philosopher but primarily as a theologian and mystic, his effect on the intellectual life of classical Islam was monumental. His treatises defined the place of reason in Islamic intellectual life and the role of foreign sciences in the curriculum of higher education.[48] After him, formal education diverged from the trunk of Greek philosophy and science, passing that particular tradition onto Western Europe. Al-Ghazzali's writings and example solidified the religious sciences as the main body of studies for those seeking higher education, and ended the influence of Falsafah on the curriculum in formal schools. Henceforth, only a few scholars pursued the foreign sciences—and those only in private—with a resulting loss of scientific advancement in Islamic culture.

Al-Ghazzali—perhaps the greatest Muslim theologian[49]—was born in Tus, a small town in northeast Iran in the province of Khorasan. Drawn to Sufism, he traveled to Nishapur to study under a famous Islamic theologian, al-Juwaini. The Vizier Nizam al-Mulk offered him the head teaching position in his newly founded madrassah, the Niza-miya—the most noted institution of higher learning in Baghdad and perhaps all the Islamic world in the eleventh century.

While residing in Baghdad, al-Ghazzali was confronted by scholars well versed in the foreign sciences and philosophy—areas of knowledge that he could not rationalize with his basic faith. A conscientious scholar, he could not ignore this information but was unable to accommodate his own faith to it. Al-Ghazzali suffered a deep spiritual crisis that had obvious psychological effects on his personality. He gave up his position at the Nizamiya and retired to a life of prayer and ascetic living—a retreat from the world during which he attempted to resolve his own belief system. He returned from that adventure and took on himself the role of renouncing foreign philosophy and science where he could not rationalize them with revealed Islamic tenets.[50] His most noted manuscripts on this matter—*The Incoherence of the Philosophers* and *The Revivication of the Religious Sciences*—employed the methods of logic and dialectic derived from the Greeks to attack the positions of the philosophers. Through his writings and his example, he sanctified and gained legitimacy for the teaching of Sufism in the curriculum of formal institutions of higher learning.

Al-Ghazzali forcefully argued against the philosopher's notion of causation in natural phenomena, adopting the Asharite posture that all occurrences in heaven and earth are the manifestation of the Will of God only, and that the behavior of each object is individually enacted by Divine Will.[51] Further, any observed relationship between the behavior of two objects is coincidental and not explanatory. This position had a devastating effect on the pursuit of scientific explanations of natural phenomena. Its wide acceptance curtailed further advances in the scientific world—which depended on experimentation for verification—and seriously questioned the use of observation when its intent was to show causation between two natural events. As Sayili has stated, "But for al-Ashari and al-Ghazzali the Arabs might have been a nation of Galileos, Keplers, and Newtons."[52] While warning that the sciences had only a restricted role to play in understanding reality, al-Ghazzali allowed that mathematics was important in calculations and for explaining the movement of the heavenly bodies; but he cautioned that faith in mathematics might lead to greater acceptance of rational proofs of natural phenomena and could lead to heretical views on causation.

Al-Ghazzali accepted logic as a method of demonstration through which statements were categorized and objects could be placed in hierarchical order. He held a neutral attitude toward its employment in more practical everyday matters, but argued that it could not be used to prove or disprove matters of revelation or faith since such information comes through intuition and imagination, which lay beyond the reach of reasoning. With regard to the natural sciences, he relegated their value to description and dismissed their validity in offering explanations of causality.

After al-Ghazzali, Peripatetic philosophy survived only to a limited degree in Islam, primarily in Shiite schools. Sunni Islam—with its strong adherence to Asharite views—rejected it. For the most part, the foreign sciences and philosophy disappeared from formal instruction, and those who engaged in them—even in private—were suspect. These studies did, however, emerge in al-Andalus, particularly in the works of Islam's greatest commentator on Aristotle, Ibn-Rushd—known in Europe as Averroës.

The purest Aristotelian in Islam and the most recognized Islamic philosopher in the West, Ibn-Rushd (1126–1198) was born in Cordova of an influential family of jurists and religious scholars. A true polymath, he studied law and medicine as well as philosophy and served the caliph as both judge and physician for most of his life. He drew his scholastic roots from the Andalusian school of philosophy supported by the Umayyad caliph Muawiyah II. It was rooted in Kadarite beliefs, and relied more on the views of al-Farabi than those of Ibn-Sina and basically opposed the anti-intellectual stance of al-Ghazzali. This philosophical stance can be attributed in part to the distance that lay between the Iberian peninsula and the Middle East and the weakened influence of Asharism on religious life in Moorish Spain.

Ibn-Rushd's interest in philosophy drew him not only to Peripatetic texts, but also to the original translations of Aristotle's works now more readily available. Thus, he did not rely totally on the commentaries of al-Farabi or Ibn-Sina for his understanding of Greek philosophy.[53] He produced some 38 volumes in addition to numerous shorter treatises, covering all of Aristotle's works known to him. He also wrote on astronomy, physics, and medicine and offered a major refutation of al-Ghazzali's work *The Incoherence of Philosophy*. Ibn-Rushd entitled his own work *The Incoherence of the Incoherence*. When the philosophical manuscripts of Ibn-Rushd were first introduced in Paris, they drew charges of heresy because of their rationalistic and allegedly antireligious biases. The derogatory term "Averroism" became attached to his interpretation of Aristotle as echoed by enthusiastic students and faculty who championed them intemperately. In time, however, the philosophy faculty and church officials accepted them as a means to substantiate Christian doctrine through logical arguments. Along with translations of Ibn-Sina's works on Aristotelian thought, those of Ibn-Rushd became standard resources—in both Latin and Hebrew translations—for the study of philosophy in Paris and other medieval universities in the West.[54]

The main goal of Ibn-Rushd's intellectual life was to harmonize philosophy and religion. He espoused that both reason and revelation are sources of knowledge and firmly believed that philosophy offers the best means to resolve inconsistencies in Islamic theology. He adhered to Aristotle's ontological beliefs, with the exception of the relationship of God to the universe—in which case he acceded to Islamic tradition. He defended Aristotle's position on causation and the importance of purpose and function in defining existence: To do otherwise would deny the importance of observation and reason. Ibn-Rushd criticized Ibn-Sina's approach to philosophy because he thought it yielded too much of a concession to the Asharite view. As such, Ibn-Rushd gave a forceful refutation of al-Ghazzali's stand on the role of philosophy as being irrational and, therefore, not acceptable.[55]

With the banishment of Ibn-Rushd and the burning of his books (by order of the Emir Abu Yusuf Yaqub al-Mansur) at Seville in 1194, Falsafah as an active school of thought disappeared from Islam. Greek rational methods survived only in Kalam, as a means to support orthodox religious views. From then on Hellenistic intellectualism would pass to Christian Europe and determine the course of higher education and the evolution of knowledge in a distinctly different fashion from that of Islamic countries in North Africa and the Middle East.

Notes

1. Mehdi Nakosteen, *History of Islamic Origins of Western Education* (Boulder: University of Colorado Press, 1964), 13–35.

2. F. E. Peters, "The Origins of Islamic Platonism: The School Tradition," in *Islamic Philosophical Theology* (Albany: SUNY Press, 1979), 14–17.

3. Will Durant, *The Age of Faith,* The Story of Civilization Series, no. 4 (New York: Simon and Schuster, 1950), 123.

4. F. E. Peters, *Aristotle and the Arabs* (New York: New York University Press, 1968), 3–4.

5. Richard Waltzer, *Greek into Arabic* (Oxford: Bruno Cassirer, 1962), 6.

6. Peters, "The Origins," 25–26.

7. Edward T. Withington, *Medical History* (London: Holland Press, 1964), 102.

8. Donald Campbell, *Arabic Medicine* (London: Kegan, Trench, 1926), 6–7.

9. Fielding H. Garrison, *An Introduction to the History of Medicine,* 3rd ed. (Philadelphia: W.B. Saunders, 1924), 103ff.

10. Ali Abdullah Al-Daffa, *The Muslim Contribution to Mathematics* (London: Croom Helm, 1978), 33.

11. Daniel J. Boorstin, *The Discoverers* (New York: Random House, 1983), 11; Seyyed Hossein Nasr, *Islamic Science,* World of Islam Festival Publishing (Westerham, Kent: Westerham Press, 1976), 78.

12. Nasr, *Islamic Science,* 36.

13. Boorstin, *Discoverers,* 79.

14. Gerald R. Hawting, *The First Dynasty of Islam* (Carbondale and Edwardsville: Southern Illinois University Press, 1987), 11–18.

15. Ignaz Goldziher, *Mohammed and Islam* (New Haven: Yale University Press, 1917), 53.

16. Peters, *Aristotle and Arabs,* 64.

17. Franz Rosenthal, *The Classical Heritage of Islam* (Berkeley: University of California Press, 1965), 17.

18. Peters, *Aristotle and Arabs,* 60.

19. Philip K. Hitti, *History of the Arabs* (London: Macmillan, 1956), 313.

20. Ibid., 315.

21. For a more complete discussion of this theme, see Nasr, *Islamic Science,* 5ff, and *Science and Civilization in Islam* (New York: New American Library, 1968), 21ff.

22. Nasr, *Science and Civilization in Islam,* 93–94.

23. Ibid., 33–34.

24. Goldziher, *Mohammed and Islam,* 100–101.

25. Morris S. Seale, *Muslim Theology* (London: Luzac, 1964), 6–7 and 26.

26. Hitti, *History of Arabs,* 245.

27. Seale, *Muslim Theology,* 43–86.

28. Marshall G. S. Hodgson, *The Venture of Islam,* vol. 1 (Chicago: University of Chicago Press, 1974), 437ff.

29. Peters, *Aristotle and Arabs,* xxi.

30. Goldziher, *Mohammed and Islam,* 136.

31. Peters, *Aristotle and Arabs,* 144.

32. Nasr, *Science and Civilization in Islam,* 294.

33. Goldziher, *Mohammed and Islam,* 127.

34. Seyyed Hassein Nasr, *Three Muslim Scholars* (Cambridge, Mass.: Harvard University Press, 1964), 10.

35. Ibid., 11.

36. Waltzer, *Greek into Arabic,* 13.

37. Ibid., 14.

38. Nasr, *Three Muslim Scholars,* 14.

39. Waltzer, *Greek into Arabic,* 19–22.

40. Nasr, *Three Muslim Scholars,* 15.

41. Ibid., 15.

42. Nasr, *Science and Civilization in Islam,* 60–62.

43. *The Life of Ibn Sina,* critical ed. and annotated trans. William E. Gohlman (Albany: SUNY Press, 1974).

44. Waltzer, *Greek into Arabic, 25.*

45. Nasr, *Three Muslim Scholars,* 29.

46. Ibid., 27.

47. W. M. Watt, *Islamic Philosophy and Theology* (Edinburgh: Edinburgh University Press, 1962), 114–24.

48. Nasr, *Science and Civilization in Islam,* 307–12.

49. Hitti, *History of Arabs,* 431; Watt, *Islamic Philosophy,* 114.

50. J. R. Hayes, ed., *The Genius of Arab Civilization* (Cambridge, Mass.: MIT Press, 1983), 60.

51. See al-Ghazzali, "Deliverance from Error," trans. W. M. Watt in *The Faith and Practice of Al-Ghazali* (London: George Allen and Unwin, 1953), 30–36; Nasr, *Science and Civilization in Islam,* 35 and 311–12.

52. Aydin Mehmed Sayili, "Islam and the Rise of the Seventeenth Century Science," Ankara, Turkey, *Bulletin* 22, 87 (July 1958): 353.

53. Peters, *Aristotle and Arabs,* 216–18.

54. Waltzer, *Greek into Arabic,* 26–27.

55. Ibid., 27.

4

The Flowering of Islamic Science

He has subjected to you what the heavens and the earth contain; all is
from Him. Surely there are signs in this for thinking men.

The Quran 45:12

Until recent decades, the majority of Western writers viewed the
Islamic contribution to science primarily as one that served as a bridge
between the attainments of the Greeks with those of Medieval Europe.[1]
Despite recent efforts on the part of scholars from Islamic countries to
challenge that position, debate still continues over the quality and
volume of contributions during this period.[2] In recent years—certainly
since the end of World War II—Muslim scholars have made significant
advances in understanding the growth of science during the Classical
Age of Islam by translating and preparing commentaries on a great
number of manuscripts from that early period. In particular, those
trained in the Western tradition of research have received greater
credibility as experts in the field of Middle Eastern studies in non-
Islamic countries. Nasr argues persuasively that Arabic-speaking
scientists from the earlier period did not simply transmit Hellenistic
science to Medieval Europe but expanded that body of knowledge
before it entered the Christian West in Latin translations.[3] More
traditional Western scholars have tended to negate the creativity of
scholars of this era, commenting that such men added very little depth
to the level of science already generated in the later Hellenistic period.

The disagreements between Islamic and Western scholars have roots
in national and ethnic pride: Each is bound by a different perspective

when evaluating contributions of that transitional stage in the long history of science. Western scholars judge the discoveries of that time in light of what occurred later, during and following the Renaissance of Western Europe. Because of the sequential and utilitarian nature of scientific discovery, the state of the art in any particular scientific endeavor tends to erode interest in all that has preceded it, or—as some have judged—the value of any scientific discovery is measured by the number of previous discoveries it renders obsolete. Certainly, if this is one's perspective, much of what developed in the classical ages of both the Greek and Islamic cultures is no longer functional or relevant to modern science and remains of interest primarily to historians.

This chapter will focus on the advancement of scientific knowledge as it relates to the higher learning of the classical period of Islam—discussing the influence of its contributions on higher educational institutions and curriculum not only in classical Islam, but in Medieval Europe as well. Western readers of scientific studies from this early period tend to lament the fact that Islamic scholars and scientists did not penetrate further in unveiling the mysteries of the physical world, given the distinguished heritage of Greek knowledge available to them through the translation of Greek manuscripts into Arabic. In addition, they had benefited from the great body of knowledge compiled at Jundi Shapur—which combined elements of Oriental astronomy, mathematics, medicine, and natural science. The discoveries of Arabic-speaking scholars and scientists of this age must be viewed in context and judged accordingly. Rather than criticizing them for what they failed to do, they deserve praise for what they did accomplish, especially considering the parameters placed around scientific inquiry by the prevailing faith system of Islam. One might argue that Western scholars during the Middle Ages did even less with their Greek heritage.

In many ways, Medieval Europe resembled Islamdom during its classical period. During both eras, the metaphysics of Greek philosophy dominated intellectual life and retarded scientific observation and experimentation. In the case of Islam, however, this was a more gradual process—allowing for several centuries of openness and freedom, and facilitating a fruitful period of advancement in knowledge about the physical world. The brilliance of intellectuals in Islamic lands appears no less dim than that of scholars of any age. Ample evidence exists that hakims such as Ibn-Sina and Ibn-Rushd rank among the greatest intellects of any age or period. As the basic religious and metaphysical truths of his environment confined Thomas Aquinas, so too did the values of their theocentric society circumscribe Islamic scholars.

In the context of higher education, the present study interests itself with the growth of knowledge and—particularly in this section on scientific advances—with how that knowledge entered or was excluded from the curricula of higher educational institutions. The events offer a fascinating case study of how and why specific decisions were made regarding curriculum in a society that was maturing in many aspects of knowledge while attempting to harmonize its faith in a predetermined cosmos with natural phenomena and secular values—in what anthropologists term the process of "enculturation."

People who deal with the elements and evolution of curricula generally agree that three major factors determine the curriculum of any school system: societal values, the needs and desires of learners, and the status and dictates of a subject matter (now referred to as a "discipline"). Chapter 3 discussed the role of philosophy and theology in Islamic education, and defined its major values for learning. During the period that learned men attempted to define and describe the theosophy of Islam, those same individuals encountered scientific knowledge from prior cultures and sought to incorporate it into the Islamic cosmic overview. The tenets of Islam had not at that time been codified, and a spirit of genuine exploration prevailed as the Quranic revelation was made more understandable and manifest over a period of several centuries.

Islamic Perspectives on Science

Arab scientific knowledge was scant and based primarily on mythology. Inquisitive men, newly converted to Islam, were impressed—even fascinated—by what they found in the centuries-old knowledge that suddenly came into their scope of awareness. They immediately perceived the usefulness that knowledge would hold for them—particularly the mandate of the new religion to probe the universe and discover the reality of God's creation. The Quran did not forbid exploration of the natural world; in fact it encouraged such activity, since nothing but good could result from the proper use of knowledge and reason. Thus, early scholars openly embraced the new knowledge and incorporated it into their intellectual framework.

Following in the tradition of the Greek polymaths, scholars in Islamic territories also undertook the study of all areas of knowledge.

Their interpretation of the Quranic edict to understand the universe propelled them in the search. After absorbing the translated writings of both the Greek and Persian world, Islamic scholars exercised much freedom in their studies. This concept of intellectual freedom has come to us through the German university with its promotion of *lehrfreiheit* (freedom to teach) and *lernfreiheit* (freedom to learn), which have evolved into the modern conception of academic freedom. As in modern societies, the Islamic community honored the pursuit of knowledge and accorded those who engaged in it the status of a profession—one that provided an avenue of upward economic and social mobility for many not born to higher status. The brightest minds in Islam were drawn to intellectual pursuits—a position not only honored in Islamic society, but one of power and influence with rulers.

Initially the Islamic attitude toward the relationship of knowledge and truth lacked clear definition, yet some basic premises about the role of knowledge emerged very early in the minds of learned men, as interpreted from the Quran and hadith.These attitudes toward knowledge clearly set the parameters under which investigation of worldly matters could take place. They set the direction for scholarly endeavors and greatly influenced later decisions as to what kinds of information and cognitive skills would be transmitted to future generations through the structured system of higher education. The most basic tenets guiding Islamic scientific thought proclaimed that the Quran contained all truth and knowledge: First, the principles of all scientific knowledge—but not the details—are found in the Quran; and second, the Quran and hadith define the environment and values inherent in the cultivation of the sciences.[4] These two basic premises underscore the Islamic viewpoint that all knowledge confirms the Divine Logos (Cosmic Mind) and ultimately God. Thus, religious belief—the true knowledge of God and the supernatural—always supersedes specific knowledge about objects of the terrestrial world.

Throughout the cosmos created by God, the unity of knowledge prevails: that is, all objects—whether material or supernatural—interconnect in a grand design. Their relationship is prescribed in hierarchical fashion by the Divine Will. Knowledge about any object in the world ought to—by its association with other objects in the terrestrial world and in the supernatural world—lead to the Divine Logos and God. One's engagement in the pursuit of knowledge, then, is really the search for the nature of God and the ascent of an individual's soul—which incorporates intellect—toward the Divine Essence. Since all objects interrelate and eventually lead to an understanding of the

Divine Logos and of God, the challenge to the individual is to perceive knowledge in a universal way; that is, one's pursuit should engage an inquiry of all intelligible objects, natural and supernatural. To understand an object without realizing its interrelatedness to other objects in the cosmos leads to futility or, worse yet, idolatry—that is, the reverence of the object for its own sake and not for its relationship in the ascending hierarchy of objects to the Divine.

In reference to our ability to understand the Divine Logos and the cosmos, the Quran enjoins one to pursue knowledge as a means of salvation. God endowed humans with intellect by which we can use our senses and reasoning to discover more about the natural and supernatural worlds. While the senses provide the means for expanding one's knowledge of the terrestrial world, the intellect endows an individual with power to analyze the essence of material objects, which includes their relationship to supernatural objects and the Divine Will. As discussed in previous passages on philosophy, traditional Islamic belief maintained that intuition defined the capacity in human intellect that allowed one to cooperate with God's mystical being and thus learn more about the supernatural world, facilitating ascent to a higher sphere and to an understanding of the Divine Will. The purpose of knowledge is to lead man to God and to further harmony within the cosmos.

Given these predilections and background, how did scientific intellectualism evolve during the classical period of Islamic society? The first task of Muslim scholars was to rationalize and justify the new knowledge encountered in the conquered lands with their Islamic faith. Because Greek natural science based on Aristotelian and Neoplatonic views had common roots with Middle Eastern notions about the physical world, this proved not difficult. The perception of the cosmos as part spiritual and part material—deeply ingrained in Neoplatonic philosophy—complements the Quranic vision of the cosmic world. Also, the Quran encouraged use of rationalism—the hallmark of Greek thought—and mandated that all should explore creation to understand more fully how its interrelated parts manifest the harmonious nature of God. Since the Quran and hadith, as understood in this earlier period, assigned no proscriptions against scientific knowledge, Islamic scholars—stimulated by what they learned from other cultures—embraced the knowledge they found useful and in harmony with their own world view.

Intellectualism had a long tradition in Persian lands, going back to Hellenistic times, and in places—notably Jundi Shapur—the collected knowledge of both the Orient and Greece were honored and disseminated. Initially, Persian scholars—neither repressed nor persecuted by their Arab conquerors—would lead the Islamic world in the pursuit of knowledge. The world view of the Islamic revelation imposed on them did not contradict their own experience, nor did it forbid them from pursuing their interests. Learning flourished in the fertile soil of Persia, and here primarily the fruits of the Islamic intellectual renaissance ripened and spread throughout other regions of Islamdom and later into Western Europe.

In their encounter with knowledge from both Oriental and Greek sources, Muslims sought only information useful to them—not adopting those aspects of the Greek and Oriental intellectual and cultural tradition that conflicted with Islamic revelation or that did not emphasize the morality and values dictated by the Quran and hadith. Scientific knowledge as encountered in upper Mesopotamia and Jundi Shapur seemed to them unbiased, and they adopted it readily. In mathematics, they recognized a key to understanding the symbolism of the physical world. In both the Hellenistic and Oriental traditions, numbers incorporated both qualitative and quantitative meaning. Learned men envisioned in mathematical systems an analogical method to understanding the supernatural world through the symbolism of numbers. The newly acquired mathematics provided Islam a means of measuring, defining a calendar, and dividing inheritances. It gave Arabs the means to improve on their own rudimentary system of counting and fostered a sophisticated geometric approach to astrology.

Astronomy provided a functional means of noting the movement of heavenly bodies—not only to denote time, but also to understand worldly events. Those who converted to Islam continued the Middle Eastern presumption that the heavenly bodies—moved by divine power—could reveal messages to humankind, if only one could interpret them. In a more practical manner, the study of astronomy provided the means for Muslims to establish a religious calendar as dictated by the Quran, and to set the time for the required prayers of the Islamic liturgical cycle and find the direction to Mecca for daily prayers and pilgrimages. Mathematics and astronomy allowed Muslims to transcend the terrestrial world and investigate the celestial bodies of the upper cosmos, which they considered to be possessed of mystical powers.

The Hellenistic and Oriental methods of healing encountered by the earlier Arabic conquerors surpassed their simple tribal remedies. Islamic polymaths quickly assimilated Greek perspectives of the healing arts and combined this with the pharmacology of the Middle East and Orient. In practicing the role of physician, Islamic polymaths did not assume that they brought about a cure; only God could accomplish that. The Quran did state, however, that a cure for every disease existed; and it empowered humans to cooperate with God in affecting the return of an afflicted person to a state of health. The healing arts were allied closely to all other sciences; the study of medicine involved engaging all areas of knowledge. Here again, the Islamic view acknowledged both material and spiritual dimensions to each object created by God. The true scientist pursued not only the quantifiable characteristics of any object, but its qualitative aspects as well; both were equally important for a full understanding of the created universe and a spiritual communion with the Divine Will.

On a more technical level, exploration of natural phenomena yielded Islamic scholars important information about metallurgy, architecture, engineering, animal husbandry, and agriculture. In the Islamic framework, all these studies were considered good and worth pursuing, because they benefited man and allowed him to live in harmony with God's plan for the cosmos.

Debate on the use of ratiocination affected the scientific explorations of Islamic scholars. During the ascendency of the Mutazilite movement and the acceptance of rationalism as the path leading to truth, science was pursued with the same freedom that accompanied the development of philosophy and theology. During the time when the Abbasid caliphs in Baghdad supported the Mutazilite movement, the translation period reached its zenith, and the caliphs themselves encouraged the adoption and development of the natural sciences along the rationalistic pattern set by the Greeks. With the eradication of the Mutazilites as a dominating influence in Islam during the late ninth century and the dampening of its spirit throughout the Middle East, rationalism began to weaken as an effect on intellectualism, teaching, and higher educational institutions. Parallel to this period of fluctuating interest in science, jurisprudence and the religious sciences emerged as the major focus of Islamic education.

As outlined in the section on philosophy, devotion to rationalism as the primary tool of discovery devolved to only a few members of intellectual society: the Faylasifah. Scientific endeavors were confined to only a few institutions and individuals. During the period of openness, however—before the religious influence of Asharism and Sufism would dominate Islamic society—polymaths made their greatest discoveries and contributions to scientific thought. Although devout Muslims considered the pursuit of all knowledge to be a religious quest, some more than others possessed the ability and desire to focus their energies in the exploration of natural phenomena rather than the task of synthesizing physical data with supernatural knowledge. While one group of scholars—such as al-Kindi, al-Farabi, Ibn-Sina, and Ibn-Rushd—became authors of great tomes incorporating all knowledge known to them, another group concentrated on scientific inquiry. This is not to say that they did not engage in philosophic and theological discussions, for to ignore such matters would place them out of harmony with the prevailing values toward knowledge; but in large part they emphasized science, and thereby made greater advances in the exploration of physical phenomena and mathematics.

The truly scientific minds of the classical period relied on observation, experimentation, and analysis of results to a much greater extent than their contemporaries who—under the influence of the Neoplatonists—accepted Greek authority for descriptions of the natural world and the rational and logical tools stated by Aristotle to explain them. Jabir ibn-Hayyan (ca. 721–815)—known in the West as Geber, and considered the greatest name in Islamic alchemy—clarified the early position of Islamic scientists well when he said, "The first essential is that you should conduct experiments. For he who does not conduct experiments will never attain to the least degree of mastery. It must be taken as an absolutely rigorous principle that any proposition which is not supported by proofs is nothing more than an assertion which may be true or may be false."[5]

Following in Geber's footsteps were al-Haitham (ca. 965–1039), whose works in optics surpassed those of the Greeks and provided the seminal influence in the development of physical science in Medieval Europe; al-Khwarazmi (d. ca. 863), the greatest mathematician of the Middle Ages; al-Razi (865–925), whose understanding of healing derived from clinical observation; and al-Biruni (ca. 973–1051)—perhaps the greatest natural scientist of Islamdom—whose studies in all the areas of the natural sciences were transported to Western Europe, spawning further scientific investigations. While each of these hakims also expounded his views in the areas of philosophy, mathematics, and medicine, they are more honored for their scientific endeavors and would be recognized as scientists even by contemporary criteria.

After al-Biruni, Islamic scientists (except astronomers) employed experimentation and observation less and less. By the time of al-Biruni, the prevailing pietistic approach to theosophy dominated the intellectual life within Islamdom. Scholasticism, with its foundations in dialectics and logic, controlled the thinking of most polymaths. At the same time, Asharism and the other more traditional Islamic views, which reasserted the value that earthly knowledge was of much lesser importance than supernatural knowledge, governed the instruction of young men in mosque schools and in the newly created madrassahs. Soon, even the works of Ibn-Sina and the Peripatetic philosophers were no longer in vogue; some were banned, as in the case of Ibn-Rushd.

Umar al-Khayyam (1050?–1123?)—whose hierarchy of knowledge was described in Chapter 3—clearly supported the Sufi view that the pursuit of knowledge calls one to a life of purification and contemplation. He considered his work in mathematics as merely supplementing his more important goal in acquiring truth through meditation and ascetic living. In this atmosphere, natural philosophy could not be removed from metaphysics, and nothing in the natural order could be isolated from its place within the hierarchical cosmos that unified knowledge about all objects created by God. The quest for unity of knowledge, for a harmonious explanation of all the data about the world, and for revelation outweighed the curiosity of learned men to seek out specific facts and to pursue narrow phenomena in any given scientific field.

In the century following al-Khayyam, Islamic cosmology took its final form in works similar to those by Ibn el-Arabi (1165–1240) and his students who related numbers, letters, objects, parts of anatomy, and celestial bodies into complex, circular, cosmological diagrams.[6] These depictions represented the symbolic relatedness of all known objects within the cosmos and defined the hierarchical relationships among them. To Western eyes, such intriguing diagrams appear more mystical than scientific. But in the Middle Eastern tradition and the theosophic grounding of Islam, they depicted the essence of reality and—despite their lack of verification by observation or experimentation—were widely accepted as representing the true nature of the universe.

This world view—part mystical, part physical—determined the curriculum of higher education institutions from the eleventh century. Scientific knowledge, as we currently understand it, took its place in the curriculum at an elementary level that was preparatory to advanced studies. Scientific information relayed to young men was rudimentary, akin to that contained in the medieval West's quadrivium: geometry, arithmetic, astronomy, and music. As the great intellects of an earlier Islamic age were drawn to the Greek and Oriental sciences because their interpretation and understanding of it was important to the evolving intellectual trends of the time, bright minds in later centuries pursuing influence and an academic life followed the call of jurisprudence and the religious sciences as the most promising avenue to a position of influence and power.

By the twelfth century, the primary characteristics of Islamic science were defined and clarified. These have continued to the present. In part they explain why scientific endeavors ceased to advance beyond that century—except in astronomy—and why now in the twentieth century Islamic societies have great difficulty in accepting Western science and technology. Even students from contemporary Islamic countries who study in Western institutions retain an attitude quite different from their non-Islamic peers. The difference in viewpoint can occasion schizophrenia on the part of students who must learn science according to the value systems of two cultures.

In sum, the Islamic view toward science as it evolved during the classical period and was defined at the end of that era can be explained by the following assumptions: Scientific inquiry is bounded by two principles: unity and hierarchy. Nothing exists that is not related physically or symbolically to everything else in the cosmos, and that relationship is defined through a religiously inspired hierarchy. Truth and reality reside totally in the Divine Will as manifested in the cosmos in symbolic form only. Hence, all objects within creation have both a qualitative and quantitative essence. In the cosmological order of things, the qualitative essence holds a higher value and priority than any physical dimensions or characteristics.

Scientific knowledge must be used primarily to define and describe the cosmos. It ought not be employed to control the natural order of things. The formation of hypotheses and the seeking of causation to explain natural phenomena hold little value in the cosmology of Islam. Events in nature occur because God wills them; only coincidentally do they occur in close proximity to other actions. The Quran and hadith contain all truth about the cosmos. Explorations into the natural order of things and the physical dimensions of an object merely add details to its essence as created by God. These details are of lesser importance than the ultimate truth about the object. Knowledge about the supernatural world is more valued and ultimately more useful to humanity than that of the terrestrial world. The true seeker of knowledge will pursue *sapientia* (wisdom) rather than *scientia* (scientific knowledge). Knowledge of terrestrial matters is valuable if it facilitates one's understanding of the supernatural world and the ascent of the soul to

God. Thus, scientific knowledge for its own sake had little meaning in this Islamic framework. Knowledge about terrestrial matters and objects matters only if it facilitates the search for God and improves the potential for transcending the world and attaining a life in the hereafter. Knowledge about things and objects of the world that deflect individuals from that direction pervert the use of knowledge. When doubt exists about the right use of knowledge that does not originate from revelation, the Quran and hadith as interpreted by religious scholars must illuminate the proper course of action.

Achievements of Islamic Scholars in Science

Remaining constant to Islamic principles of the unity and hierarchical nature of all knowledge, scholars throughout Islamdom pursued studies in a catholic manner. In writing the results of their investigations, they did not organize information and theory into the categories recognized today as disciplines. Our present division of knowledge into specific disciplines stems from a nineteenth-century convention, emerging from the focus on research and specialization of the German universities. Scholars of the German university system elected to channel their energies into the exploration of specifically defined areas of knowledge, bound together by similar properties and a method of inquiry. For the Islamic scholar, knowledge was ordered hierarchically from the terrestrial—centered on the earth and its immediate environs—up through the various spheres of the supernatural world, and culminating in the Divine Logos.

As regarding the terrestrial realm, all studies were considered interrelated; and each object of study was comprised of both a physical nature and a spiritual property that linked it to all the other objects in the universe. This applied equally to celestial bodies, minerals, plants, animals, natural processes, and humans. The Western mind has difficulty viewing knowledge from this perspective and may indeed become impatient in wading through manuscripts written during the Islamic Golden Age that combine the spiritual, the magical, and the physical properties of the natural world. Also, the manner in which Islamic scholars organized and related their information may confuse the Western academic whose background divides the intellectual world into accepted disciplines within the parameters of the natural sciences, the social sciences, and the humanities. Nonetheless, patience and persistence in the study of manuscripts written during this period can render great rewards. The manuscripts written between the eighth and twelfth centuries evidence aspects of all the present-day disciplines. Not only did Islamic scholars translate and comment on Greek and Oriental sources, but they added much to our understanding of the natural world, despite their penchant for intertwining its spiritual and material characteristics.

A number of Islamic scholars of this period have been discussed earlier, primarily because of their manuscripts on philosophy and theology. Their contributions to scientific thought were also noted, for their names appear again and again in treatments of Islamic sciences. To supplement those honored polymaths whose primary focus lay in theology and philosophy, individuals most noted for their scientific achievements ought now receive their due. They, too, exemplify the universality of the polymath in Islamic intellectual history, despite their renown in Western histories for their scientific writings.

Among the earliest known scientists of the classical period was Jabir ibn-Hayyan—the Latin "Geber" (ca. 721–815)—the founder of Islamic alchemy. Supported in Baghdad at the court of Caliph Harun al-Rashid, he wrote some 3,000 treatises—the majority on alchemy but also on logic, philosophy, medicine, the occult sciences, physics, mechanics, and other areas of then known knowledge.[7] Confusion surrounds the Latin translations of Geber's work, and it is difficult now to distinguish his original writings from those compiled by his disciples.[8] In any case, he made an indelible mark on the study of alchemy—the foundation of chemistry.

Ibn-Hayyan was both a Shiite and a Sufi, and it was from the latter that he was strongly influenced by mysticism and spirituality. Many Sufis believed that a parallel relationship existed between the transcendence of the soul to the heights of the celestial world and the transmutation of base metals such as lead into pure metals, such as gold. Because of the mystical nature of Sufi teaching, ibn-Hayyan experimented with metals and elements and prepared lengthy manuscripts on their spiritual and supernatural qualities. While primarily occupied with the process of transmutation, he did develop chemical precedures that have endured. He was familiar with the properites of acids and bases and was able to isolate nitric acid, aqua regia, sodium hydroxide, corrosive sublimate, antimony, bismuth, zinc, ammonia, and phosphorous. He also wrote widely on the physical and chemical properties of compounds.

We owe the term "algebra" to the ninth-century scholar Musa al-Khwarazmi (d. ca. 863), who traveled to the Orient to study mathematics. Upon his return to the court of al-Mamun, he synthesized the mathematics known to him and presented it in a volume entitled *al-Jabr wa'l-Mugabalah,* shortened to *Algebra.*[9] The Latin text of his *Algebra* was used into the sixteenth century as the principal textbook on mathematics in Europe. More than any other scholar, he was responsible for the introduction of Indian numerals to the West. These imports from the Orient greatly simplified computation and constituted a basic vehicle for the continued development of more sophisticated mathematics in Islam and later in Europe. By this time, Islamic mathematicians had introduced the concept of zero, and had created a system of numbers based on multiples of ten. Our mathematical term "algorism"—defined as the act of calculating by means of nine digits and a zero—is derived from al-Khwarazmi's name. He developed algebra as a practical tool in solving problems in inheritance, lawsuits, and commerce. His contributions to mathematics also included tables of sine and cotangent values. The Caliph al-Mamun employed him as an astronomer in the royal observatory, in which capacity al-Khwarazmi charted the heavens and improved the geographic maps of Ptolemy. Additionally, he developed astronomical tables and introduced the concepts of latitude and longitude into cartography.

The *Fihrist* of al-Nadim lists 113 major and 28 minor volumes authored by Muhammed al-Razi (844–926), a physician practicing in Baghdad.[10] Nasr attributes to al-Razi some 184 volumes—56 of them dedicated to medicine and healing.[11] He wrote on chemistry, alchemy, and medicine, but was noted more for his skills in healing. Al-Razi was considered the greatest practitioner of medicine in Islam and introduced the use of animal gut for sutures and mercury as an ointment in treating skin diseases. His treatises on smallpox and measles stood as the standard treatment of those diseases until the middle of the nineteenth century—some 40 English editions having been distributed between 1498 and 1866.[12]

Al-Razi is considered second only to Ibn-Sina in his knowledge and writings on medical matters. He received direct experience in the art of healing as director of hospitals at Rayy and Baghdad. Under al-Razi's tutelage, the hospital and clinic became a medical school; and it is noted that he taught both through lectures and clinical experiences, assigning patients in the hospital to his students and supervising the treatment. His writings included many case studies and medical histories from which he had been able to draw conclusions about the art of healing. He is considered the "Father of Pediatrics" because of a monograph in which he discussed diseases of childhood. Some of the topics of more than usual interest addressed in his writings include frostbite, first aid, homosexuality, arthritis, and diabetes, as well as the ethics and morality of the physician. Translations of his manuscripts were well known in the Middle Ages and comprised a large part of the curriculum of medical schools in Salerno and Paris.

The greatest of Muslim physicists, Abu ibn al-Haitham (ca. 965–1039), lived in Basrah and Cairo.[13] Alhazen—his Latin name—was summoned to Cairo by the Fatimid caliph in order to control the Nile's flooding. In this endeavor, he was unable to offer a proper explanation, much less a remedy. But his legacy in physics, particularly in the area of optics, has secured for him a place among the elite of physicists. His approach to science was more mathematical and less qualitative than his contemporaries, and he devised numerous experiments to test his theories. In the area of optics, he measured angles of incidence and refraction—involving the solution of fourth-degree equations—and introduced the use of the camera obscura as a device for observing eclipses of the sun. He was familiar with the properties of spherical aberration and designed lathes on which he was able to manufacture both lenses and curved mirrors for his experiments.

Al-Haitham conceived of light as a substance that traveled from an object to the eye and conceptualized that it traveled at different speeds through different mediums, such as air and water. He was interested in studying the phenomena of dawn and dusk, which he stated occurred until the sun was 19 degrees below the horizon.[14] The first scientist to conceive of the eye as a lens, he described vision as a product of rays being transmitted through it. This led him to examine and publish several tracts on diseases of the eye. His works in Latin translation ignited interest in exploring physical phenomena in Western scholars, including Grosseteste, Wittlo, and Galileo.

Many in the Islamic world consider Abu Raihan al-Biruni (ca. 973–1051) as the greatest of Muslim scientists.[15] He traveled through Persia and India and recorded his experiences in several volumes. His manuscript entitled *India* offered the best account of the Hindu religion and culture known in the Middle Ages in both Europe and the Middle East. He wrote the standard text on astronomy used both in Islamic institutions of higher learning and later as part of the quadrivium in Latin schools. A true polymath, he wrote scientific works in physics, mathematics, geography, mineralogy, and nearly every branch of mathematics, astronomy, and astrology. He was able to measure the specific gravity of metals and precious stones and explained springs and artesian wells through the principles of hydrostatics. Despite authoring some 180 known works, his name is little recognized in the West since, unfortunately, his scholarly findings entered Europe in compilations and not as specifically identifiable books. Still, in the Middle East, al-Biruni is considered one of the great intellectuals and scientists in the history of Islam and much of the scientific curriculum still used in Islamic schools is attributed to his genius.

As mentioned earlier, perhaps the most famous Muslim scholar and poet known in the West is the Persian Umar al-Khayyam (1050?–1123?). Little is known about his life and travels, and the dates of his birth and death are mere approximations. Evidently, he spent most of his lifetime near Nishapur—his birthplace. Best known in the West for his poetry, among Muslims he is honored as a famous mathematician and reformer of the calendar still used in parts of Iran and Iraq. He prepared works in algebra, geometry, and physics, as well as metaphysics. His algebraic treatises advanced the solution of cubic equations, which he solved geometrically.[16] While the *Rubaiyat* in its Romantic translation by Fitzgerald has the aura of "eat, drink, and be merry," the Persian original reflected more of al-Khayyam's theological roots in Sufism.

Finally, we consider the polymath Nasir al-Din al-Tusi (1201–1274). Al-Tusi was born in Tus during the time of the Mongolian invasions, and he is attributed with saving part of the intellectual heritage of Islam by rendering his services as an astrologer to the Mongol leader Hulagu.[17] He established the great observatory and scientific institution at Maraghah—considered to be the most sophisticated astronomical observatory then constructed. He contributed greatly to the writings of his day with commentaries not only on original Greek scientific works translated into Arabic, but also on many of the Islamic scholars and their works. Al-Tusi is most noted in the West for his work in astronomy and the development of the Maraghah observatory and its astronomical instruments. He criticized Ptolemy and offered a new planetary model labeled the "Tusi Couple." Through his leadership, the astronomers at Maraghah devised the most sophisticated and accurate astronomical tables of the Middle Ages. These greatly influenced the work of Nicolaus Copernicus, Johannes Kepler, and Tycho Brahe in the fifteenth and sixteenth centuries. As a devout Shiite, he also turned his intellectual energies toward the questions of ethics and theology. His manuscripts in these areas are still used in religious schools in the Middle East as part of the training of Shiite Muslims.

In the West, we know only the most outstanding scientists of the Islamic world. Regretfully, many of their manuscripts have disappeared in both their Arabic and Latin forms. As in any intellectual sphere, these men borrowed from and were stimulated by other scholars who, though of lesser stature, nonetheless contributed major advancements and insights in the sciences, arts, and professions during the period A.D. 700–1300. A summary of Islam's technological, scientific, and intellectual achievements indicates clearly the advances contributed by them to all these areas of knowledge after the Hellenistic period. These accomplishments remained the high point of the scholarly world until the Renaissance and Enlightenment of Western Europe. In the sciences, particularly, Islamic scholars wrote what were considered definitive works until the Scientific Revolution and the establishment of the German research university in the nineteenth century.   Continuing in the tradition of Ptolemy, Islamic scholars knew and plotted the movements and positions of the planets and stars. They constructed astronomical instruments to improve the accuracy of sightings that have been preserved for us in writings, drawings, and in the instruments themselves located in observatories. According to Nasr,

> The most important Islamic astronomical instrument is of course the astrolabe, which consists of the stereographic projection of the celestial sphere on the plane of the equator taking the pole as the viewpoint. The circle of declination and the azimuthal co-ordinates appear on the plates of the astrolabe, while the asterisms are on the spider or net. This multifunctional instrument can determine the altitude of the stars, the sun, the moon, and other planets in much the same way as a sextant or quadrant. The astrolabe can also be used to tell time and to measure the height of mountains and the depth of wells.[18]

In addition to the astrolabe, Islamic scholars constructed the azimuthal quadrant—predecessor of the theodolite that was later used by Tycho Brahe in his observations. They also manufactured zodiacal armillaries and celestial globes as models of planetary movement—examples of which still exist. The culmination of Islamic instrument production occurred at the observatory at Maraghah. Examples of the mural quadrant can still be seen on the walls of buildings used for observatories throughout the Middle East and the Orient.

Some mention should be made of the relationship between astronomy and astrology in the last centuries of the first millennium. The two were considered one body of knowledge since, in the tradition of Islam, the properties of celestial bodies were both supernatural and physical. The stars and planets, imbued with supernatural intelligences, offered insights into the Will of God. Thus, their observed placement in the sky and proximity to other bodies—although predictable—provided a means for understanding earthly events. Islamic writings and theories on astrology have come down to the present day as evidenced in astrology columns in newspapers and the honor still accorded astrologers in Eastern cultures, who are consulted in regard to the most propitious and ill-fated timings for certain events to occur.

Islamic scholars invented and used trigonometry and geodesic geometry to plot the movement of the stars and planets. They introduced the use of sine and cotangent instead of the less sophisticated measurement by chords, in order to give greater accuracy to their sightings. Because of this greater precision in astronomical measurements, Islamic cartographers improved on earlier Greek celestial charts and earth maps. They were surprisingly accurate in their invention and use of latitude and longitude as means of locating geographic features and cities.

In attempting to refine the Ptolemaic system of planetary motion, Islamic astronomers theorized that the sun—and not the earth—could lie at the center of the universe. They perceived a flaw in the Ptolemaic planetary system because it could not place the earth exactly at the center of the universe. This prompted them to devise a new system of planetary movements that would do so. It also allowed them to hypothesize that planetary movement could be explained if the sun were placed at the center and the planets orbited around it. Despite having the prerequisite information to advocate a heliocentric system, Islamic scholars chose not to do so because such a system would undermine the cosmology and faith of Islam as stated in the Quran.

According to Nasr, the most enduring Islamic contribution to astronomy was to view celestial bodies as having physical attributes.[19] In the Greek system, heavenly bodies were perceived as abstractions and portrayed through mathematical models. Islamic astronomers maintained that the stars and planets did have a material composition, and thus asserted that their observations did indeed record movement of tangible bodies.

Astronomy constituted a useful science for Muslims; through its concepts they had the capability of organizing the religious aspects of their faith. The Quran commands prayer five times a day at specified periods of time, and that the direction of prayer should always be toward Mecca. Further, it commands that one of the months of the year should be dedicated to prayer and fasting. Their knowledge of astronomy assisted believers in implementing this for the variety of latitude and longitude existing throughout Islam's vast landholdings. Muslims chose to remain with a lunar calendar, because they judged it would be more fair in the practice of religious rituals in various latitudes. Using the lunar calendar over a long period of time, religious holidays—especially the month-long celebration of Ramadan—would occur in every season of the year; thus no Islamic community would be favored or burdened by always having to observe the daily fasts in the same climatic conditions or length of daylight. As Nasr argues,

But the Holy Quran forbade the intercalation of the lunar year into the solar one according to the well-known verse: "Postponement (of a sacred month) . . . is only an excess of disbelief whereby those who disbelieve are misled . . ." (IX;37).

This injunction is itself an explicit proof of the nonhuman origin of the Holy Quran, if proof be needed, for it means that the Holy Book foresaw long before the problem arose that the only way to preserve justice among Muslims was to forbid intercalation. The major Muslim rites, such as the daily prayers and fasting, are related to the times of sunrise and sunset. Moreover, Islam is a worldwide religion with adherents living in various geographical locations where the length of day and climatic conditions differ greatly. Had the lunar year been fixed within the solar year—as some modernized Muslims unaware of the consequences of their proposals suggest it should be—a grave injustice would be incurred in that some people would have to fast longer days or perform other religious rites under more difficult conditions throughout their lives. Only the forbidding of intercalation could ensure divine justice for all believers. In this verse the Holy Quran took into consideration the future state of the Islamic community far beyond the geographical confines of that small community in Arabia to which the message was originally addressed.[20]

Islamic astronomers like their colleagues until the time of the Copernican Revolution expended much energy attempting to justify the lunar and solar calendars. While remaining with the solar calendar in dealing with climate and growing cycles, they selected the lunar calendar as the base for religious practice and assignment of the months of the year.

Mathematics held a particular interest for Islamic scholars because of its symbolic representation of nature. They viewed it as the avenue of transcendence from the physical to the supernatural world. At the base of mathematical theory lay the concept of unity, which is—indeed—the central theme of all Islam. Mathematics symbolically represented both the unity of the cosmos and its subsumed parts. Islamic mathematicians adopted the geometric theorems inherited from the Greeks, but soon engaged in more advanced solutions to many problems unknown to their predecessors. They related geometry to algebra and used geometric means to solve for unknowns in complex algebraic equations. Geometric figures provided their greatest inspiration in art and architecture. Forbidden to depict the human figure in religious art, artisans relied on geometric patterns to portray unity and harmony in the design of buildings, carpets, and other objets d'art.

Islamic scholars perfected algebra as we know it today, and derived the means to solve not only linear and quadratic equations but those of third- and even fourth-degree unknowns. Algebra provided Muslims with a practical mathematical tool for solving problems in commerce, science, and the division of inheritances. Al-Khwarazmi's approach particularly stressed the use of algebra for solving practical problems in everyday life. Islamic mathematicians devised an algebraic method for extracting square roots and for finding the altitude of a triangle when the three sides are known. Islamic mastery of algebra culminated in the noted eleventh-century treatises of Umar al-Khayyam, who described a more advance treatment of the subject than those of al-Khwarazmi.

The other branch of mathematics that bears the inventive stamp of Islamic scholars is trigonometry. Greek mathematicians had used the concept of chords to study the relationship between the angles and sides of a triangle. To this base, Islamic mathematicians constructed a system of functions that have survived to the present—the sine, cosine, tangent, cotangent, and secant—and greatly simplified trigonometric calculations. Astronomers as early as the ninth century employed such functions in their observations and calculations of the planets. Tables of trigonometric functions applied by students today date from this period. Al-Biruni prepared a masterful work in spherical trigonometry—discovered quite recently—as well as a popular canon on the subject.

Islamic scholars introduced the so-called Arabic numbers to the West, greatly facilitating computation. With the introduction of zero, the numbering system allowed for the generation of decimal fractions. This ease of calculation allowed them to compute the numerical equivalent of pi and of other constants used in both geometry and astronomy, such as trigonometric functions. Intrigued with the abstract qualities of numbers, the Islamic mathematicians also invented numbers theory and debated the points of a continuing progression of numbers to eternity.

Evidence of their architectural skills exists today in the beautiful mosques and public buildings still functioning in the Islamic world. Artisans excelled in the use of geometric figures and interlacing lines to decorate the buildings. Because the Quran expressly forbade the use of images, they concentrated their efforts on that form of ornamentation rather than on statuary, as the Greeks had. The most elaborate form of the use of geometric figures and lines we now term "arabesque." Western architects have adopted its form since the Middle Ages.

Except in optics, advances in physics were greatly restricted because Islamic scholars for the most part adopted Aristotelian concepts of natural philosophy that linked both physical and metaphysical properites together.[21] Those scholars, such as Ibn-Sina, who accepted almost completely the Peripatetic philosophy occupied their time dealing with physical properites of matter in a speculative way and did not undertake observation and experimentation of physical phenomena. A few Islamic scholars—such as al-Biruni, al-Haitham, and al-Biruni—did reject the Peripatetic view. Their experimentation and observation added to our knowledge of the physical properties of nature. The non-Peripatetic scholars conceived of material as being comprised of atoms. Such atoms, created by God, received their impetus and movements from Him. The non-Peripatetics rationalized Aristotelian views of motion and inertia with their atomized view of the world, but added very little precision to the understanding of motion and force. They did, however, anticipate Galileo's Pisan experiments with weights and theorized that objects fall not in relation to their weight, but according to a power that draws them through their medium of descent—air or water. The non-Peripatetics did not aspire to measure gravity; however, they did understand the concept of specific gravity and had determined its numerical equivalent for numerous metals and precious stones. Islamic physical scientists perceived of sound as a vibration in the air and were also aware of the concepts of capillary action and the laws of the pendulum.

Islamic craftsmen built sophisticated balances by which to measure specific gravity; and they were familiar with the laws of levers, pulleys, and hydrostatics. In applying the laws of mechanics, Islamic inventors constructed windmills, waterwheels, balances, water clocks, purification systems, and roads; metallurgists had the technical skills to manufacture many alloys of iron and steel. Both Ibn-Sina and al-Biruni contributed to our knowledge of mineralogy by writing books that described metals, minerals, and their physical and supernatural properties.

Through experimentation and observation, al-Haitham measured the angles of incidence and refraction of light in various media. Al-Haitham anticipated Snell's Law of Refraction by calculating the ratio of the angle of incidence and refraction using the chords of each to derive the constant relationship between the two angles. Snell in 1621 and—independently—Descartes in 1637 refined that calculation by employing the semi-chords of the angles, thus leading to a simplified formula of using the sines of the angles to derive the constant rather than the diagrammatic approach of al-Haitham.

In Islamic education, music was approached as a form of science, particularly so because it stressed harmony and the mathematical relationship of sounds and rhythm. Talented musicians invented a system of notation that designated both the pitch and duration of a note. While allowing that many different harmonic scales existed, they finally settled on the Greek Pythagorean scale, which has come down to us. Islamic craftsmen excelled in the production of fine musical instruments, such as lutes, flutes, rebecs (early violins), drums, horns, harps, and organs. While Muslims traditionally believed that the voice was the primary instrument to be used in praising God, they did enjoy musical instruments at secular functions, and formed bands under a leader or conductor who used a baton to coordinate the players and mark time.

From the ancient study of alchemy has evolved our understanding of chemistry. While Islamic alchemists isolated numerous elements and explained the properties of many chemical compounds, perhaps their greatest contribution to the study of chemistry remains in the laboratory processes they discovered and used in combining and separating chemical compounds. These included evaporation, filtration, crystallization, calcination, and reduction. They could produce important chemical compounds such as alcohol, sulfuric acid, and potash and had begun to formulate a taxonomy of chemical elements.

Islamic contributions to the study of geography included physical, cultural, and mathematical treatises. Because scholars traveled widely throughout Islamic lands, they were able to add much to the existing descriptions of lands, animals, plants, and the culture of the human inhabitants. This they did in numerous volumes that are still available—exhibiting a great desire to understand better the cultural and physical environment of the many peoples who inhabited Islamdom, from the Pyrenees to the Indus River. Al-Biruni's manuscript on India—considered the epitome of this science—depicted the most authoritative view of that subcontinent known in the Middle East or Europe until modern times. Ibn-Sina contributed to this area by forming a theory on the origin of mountains in which he spoke about many geological factors, including rock and sediment strata and land movements.

Islamic geographers excelled in cartography—drawing accurate maps of the heavens, the earth, and the seas. Because sailors had access to navigational instruments, charts of navigable waters became well known in the Middle East and Europe. Not only did learned men of Islamdom know that the world was a sphere, but some had calculated its circumference and also the length of the degree of arc at the equator. Even with rough instruments, measurements calculated during this time were quite accurate.

Islamic scientists comprehended the periodic movement of water in oceans and seas, and had calculated tide tables to predict the rise and fall of the water level at specific harbors. They understood such geological phenomena as weathering, erosion, and sedimentation. Because much of their land was arid, scientists studied the nature of underground water systems and the functioning of artesian wells. These they employed to their advantage in the study of agronomy.

Traditionally, the Orient abounded in the lore of plants as medicinal substances; thus, the study of botany meshed with the study of medicine, especially in the area of pharmacology. Islamic studies in botany dealt with classification of plants, their physiology, genesis, and modes of growth, and also a description of their parts, geographical and climatic conditions for cultivation, and medical as well as occult preperties. Zoology interested Islamic scholars because of the great array of animal life that thrived in their vast empire. The various species were classified, described in great detail, and even depicted in drawings. Specimens were transported between major centers for study. Because animals contributed so heavily to the economic well-being of Islamic society, zoology also stressed the manner in which products derived from them could be processed to increase their usefulness to humans.

Islamic contributions to medicine were monumental—as evidenced in the many volumes written by noted physicians of the classical period, including Ibn-Sina, al-Razi, and Ibn-Rushd.[22] Their concept of the physician's role went beyond mechanical treatment of physical and mental illness, but took a holistic approach that incorporated preventive medicine as well as concepts of hygiene. A physician's advice would certainly include diet and dietary matters, the importance of fresh air and exercise, and avoiding excesses of eating and drinking. Physicians recognized the importance of cleanliness; and indeed, Islamic religious practice required cleaning the body on a daily basis. Their concern with the mental health of patients led them to diagnose and treat psychosomatic illness. For them, healing was as much a spiritual as a physical process; they advised and guided their patients in acquiring a positive state of mind and encouraged them in achieving spiritual growth. This holistic approach to medical practice emanated from the basic Islamic perception of knowledge that manifested the unity and hierarchical nature of all creation. The healthy person had achieved harmony with both the terrestrial world and the supernatural world of the upper cosmos.

Despite their reliance on Hellenistic medicine—particularly that of Galen—with its false assumptions about the nature and the origin of disease, physicians in Islamdom became astute observers of symptoms and the reactions of patients to certain medical practices, thus taking a pragmatic approach to the healing arts. Paradoxically, while adhering to erroneous assumptions about the cause of disease, physicians in Islamic lands still achieved success in facilitating healing by following paractices learned through clinical experience. Their works on the nature of disease, its symptoms, its progression, and recommendations for healing comprised the medical literature of Europe during the Middle Ages on down to the ninth century and the beginning of modern medical practice. Garrison describes the method of the physician in the following manner:

> Diagnosis of internal disease is founded upon six canons: (1) The patient's actions; (2) his excreta; (3) the nature of the pain; (4) its site; (5) swelling; (6) the effluvia of the body; and further information is elicited by "the feel of the hands," whether firm or flabby, hot or cool, moist or dry, or by such indications as "yellowness of the white of the eyes" (jaundice) or "bending of the back" (lung disease).[25]

People in the Middle East seem particularly susceptible to diseases of the eye. In response to this, physicians in that region were among the first to categorize and prescribe treatment for such ailments through ointments, eye washes, and surgery. They diagnosed glaucoma and recognized its cause as an increase of pressure within the eye. They observed the existence of cataracts, which they removed surgically with a suction tube. Al-Haitham contributed much to the knowledge about the anatomy of the eye because of his interest in optics and lenses. He maintained that the eye was structured like a lens, and that rays from objects outside the person entered the lens of the eye and imprinted an image on the membrane in the back of it. He identified the optical nerve and recognized its importance to the phenomena of vision.

Despite the lingering prejudice that surgery occupied a less prestigious form of medical practice, Islamic physicians made great strides in developing surgical procedures. They were most adept in the use of cauterization to stem bleeding and to retard the growth and spread of infection. They invented instruments for all types of surgical procedures including the use of catheters for the cleansing of the urethra and bladder, and probes for cleansing the lower intestine, in addition to scalpels, forceps, saws, pincers, and suction devices. Surgeons operated not only on limbs and the abdomen, but the cranium as well. Lithotomy, tracheotomy, Caesarean section, the removal of cancers, tumors, and cataracts all lay within their capabilities. In addition, surgeons could repair harelip, amputate limbs, and remove teeth. They employed strands of animal gut as sutures and realized that incisions should be kept clean.

In surgery, they invented a form of anesthesia—the soporific sponge. To accomplish this, the surgeon soaked a sponge with opium, mandragora, and other sleep-inducing drugs and placed it over the nose and mouth of the patient. These could be prepared in advance and dried for storage. The surgeon would then activate the sponge by immersing it for a moment in water just prior to application. In addition to administering drugs as a method of anesthesiology, surgeons also employed hypnotic suggestion to reduce the pain of incision. These methods still survive in Eastern cultures—and in the case of hypnotic suggestion, have even proved useful in the hands of Western practitioners. Physicians understood the mechanics of setting bones properly, and devised an effective means of immobilization. They had success in setting bones and joints in arms, legs, and hips and also attempted to work with the spinal column. In dental surgery, they practiced the removal of teeth and abscesses from the mouth. They could manufacture false teeth out of bone and wood.

Western authorities tend to agree that dissection of human corpses did not occur, because of the Islamic prohibition against mutilation of bodies and the lack of corroborating evidence that Islamic understanding of anatomy went beyond that of Galen. Some Eastern authors contend that dissection under special circumstances did occur, and that those attending the wounded and injured also used that opportunity to observe the anatomical structure of the human body. According to Hamdani, Abdul Latif Baghdadi did dissect the human body, discovered that Galen was wrong in many instances, and published his findings in several volumes.[24] Hamdani defends the use of dissection on Quranic grounds that the pursuit of knowledge through reasoning is an important mandate of the scholar. He cites the Quran: "Do not follow that of which you have no knowledge. Indeed the ear, the eye, and the mind shall be held answerable for that." Whether or not dissection was indeed performed by a few Islamic physicians, evidently information about it was little known in the Middle East during this era, nor did it enter Western Europe with the other medical texts that became so popular in the Middle Ages.

The use of drugs, herbs, and other vegetable material in the cure of disease had a long-standing tradition among the Arabs and the Middle Eastern and Eastern cultures that came into the Islamic Empire.[25] Scholars inherited a vast knowledge of pharmacology from many sources. Chapters on the use of drugs and herbs in the treatment of disease comprised an important part of any treatise on medicine. While physicians used pharmacology to a great extent in their treatments, pharmacists also had respect in Islamic society; and individuals quite often would seek advice from one of them, rather than from a physician. A large part of pharmacology was based on myth. Prescription relied heavily on the magical properties of different herbs; but, as in much folk medicine, experience had taught the value of the many natural substances used in the treatment of disease and ill health. The pharmacopoeia compiled during classical Islam listed several thousand items, giving their properties, locality, and purpose. Until the development of synthetic drugs in recent history, the pharmacopoeia in use in the Middle East remained a staple of this form of treatment in the West. In Eastern societies, much of it remains intact, offering popular remedies for many described illnesses.

The efforts of Islamic polymaths to advance knowledge of the universe in both its conceptual and materialistic aspects yielded a great harvest, as is revealed in the multitudinous volumes authored by them on every subject during the Classical Age. Much of this has entered the mainstream of knowledge that continuously flows and increases through world civilization. Ironically, the Islamic contribution in philosophy and science did not receive its impetus from formal institutions of higher education, nor did these structures serve as the conduit for that intellectual treasure to merge with that of other cultures. Rather, the fruit of Islamic engagement with these areas of knowledge drew nourishment from individuals bound together in spontaneous groupings. The emergence of these informal structures of higher learning provides the focus for the next chapter in this short history of Islamic education.

Notes

1. H. J. J. Winter, *Eastern Science* (London: John Murray, 1952), 59–60; Donald Campbell, *Arabic Medicine* (London: Kegan, Trench, 1926), 3; Giorgio de Santilla, from the "Preface" to Seyyed Hossein Nasr, *Science and Civilization in Islam* (New York: New American Library, 1968), vii–xiv.

2. Nasr, *Science and Civilization in Islam,* 21–29; Rashdi Rashed, "Islam and the Flowering of the Exact Sciences," in *Islam: Philosophy and Science* (Paris: UNESCO Press, 1982), 133–59; Aydin Mehmed Sayili, "Islam and the Rise of the Seventeenth Century Science," Ankara, Turkey, *Bulletin* 22, 87 (July 1958): 353-68.

3. Nasr, *Science and Civilization in Islam,* and *Islamic Science,* World of Islam Festival Publishing (Westerham, Kent: Westerham Press, 1976).

4. See the discussion by Nasr in *Islamic Science,* 3–5.

5. Frederick B. Artz, *The Mind of the Middle Ages* (Chicago: University of Chicago Press, 1980), 166.

6. Nasr, *Islamic Science,* 31–36.

7. Nasr, *Science and Civilization in Islam,* 42–43.

8. Ibid., 43.

9. Ali Abdullah Al-Daffa, *The Muslim Contribution to Mathematics* (London: Croom Helm, 1978), 49.

10. Al-Nadim, *Al-Fihrist* (Leipzig: Flügel, 1872), 299–302.

11. Nasr, *Science and Civilization in Islam,* 46.

12. E. G. Browne, *Arabian Medicine* (Cambridge, U.K.: Cambridge University Press, 1962), 44–47.

13. See Al-Daffa, *Muslim Contribution,* 67, 75, 83–86; Nasr, *Science and Civilization in Islam,* 49–50, 128–32; H. J. J. Winter, *Eastern Science* (London: John Murray, 1952), 72–75.

14. Al-Daffa, *Muslim Contribution,* 75.

15. See ibid., 73; Nasr, *Science and Civilization in Islam,* 50–51; Winter, *Eastern Science,* 70–71.

16. E. S. Kennedy, "The Exact Sciences in Iran under the Saljuqs and Mongols," in J. A. Boyle, ed., *The Cambridge History of Iran,* vol. 5 (Cambridge, U.K.: Cambridge University Press, 1968), 665–66.

17. Nasr, *Science and Civilization in Islam,* 54–56 and 172–74.

18. Nasr, *Islamic Science,* 118.

19. Ibid., 133.

20. Ibid., 95–96.

21. Nasr, *Science and Civilization in Islam,* 126–28.

22. Nasr, *Islamic Science,* 153–93.

23. Fielding H. Garrison, *An Introduction to the History of Medicine,* 3rd ed. (Philadelphia: W. B. Saunders, 1924), 124.

24. S. A. R. Hamdani, *Notable Muslim Names in Medical Science* (Lahore: Ferozsns, ca. 1960), 9.

25. Albert Dietrich, "Islamic Sciences and the Medieval West: Pharmacology," in Khalil I. Semaan, ed., *Islam and the Medieval West* (Albany: SUNY Press, 1980), 50–63.

5

Spontaneous Centers of the Higher Learning

Thus We make plain Our revelations, so that they may say: "You have studied deep," and that this may become clear to men of understanding.
The Quran 6:105

We have discussed at some length the intellectual awakening that occurred in Islamdom during the eighth to twelfth centuries and the evolution of sophisticated approaches to the various subject areas—theology, philosophy, natural sciences, medicine, and law. We now turn to the structures in which this burgeoning intellectual atmosphere took root. Our prior discussion was concerned with the institutions of higher learning that were situated in formal settings, attached at first only to the mosque and transforming over time into mosque-colleges and finally madrassahs. Such institutions received official sanction from the Islamic community to serve the needs of the higher learning. As detailed in Chapter 2, these schools focused somewhat narrowly on the religious sciences—primarily jurisprudence—preparing young men for positions as religious leaders, prayer leaders, and jurisconsults. The mosque-related and madrassah systems ignored the subject matter of the foreign sciences out of hand, while adopting their intellectual methodologies of logic and dialectic.

To accommodate the Islamic intellectual awakening in the nonreligious areas of knowledge, there sprang up—quite spontaneously—a number of important, informal structures that provided a fertile milieu in which learned men could explore the depths of their Greek and Oriental heritage in philosophy, theology, literature, mathematics, medicine, and natural science.

The first structures to appear in this fashion emerged from the desire of learned men and younger scholars to communicate and stimulate each other. This took form in the time-honored manners of apprenticeship and discipleship and evolved from the natural inclination of a few individuals to impart their knowledge to a younger generation. In some instances—as noted earlier—the desire to learn was stimulated by the need to hone intellectual tools so as to defend the new Islamic faith against other religions whose followers were trained in Greek philosophy and dialectic. Additionally, the thirst for knowledge was activated by the need to expand healing skills and to understand natural phenomena—particularly the movement of celestial bodies, because the Arabs considered them to be a means of communication from the supernatural realm of God to the terrestrial home of humankind.

The classification of institutions of higher learning in Islamdom into categories of formal and informal structures presents a number of dilemmas for the taxonomist. Few criteria readily distinguish between the two major divisions of institutions. Both types clearly met societal needs. Perhaps the clearest means to differentiate the two rests with their relationship to the state, which in Islamic regions was a theocracy. The mission of the formal institutions discussed in Chapter 2 was to prepare young men in assuming religious and educational roles, or in entering the bureaucracy or some other area of civil government. As such, the formal institutions of higher learning received financial support either directly from the public treasury as in the case of the halqa in mosques or the mosque-colleges, or through endowments established under the aegis of the law of waqf in the case of the madrassah. Such institutions restricted their curriculums to the religious sciences. Formal institutions of higher education were held accountable to the theocratic state for the orthodoxy of the material presented as well as for the expenditure of funds.

Informal and spontaneous institutions of higher learning—while meeting societal needs in continuing scholarship and instruction in literature (adab) and the foreign sciences—did not receive financial support directly from the state, nor enjoy any legal status within the social structure. They did have greater freedom than formal structures with regard to subject matter and instructional methodology. Such institutions were comprised of men who voluntarily committed themselves to the group's efforts. As an entity, they were not governed by the state; but the individual or individuals involved in them were responsible to society in the same way as any other citizen. Thus they could be accused of heresy, incurring punishment or banishment and their ideas and manuscripts banned. The continuance of informal institutions of higher learning depended on the personal characteristics of the hakims and their ability to attract disciples and patronage. Some supported study circles from their own means; others received stipends and living arrangements from a patron. When bound together in a structured way, the circle often acquired support from the caliph, sultan, or governor. Such communities of scholars often performed important tasks for their patron—such as translating manuscripts, observing and mapping the orbits of celestial bodies, and advising on legal and diplomatic matters. The locus of communities might be a palace, a residence, a bookstore, or perhaps even a hospital or observatory.

The most important element of these simple informal structures was the shaikh who—sitting in a chair—presided over the gathering and accepted students whom he would allow to form a semicircle on the floor around him and listen as he either read from his own writings or uttered commentaries on the manuscripts of others. Such an approach to instruction established an enduring bond between the mentor and his disciples.

The Pervasive Study Circle (Halqa)

The dictates of Middle Eastern hospitality required that an individual who invited guests to his home had to offer them some form of food and drink. This predicated that circles convening in homes would be quite small. From Ibn-Sina, we receive a description of how he met with his halqa—beginning at daybreak, and discussing and reading with it until midmorning.[1] Al-Ghazzali, as well, is portrayed as an individual who, after leaving public life, established a circle of scholars in his home to whom he gave private attention.[2] Clearly, the reputation of the shaikh determined his ability to draw students and the intellectual renown of the circle itself.

The students or *talaba* (singular: *talib*), rendered as "seekers of knowledge," sought invitations to study with a master teacher—who, if he became displeased with them, could dismiss them at will. The older, more mature, and promising students sat closer to the master and received greater attention from him in the discussions and private meetings. Talaba copied down the manuscripts that the mentor read to them, noting his asides and comments in the margin or, if they were so fortunate as to own their own copy of a well-known manuscript, they would merely write in the margins the comments made by the shaikh.[3] We recognize this activity as "glossing a text," a common form of instruction in the medieval university.

The shaikh carefully examined the notebooks of his students, correcting errors and adding appropriate comments. The authenticity of the text completed by the student was a matter of great importance, because approval from the shaikh declared to others that it contained no errors and was a complete presentation of the subject matter. The shaikh encouraged discussion among students and invited them to challenge each other and himself with probing questions. Even guests in attendance were drawn into the debates that marked the method of instruction in the halqa. Often the discussions became heated: In the search for answers, egos and sensitivites might be bruised; but dedication to elucidating the meaning of the text prevailed over these exchanges, as acrimonious as they might become. Not only were the students stimulated by such confrontational teaching methods, but the shaikh might also have to retract or alter his stated views.[4]

Presentation of material followed a basic format. The lecture first laid out the general outline of the subject. This was followed by a detailed treatment of the subheadings and a presentation of how these related to other associated topics. The focus was on analysis and synthesis of information from the perspective of the instructor. The final step incorporated an evaluative component in the open discussion of the presented material when students and visitors might probe any issues or questions with each other and the shaikh in order to clarify the topic at a greater depth. Ordinarily these formal sessions took place in approximately two-hour periods in both the morning and the afternoon.

A student's length of association with a circle depended on his own diligence and goals. Whenever he felt he had learned as much as he could or as much as he desired from a specific mentor, he would move on to another—and perhaps pursue a lifetime on the road moving from one noted shaikh to another. If he desired some formal recognition for his acquisition of knowledge, the equivalent of certification or a diploma, he would ask for and receive a letter from the shaikh stating that his copy of the master's notes were accurate and that he had developed the requisite skills to teach others from his copy of that specific work. Such a letter—the ijaza—proffered a form of license on the owner in the same way that the letter from a shaikh in a mosque-college or madrassah did so for a student in a formal institution of higher education. The more ijazas an individual earned, the more expansive his knowledge was assumed to be and the more diverse subjects he could introduce in his own instruction.

The curriculum of the study circle reflected the knowledge and interests of the shaikh, depending on his experience and perhaps the ijaza(s) in his possession. While possession of the ijaza did not constitute a requirement to teach, it attested to a scholar's credibility and provided a form of certification recognized throughout Islamdom, thus enabling a learned man to travel widely and establish himself as an instructor in a locality where he was not known personally.

Because the study of Falsafah never acquired a foothold in the standard curricula of formal schools, it achieved its home in the informal study circle and from there influenced the intellectual life of Islamic culture.[5] An introductory course of instruction in the halqa would probably commence with the "Isagoge" and commentaries of Aristotle's works and proceed through as many of the translated manuscripts of Greek philosophy in the possession of the mentor. If he were a true polymath—well versed in all areas of knowledge—his instruction would incorporate elements of natural science and medicine as well. Each shaikh had his own favorite among the foreign sciences and would become noted for his skills in teaching that particular subject matter, but certainly not to the exclusion of the others. Those circles attached to hospitals and observatories tended to stress the natural sciences and healing arts. The circles also provided the locus where young scholars acquired the skill of philosophic debate and the use of logic and disputation in defending their theses and in challenging those of other individuals.

Study circles took root throughout Islamdom and have come down to the present in Islamic countries. With the rise of the traditionalist movement and the slow rejection of philosophy and theology, the halqa in private homes provided the major means through which young men encountered Greek learning and, as mature scholars, eventually transmitted the cultural heritage into Medieval Europe. Without the halqa, it is unlikely that the works of al-Kindi, Ibn-Sina, al-Farabi, and Ibn-Rushd would have been so widely disseminated in Islamic lands.

A slight variation of the halqa manifested itself in the form of the literary salons, which appeared initially in the palaces of the caliphs—both at Damascus and later in Baghdad—but later became popular among the lesser rulers and nobility.[6] As in the case of the study circles that convened in homes, the reputation and prestige of a literary salon depended primarily on the wealth and power of the patron to attract learned men into his court. Although the social status and prestige of caliphs and governors stood unquestioned, members of the lesser nobility and of the rising mercantile class aspired to gain favor and recognition by the quality of the scholars who surrounded them and the sophistication of the discourse that took place among them. Such gatherings maintained protocol, requiring a specific dress and behavior that was primarily dictated by the social status of the host. Those invited to attend represented the intelligentsia of the day in a particular community. Astronomers, mathematicians, philosophers, theologians, religious leaders, and political appointees eagerly sought entree to the more selective literary salons; particularly desirable was a summons from the caliph or the governor of a province.

The topics for discussion were set primarily by the host and what he considered as both intellectual and topical for that day. He might seek the advice of intellectual luminaries of his court to assist in refining and preparing a topic for discussion. Quite often, recitations would precede the debate, and individuals were expected to prepare for the discussion by reading specified manuscripts. Despite the restricted behavior expected of participants in a salon, the event itself facilitated reflection on important issues and fostered the development of skills in debate. As in the individual study circles of learned men, the salons tended to encourage the reading of Greek philosophy and science and challenged guests to debate topics related to them and their role in Islamic intellectual life. Even so weighty a topic as whether or not the Quran was created received attention in the salons of Baghdad.

Honor and a special mark of favor accrued to those invited to participate in such debates and conversations. Young scholars eagerly sought invitations, hoping to receive recognition if they conducted themselves in a scholarly demeanor. The court circle of both the caliphs al-Rashid and al-Mamun were particularly distinguished for the sophistication of their discussions. Al-Mamun—particularly—delighted in staging debates and disputations among scholars of opposing views, setting those with Neoplatonic views against those who held a conservative Islamic view of philosophy. After the suppression of the Mutazilite movement and the curtailment of Greek rationalism in Islamic intellectual life, literary salons tended to reaffirm traditional beliefs—weakening the stimulus for diverse intellectual advancement. However, for a short period of time in the Classical Age, the literary salons offered a powerful means through which Greek intellectual thought and science gained entry into Islamic culture. Such spontaneous structures encouraged many individuals—teachers, bureaucrats, and merchants—to pursue advanced study in all areas of knowledge. Further, the salons gave rise to more complex and formalized structures of higher education when various court circles incorporated a library, an observatory, and a translation center.

Bookshops and Libraries

Although modern scholars might have difficulty in recognizing bookstores as centers of higher learning, they did fulfill that function in cities and towns throughout Islamdom.[7] The bedrock of Islam lies in a book: the Quran. With the compilation of the hadith stories in literary form, the basic structure of sunnah also was bound to the written word. In addition, the long oral tradition of poetry as a means of educating and enculturating people of various tribes throughout the Orient also fostered a great love of stories and epic poetry. When that legacy was placed into written language, it too emphasized the importance of literacy and the centrality of books to Islamic society.

During the Abbasid high caliphate, bookstores proliferated throughout the Middle East, and their importance spread throughout the Islamic Empire, particularly through North Africa and the Iberian peninsula. Before the Mongol destruction, Baghdad numbered more than 100 booksellers; and Sharaz, Marv, Mosul, Basrah, Cairo, Cordova, Fes, Tunis and many other cities supported multiple bookshops.[8] The buyers and sellers of manuscripts—often learned and cultured men—contributed greatly to the intellectual life of the community through their selection of volumes to be translated from Greek, Persian, or Oriental tongues and those Arabic works to be duplicated and made available to the public. Bookstores acted as a clearinghouse for ideas during much of Islam's history prior to the thirteenth century. Not only did book merchants purchase and sell books to their many patrons, they also included within their services the manufacturing of them. In this they acted much like a university press as it emerged in later centuries in Europe and the Americas. The introduction of paper from Samarkand in the eighth century greatly facilitated the proliferation of volumes available to the public. Added to the convenience of paper, however, was the beautiful hand-tooled leather binding placed around the manuscript, which constituted a work of art often quite as desirable as the publication itself as an addition to a patron's library.

Because shops provided the locus of accumulation and distribution of books, not surprisingly study circles evolved and attached themselves to specific establishments. The owner of the bookstore would act as host and sometimes leader of such a circle or would invite learned men from the community to sit and preside over discussions of intellectual and religious topics. Scholars often frequented a specific store and became associated with the literary salon located there and maintained by the book merchant. While this certainly allowed the bookseller to prosper through the sale of books discussed openly among scholars, it also served a useful purpose in disseminating knowledge and making the written word—particularly of the Greek classics in philosophy and science—available to a larger number of people. Thus, bookstores and those who owned them contributed in no small measure to the intellectual awakening of Islam.

The acquisition of private libraries accompanied the rise of study circles and the emergence of booksellers in the intellectual life of Islam. Muslims of all social strata revered books, for the Quran honored scholarship above all activities. Access to knowledge and a cultural tradition prompted a strong motive for individuals to acquire their own copies of important manuscripts—certainly the Quran; but increasingly literary, philosophic, and scientific works as well. Manuscripts were expensive; those beautifully bound, even more so. Thus initially, libraries tended to form in the homes of the wealthy, the nobility, and in the palaces of rulers. Because the dictates of the Quran required that individuals share knowledge and make available this wealth to others less fortunate than themselves, those able to afford libraries often opened them to scholars and—under certain circumstances—to the public.

From an earlier Arab writer, Shalaby extracts this quote regarding books:

> Beyond all comparison it is cheap and easy to procure. It contains the marvels of history and science, the fruit of sound minds and wise experience and reports of previous generations and distant lands. Who can have such another guest that may either make a short sojourn or stay with you as your own shadow or even as a very limb of body. The book is silent so long as you need silence, eloquent whenever you want discourse. He never interrupts you if you are engaged, but if you feel lonely he will be a good companion. He is a friend who never deceives or flatters you and he is a comrade who does not grow tired of you.[9]

Reportedly, *Al-Fihrist* of ibn Ishaq al-Nadim—the definitive catalog of books and authors of Islam in the early centuries of the empire—

originated from the listing of al-Nadim's own personal library. He states his intent in compiling this index of manuscripts and authors in the preface to the work:

> This is the Index of the books of all peoples Arabs and non-Arabs whereof somewhat exists in the language and script of the Arabs, on all branches of knowledge; together with accounts of their compilers and the classes of their authors, and the genealogies of these, the dates of their births, extent of their lives, the times of their deaths, the location of their countries, and their virtues and vices, from the time when each science was first discovered until this our age, to wit the year three hundred and seventy-seven of the Flight (987 AD).[10]

The *Fihrist* offers the most complete bibliography of manuscripts written or translated by Islamic scholars up until the end of the tenth century. In addition to listing books, al-Nadim also notes the nationality, dates of birth and death, and offers comments on the character, interests, scholarship, and personal events of many authors. His index portrays the breadth and depth of Islamic scholarship during its founding years, painting an engaging picture of the great variety of intellectual endeavors pursued by Islamic scholars. It depicts their concerns with theological, religious, philological, grammatical, moral, and philosophical themes. Tragically, the *Fihrist* also reveals the extent of the world's loss in showing the numbers of valuable contributions to knowledge that are no longer extant. Only a fragment of the titles listed by al-Nadim are presently known—the contents of the rest having long disappeared from the intellectual world.[11]

The acquisition of library materials by private citizens occasioned the formation of halqa and literary salons. In the case of caliphs, the collection of manuscripts gave rise to more structured forms of the higher learning: the palace schools—most notably, those of Baghdad and Cairo. As in present institutions of higher education, the library in Islam stood at the core of the instructional program, augmenting the material presented in lectures and discussions. A number of private libraries are reported to have housed in excess of 100,000 volumes. It is difficult to know how many different titles were included within this number, however, as collectors of books often acquired multiple copies of the same manuscript because of the beauty of its lettering or the artwork evident on its cover. Where a library of many thousands of books and a study circle reside in the same building, one finds the beginnings of an intellectual center of great sophistication. Because private libraries did not come under the scrutiny of the government and religious leaders, scientific and philosophic works of the Greeks survived during the suppression of foreign ideas that commenced during the caliphate of al-Mutawakkil in the ninth century. Ibn-Sina had special privileges in the library of the prince of his province, and made due recognition of this fact in his autobiography. Other scholars as well attribute their intellectual advancement to the availability of libraries made accessible to them by wealthier and more noble patrons.

In addition to private collections housed in the homes of the wealthy and powerful, there arose in Islam libraries that offered access to books on a wider scale. Public libraries that opened their doors to the general population and offered borrowing privileges appeared in mosques, mosque-colleges, and madrassahs. Caliphs, viziers, and local monarchs often founded public libraries in order to promote literacy and advance the level of learning within their realms. Such institutions flourished not only in Baghdad (boasting 36) and Cairo (which had five noted public institutions), but also in provincial capitals (including Bukhara, Marv, Samarkand, and Nishapur) and throughout North Africa and—particularly—the great centers of Islamic culture in al-Andalus.[12]

Not all mosque-colleges or madrassahs opened their collections to the general public; but they might still invite or approve browsing and borrowing privileges to a select group of scholars, jurisconsults, or others who petitioned for entrance. Such semipublic libraries often accommodated many other needs of scholars and students in addition to providing rooms for private study and access to a large number of books. Records indicate that wealthy patrons not only offered paper, ink, and pen, but also food, lodging, and even stipends to those with limited financial resources.[13]

According to accounts, the libraries established for public use contained rooms that were richly appointed with carpets and desks, with ink and paper provided for students and scholars. In some of the major libraries, particularly those at Baghdad and Cairo, as many as 40 to 50 rooms might be set aside to house books and to provide study space for scholars and students. The manuscripts were shelved by category and catalogued so that a patron might easily find them. According to Shalaby, the well-arranged catalog of the Nizamiya in Baghdad contained 6,000 titles, and the catalog to the great library built by the Caliph al-Hakim in Cairo filled 44 volumes.[14] Shelves were labeled to assist the browser and a notation was made as to whether or not the volume was complete. The library staff made provision for the lending of books to those scholars who desired to carry manuscripts home for more concentrated reading. The circulation department imposed certain restrictions on the procedure so as to ensure the safety and careful maintenance of volumes for which it was responsible. One library in Cairo granted lending privileges only to residents of that city. In some instances, a deposit might be required; ordinarily fines were imposed on those who delayed the return of a book beyond the specified time. Sometimes, noted scholars were allowed to remove books from the shelves, take them home, and use them without posting a deposit. A borrower could not add marginal notes, nor could he correct errors without the specific approval of the owner of the book. Lending to a third party or using a borrowed book for security was disallowed also.[15]

Libraries housed books of all description and all subject matter—from Oriental volumes written in Sanskrit to Arabic translations of Greek and Latin philosophy and science. Ordinarily, their administration and intellectual leadership resided in a head librarian who made decisions with regard to which books should be purchased, how they should be catalogued, and whether or not copies of them should be made. In regard to this last function, most major libraries incorporated both a translation center and a copy room. The personnel required to maintain libraries depended on the size of the holdings and the kinds of services offered. A staff large enough to provide all these services could number more than 100 and would include translators, scribes, and binders, as well as shelvers, custodians, and assistants to the head librarian.

The number of volumes contained in public libraries is difficult to estimate since records from those centuries tend toward exaggeration.[16] But many were reported to range between 100,000 and 1,000,000 volumes. As in private libraries, numerous copies of specific books were present, thus making it difficult to tell just how many different titles were among the holdings. In a major library, several thousand copies of the Quran might be housed.

The most noted library and center of higher learning in Baghdad during the time of al-Mamun (813–833) was the Bait al-Hikmah, the House of Wisdom. This structure combined a library, a literary salon, study circles, and an observatory—all under the patronage of the caliph. Generally, historians attribute its founding to the Caliph al-Mamun; but Shalaby argues that it originated during the reign of his predecessor, al-Rashid (786–809).[17] Certainly, the Bait al-Hikmah reached its zenith of intellectual activity under al-Mamun and his caliphate. Caliphs during this time were particularly intent on acquiring manuscripts of Greek works, either from Byzantium or in translation from Jundi Shapur. The Bait al-Hikmah housed Islam's major center of translation. Headed by Hunain and his son Ishaq, the center fostered a brilliant circle of scholars by providing access to new and rare manuscripts as well as a well-equipped astronomical observatory.

At the Bait al-Hikmah, al-Kindi founded the Arabic school of Peripatetic philosophy that was later to be taken up by al-Farabi, Ibn-Sina, and Ibn-Rushd. Here too al-Khwarazmi not only contributed to philosophy, theology, and mathematics, but also undertook major investigations at the astronomical observatory. The importance of the Bait al-Hikmah declined after the suppression of the Mutazilite rationalistic movement. The traditional position taken by caliphs following al-Mutawakkil dampened the intellectual fervor of the Bait al-Hikmah, and it never again equalled the level of openness and intellectual curiosity that it had experienced under the patronage of al-Mamun. The House of Wisdom continued as part of a palace school until the time of the Mongol invasion; the troops of Hulagu burned it during the destruction of Baghdad in 1258.

The other eminent example of an outstanding library and intellectual center—the Dar al-Hikmah, the Place of Wisdom—took shape in Cairo in 1004 under the patronage of the Fatimids. The Dar al-Hikmah received acclaim especially for its sumptuous accoutrements. The largess of its patrons made available ink, paper, desks, and study rooms for scholars and students alike. Accounts of the period attest that impecunious scholars received a stipend to sustain them during their time of study there. The Dar al-Hikmah survived for more than a century as a major center of higher learning in Egypt—until the Sultan al-Malik al-Afdal closed its doors in 1122, when he discovered that two visiting scholars were delivering "heretical" lectures within its precincts.[18] Afdal's successors later reopened the Dar al-Hikmah, but decreed that only readings and sermons judged to be thoroughly orthodox could be uttered within its walls.

The destruction of the vast library collections of Islam occurred over a lengthy period of time and cannot be attributed to a single cause. Many persons and events conspired to deprive the world of this great treasure. Certainly, personal collections fell to the vagaries of family fortunes and—in some cases—neglect. Not every father's son valued the manuscripts acquired at great cost over several generations. By far, however, the loss of the Islamic corpus of so many volumes can be laid to political and social events. During their invasions of the Middle East in the thirteenth century, the Mongols displayed no love for learning nor respect for property. They destroyed cities wholesale and library collections disappeared in the flames—quite literally, for the members of that invading horde used the manuscripts for fuel. The great library of Tripoli fell to the destructive instincts of the Crusaders on command of a monk who was displeased with the number of copies of the Quran housed on its shelves.[19] The number of volumes destroyed in the religious zeal of the Crusades cannot even be estimated. The great libraries of Moorish centers of culture also succumbed to the enthusiasm of Christians for destroying what they considered the dangerous heretical books and mystical knowledge of the infidels. Little remains of the great private and public collections of Cordova, Granada, and Toledo. Fortunately, much of the best of Islamic thought had already been translated into Latin prior to these devastating events and were rescued from oblivion to enlighten the nascent scholars of the Western World. Still, we scholars of later generations can only speculate on the extent of the loss. In scientific fields, whatever void existed has certainly been bridged. But in philosophical and literary areas, there is no way to calculate the benefit that subsequent generations might have gained from the insights of the brightest minds of those centuries.

Observatories, Clinics, and Hospitals

While observatories did not constitute a part of many palace schools, they did take shape in major ones such as the Bait al-Hikmah founded in Baghdad.[20] Caliph al-Mamun established the astronomical observatory and in 828 employed the brilliant mathematician al-Khwarazmi to lead research studies there. After the tenth century, observatories enjoyed the patronage of many rulers who built them to further celestial exploration—especially investigations into the organization of the calendar and as a means of determining the most propitious and the least advantageous days to undertake specific political activities. Around the year 1023, Prince al-Daulah of Hamadan in Persia commissioned the building of such an observatory for Ibn-Sina. Also, the Seljuk rulers in Baghdad constructed a major observatory for Umar al-Khayyam and his colleagues, with a mandate for them to formulate a more precise calendar. This they did around the year 1100.

Perhaps the most renown of all the observatories in Islamic lands took shape in the Persian town of Maraghah in 1261. Ironically, its construction was ordered by the same Hulagu—grandson of Genghis

Khan and leader of the Mongol hordes—who laid waste the major cities of Islam in the Orient, including Baghdad. This observatory housed the most advanced equipment for astronomical observation then known and was placed under the administration of the great polymath al-Tusi, whose scientific acumen we have previously discussed. The observatory was noted for the accuracy of its mural quadrant—with a radius of 430 centimeters, the largest of its kind. Among its many instruments the observatory also included armillary spheres, solstitial armilla, equinoctial armilla, and azimuth rings—all essential for mapping the orbits of celestial bodies. The library associated with the observatory housed some 400,000 volumes in all areas of knowledge. Study circles also flourished at Maraghah—allowing scientists and scholars there to instruct students, pass on the known scientific writings of the day, and cooperate with them in further investigations.

Hospitals and clinics also served as centers of higher learning during the high caliphate of the Abbasids. Hospitals—as in the case of lending libraries and observatories—received support from public funds and the patronage of the caliphs, governors, and sultans. In addition, wealthy patrons endowed hospitals with property and other assets, the earnings of which provided for the construction of the buildings and the salaries of medical staff. Islam can take great pride in the quality of health care available in such facilities during this period. Baghdad at one time licensed some 860 physicians; in the year 1160, it maintained about 60 medical institutions.[21] Cairo, as well, had five hospitals; and Damascus and the Andalusian cities of Cordova and Seville were equally known as great medical centers.[22] A hospital complex might include a library, a kitchen, study halls, ornate waiting rooms, as well as pharmacies, baths, treatment rooms, and patient accommodations. Physicians assigned patients to wards according to their symptoms or their diagnosed disease. Housekeepers assured that wards and rooms remained well ventilated and clean.

Through the patronage of either the government or endowment, hospitals provided all of their treatment free of charge. This included drugs, food, and—in some cases—performers who would help to calm patients and entertain them during their convalescence. Appointees of the caliph or governor inspected hospitals and clinics and awarded those who met specific criteria with the necessary licenses to continue in operation.

Medical education as conducted in the hospital setting would employ noted physicians who admitted aspiring physicians into their intimate circle.[23] The former would work with their students individually, assign them patients in the ward and clinics, evaluate their progress, and include them in clinical procedures—surgery, among others. The intention of the mentor was always to combine theoretical and practical studies into an integrated learning experience for the student. A physician teaching in such a clinic or hospital—surrounded by his students—would resemble the modern internship and residency system in which a physician conducts grand rounds with his students.

According to Hamdani, the course of study was as follows:

> First year's course consisted of "Aphorisms" of Hippocrates, "Questions" of Hunayn bin Ishaque, and the "Guide" of Rhases. Second year's course included the "Treasury" of Sabit ibn Qurra, the "Liber Almansoris" of Rhases, "Aims" of Ismail Jurjani, "Direction" of Abu Bakr Ajwini, or the sufficiency of Ahmad ibn Faraj. The higher classes courses consisted of "Continent of Rhases" or "Liber Regius" of Haly Abbas or "Canon" of Avicenna and "Thesaurus" of Ismail Jurjani. "Canon" was the most popular. These books related to anatomy, physiology, pathology, pharmacology, hygiene, forensic medicine, medicine, surgery, gynecology, obstetrics, eye, ear, nose, and throat diseases.[24]

At the end of the course of study, students were subject to examination by a representative of the government who would test their medical knowledge and evaluate their skills in practicing medicine. In addition to the license granted through the civil system, a student would also receive a letter of authorization (ijaza) from his mentor upon completion of the course. In the tradition of scholarship in the Middle East, a physician's knowledge was not limited to the study of medicine. As an aspiring polymath, one who pursued the physician's license also engaged in the study of philosophy, science, and religion. For instruction in these fields, he would attend the halqas of other learned men—either in mosques or private homes—where again he would receive an ijaza.

Adab—Liberal Education in Islam

Those desiring to increase their education through informal means were not restricted to the pursuit of the foreign sciences. The concept of a general education took form in Islam through that literary curriculum named *adab,* often translated as belles lettres or polite learning.

Bosworth maintains that such generalizations limit the meaning of the concept. According to him, the translation of *adab* "seems to denote 'custom, mode of life, rule of conduct,' and in practice it meant the sharpening of the mind through humanistic studies."[25] As such, adab supplemented the religious education of many individuals—particularly those in the middle and upper socioeconomic classes who sought knowledge of worldly matters to give them a necessary sophistication in their daily activities, whether government service, business, or merely participation in intellectual and cultural affairs.[26] One who possessed such polite knowledge of cultural and civic affairs acquired the title *adib*—the well-rounded, or the liberally educated, person.[27] The lessons of adab were useful particularly for those who served as administrators and secretaries in the state bureaucracy. As quoted by Bosworth, a secretary serving under the last Umayyad caliphs admonishes his colleagues thus:

> O secretaries, strive to become proficient in the various branches of *adab!* Become learned in religion, beginning with the study of God's Word and the prescriptions of Islam! Then perfect yourself in the Arabic language, for it gives an incisive edge to your tongues. Then become skilled in calligraphy, for it constitutes the adornment of your writings. Be able to relate poetry, and be conversant with its striking features and meanings. Learn about the battles of the Arabs and Persians, and the tales and exploits connected with them, for all this will be an aid for you in whatever your ambitions may aspire to.[28]

To assist those seeking adab, a few Islamic polymaths authored texts elucidating basic information about all areas of knowledge. Mention was made in Chapters 2 and 3 about the efforts of al-Farabi in *The Enumeration of the Sciences* and about the Brethren of Sincerity, who edited a compilation of *Epistles* in this regard. A most useful encyclopedia of knowledge appeared shortly after Hellenistic influences had reached their apogee, written by Abu Abdallah al-Khwarazmi (not to be confused with the noted mathematician, Musa al-Khwarazmi) and entitled *The Keys of the Sciences*.[29] Evidence indicates that the *Keys* took final form sometime after 977, when the governance of Islamic lands under the Abbasids had reached a high level of sophistication and departmentalization. At that time, much of the day-to-day business of administering government bureaus resided in the hands of civil servants employed by each *diwan*—one of the bureaucratic departments established by the Abbasids to provide specialized and efficient administration of various public services.

Khwarazmi's aim was to bring together a great encyclopedia of knowledge, skills, terms, and processes both essential and helpful to the ministers and secretaries in the diwans. In doing so, Khwarazmi also portrayed an exacting view of the departmental structure of provisional government under the Abbasid caliphate. In this case, the particular bureaucracy under discussion belonged to the Saminids who governed in Bukhara, Transoxiana, during the ninth and tenth centuries. According to Khwarazmi,

> My spirit impelled me to put together a book which would include the keys of the sciences and the basic principles of the various skills which would contain all the conventional and technical terms that each group of specialists uses and that the textbooks, limited as they are to the sciences of grammar and language, fail, either wholly or in part, to deal with.[30]

The humanistic studies included in adab introduced the student to basic information of the religious sciences, the foreign sciences, and Arabic literature. It would not suffice that a secretary or minister knew literature and grammar as well as the rudiments of the Muslim faith; he must also familiarize himself with concepts of jurisprudence, religious studies, history, and all the recognizable natural sciences of that era. Practical information greatly facilitated the functions of administration, and those employed in such activities had to be cognizant of details in a wide range of intellectual and economic life. Financial accounting and the preparation of tax statements required arithmetic skills. Algebra provided the formulas for dividing inheritances according to Islamic law. Drafting cadastral surveys in order to compute land taxes employed both geometry and trigonometry. They also constituted necessary tools to measure the volume of water allotted to each farmer for irrigation. Knowledge of astronomy/astrology was prerequisite for setting dates on both the religious and agricultural calendars.

The curriculum set forth by Khwarazmi differed from that of al-Farabi and the Brethren of Sincerity in that it emphasized the practical nature of knowledge in performing one's functions as a minister or secretary. It went further than the other two broadly conceived curricula in presenting information in the format of a handbook, easily understood and found. Similar to the others, however, *The Keys of the Sciences* did aspire to present a comprehensive view of necessary available knowledge, which was considered by Muslims to be finite and therefore subject to an all-encompassing classification.

The organization of Khwarazmi's book reflected the two major classifications of the sciences firmly entrenched in Islamic culture: knowledge indigenous to Islamic society and the Muslim faith and knowledge absorbed from other cultures, primarily Hellenistic. In combining the two divisions in one corpus, Khwarazmi followed in the path of the other great Islamic polymaths who had embraced Greek philosophy and science. The incorporation of the foreign sciences into his opus distinguished his curriculum from that offered in formal structures of higher learning, the mosques, mosque-colleges, and madrassahs. Khwarazmi conceived his book as a study guide, intended for those pursuing knowledge under informal circumstances—most likely, outside a study circle. It serves as a general approach to areas of knowledge—readily understood by literate individuals with an elementary education, but not a definitive text in any specialized area of study.

In the first chapter of the book—which highlights aspects of Islamic law—Khwarazmi describes the sources of the law, with some attention given to noted jurists and the founders of the various orthodox schools. The chapter then deals with ritual cleanliness, daily worship, fasting, taxation, pilgrimages, the ethics of sales and purchases, punishment for crimes, and division of inheritances.

The second chapter focuses on Kalam and offers a glossary of terms used by philosophers and theologians. The traditional division of knowledge between the purely Islamic and the foreign sciences did represent a dilemma for scholars desiring to offer an encyclopedic view of knowledge. While both logic and Greek philosophy were adjudged foreign, both had become integral to the study of religious sciences—especially jurisprudence and Kalam. Most scholars considered logic as preparatory to the understanding and pursuit of any advanced curriculum. Aristotelian categories of knowledge and intellectual faculties grounded the study of speculative theology as it took form in Islamic circles. Thus, Khwarazmi includes both logic and Kalam as part of his discourse on Islamic sciences. In a more practical vein, the author describes the many sects and heresies within Islam; divisions of Christianity under the headings of Melkites, Nestorians, and Jacobites; and six Jewish sects. The text also makes brief mention of various Oriental religions—particularly those that had their roots in Persia. The second chapter concludes with a catechism of questions and answers commonly raised by Islamic religious leaders and considered important to an understanding of the Muslim faith. Chapter three presents the rudiments of grammar—a science that since the eighth century had evolved into a highly sophisticated approach to language, as exemplified by two famous schools at Basrah and Kufah.

Chapter four—dedicated to the art of the secretary—offers a unique sketch of a provincial bureaucracy and of the terms and processes employed by the administrators of each diwan. The first section, "On the Technical Terms Employed in the Diwans and Pertaining to Records, Registers and Financial Documents," describes the cadastral survey used for computing taxes, the register showing the balance of taxes owed, a record of installment payments, a financial balance sheet, items of expenditures and receipts, and other documents prepared to assure the appropriate levels of taxation and payments for land holdings.

The second section of the chapter reviews the "Technical Terms of the Secretaries in the Department of Taxation." It defines various forms of assets—both property and real estate—including territory surrendered through peace treaties, goods and lands gained through plunder, disposition of property of a person who dies without heirs, animals let to pasture, money paid to expatriates, and so forth. Section three outlines the technical terms for secretaries in the department of the treasury.

In section four—titled "On the Expressions Used in the Department of the Postal Service"—such details as the care and treatment of mules, their assignment, and their appropriate riders are clarified. Section five, "On the Technical Terms of the Secretaries in the Department of the Army," presents guidelines for the movement of troops, payment schedules, and allowances provided for various members of the armed forces.

Section six, "On the Expressions Used in the Department of State Lands and Resources," discusses land surveys and the various standard measurements employed to describe areas of land. Section seven focuses "On the Expressions Used in the Department of Water Regulation." Water—a scarce and essential resource in the Middle East—fell under strict regulation by the civil government. A special diwan was established to ensure the equitable distribution of irrigation water to landholders. The terminology defined in this section includes conduits, pools, dams, and liquid measurements.

The final section describes technical terms and methods employed by secretaries who indite correspondence as part of their official duties. It elucidates the proper forms of address and organization of letters, and advises on achieving a professional and accurate style in written communication. Khwarazmi suggests when to write in an ornate rather than a restrained style and cautions on the use of words that might be misleading to the reader if used in a certain context.

The final chapter of the first discourse covers a history of the world—or at least the part that influenced the evolution of the Islamic Empire. Khwarazmi outlines not only a history of the Arabs, their conquests, and the establishment of Islamdom, but also antecedent events in neighboring cultures—Greek, Roman, Persian, and Oriental. An unusual section in this chapter discusses the various sociopolitical classes of people in the regions surrounding Islamdom. It lists the proper titles for officials, mores and customs, and dialects spoken by various groups within the larger social structure.

The entire first discourse amounts to 130 pages out of a total of 290 (pagination reflects the German translation by Edward van Vloten), with 26 pages devoted to chapter four, "The Art of the Secretary." The treatment of any one subject was limited and merely offered an overview of the topic. The encyclopedia did indeed serve as a handbook and guide, and not an exhaustive—or even very sophisticated—treatment of any individual subject matter.

In the second discourse, Khwarazmi concentrates on the foreign sciences—primarily those introduced from the Hellenistic tradition. The first two chapters instruct in philosophy and logic, introducing Neoplatonic and Aristotelian theories adopted by Islamic scholars. Khwarazmi reviews the Aristotelian classifications of knowledge: philosophy, mathematics, and the natural sciences. He follows this with a section on "the supreme, divine philosophy," which attempts to define God in philosophical terms. Definitions of the various faculties of the intellect and how they are employed in the pursuit of both material and spiritual reality conclude this chapter. The chapter on logic is based on the "Isagoge" of Porphyry of Tyre, ending with a discourse on rhetoric. As reaffirmed by Khwarazmi, logic functions not only as an intellectual tool but as an ethical one, as well—enabling one to pursue both truth and morality and to distinguish between good and evil actions. The study of logic provides the means to lead a good life and achieve true happiness.

The third chapter offers a brief summary of tenth-century medical practices—many of which were drawn originally from Greek sources and interpreted by Islamic physicians. In the final section of the chapter, Khwarazmi discusses the theory of balance among the nine temperaments of the body and concludes with recommendations for the use of drugs and other natural substances to facilitate equilibrium among the temperaments and thus acquire physical well-being.

Chapters four and five concentrate on various theories and formulae of mathematics, beginning with simple arithmetic computations. In one section, Khwarazmi discusses the common numbering systems in use: the Arabic-Indian digits based on the decimal system; and the lettering system adopted from the Greeks, mostly used by accountants and astrologers. He does not mention the sexagesimal system favored by al-Biruni and other scientists. A presentation of algebraic methodology concludes the fourth chapter. In the next chapter Khwarazmi reviews geometry, drawing from Euclid's *Elements*. The mathematics of parabolic mirrors and Ibn al-Haitham's theories in optics receive only brief treatment in this discussion on mathematics.

Astronomy/astrology appears in the sixth chapter, which emphasizes the significance of the movements and conjunctions of heavenly bodies. This chapter covers "the names of the moving and fixed stars; terms relating to the structure of the heavens and earth and the rotation of the seasons; the transits of the stars; and the instruments used by astronomers, such as the flat or planispheric astrolabe, the spherical astrolabe, and time keeping instruments."[31]

In the seventh chapter, Khwarazmi turns his attention to music, musical instruments, and theories of harmony and rhythm. He describes the great variety of instruments available in the Middle East. In his section on harmonics, he draws heavily from the previous works of al-Kindi and al-Farabi. Chapter eight—in a return to more practical matters—describes mechanical contrivances and hydraulic and pneumatic machinery. Khwarazmi's sources here are decidedly Greek in origin—deriving in particular from the writings of Hero of Alexandria on hydraulic devices, levers, and pulleys. Khwarazmi emphasizes methods used to move heavy or difficult objects with minimal force. The first section deals with levers, wedges, drills, and machinery of war such as mangonels and ballistas. In the second section he writes of siphons, barrel taps, tubes, pumps, devices for hurling flaming naphtha, equipment such as waterwheels and sprinklers used to raise and direct water for irrigation, and chronometers driven by the measured falling of water or sand.

Khwarazmi concludes *The Keys of the Sciences* with a chapter on alchemy—the antecedent of chemistry. The initial paragraphs describe the apparatuses employed in distilling, melting, and baking substances—such as stills, alembics, and furnaces. Next follows a discussion of metals and metallurgy, evaporating agents, and catalysts. This final chapter ends with an outline of various chemical processes: distillation, liquification, sublimation, and calcination.

Similar to his treatment of the Islamic sciences, Khwarazmi's text on foreign sciences emphasizes popular information—intended for an audience desiring a general understanding of various academic subjects, rather than intellectual depth. He places the focus on useful information, not esoteric knowledge. The entire book—some 290 pages in the German translation—constitutes a general education for those who served in the bureaucracy, or for a private master. *The Keys of the Sciences* provides us with a unique view of the breadth and depth of knowledge expected of an educated person in Islamic society.

As the classical period of Islam drew to a close, the importance of spontaneous centers of the higher learning also faded. While many aspiring scholars would continue to further their intellectual growth at the feet of a shaikh, the prevailing atmosphere of conformity and a return to a more religiously grounded education prompted most young men to matriculate in formal structures of higher education—the mosque-colleges and madrassahs. Through them and their prescribed curriculum, promising and secure positions could be found in government, religion, and education. We hear less about intellectually exciting palace schools or the halqas of noted scholars after the demise of the Abbasid caliphate and the emergence of many petty dynasties throughout Islamdom.

Notes

1. S. A. R. Hamdani, *Notable Muslim Names in Medical Science* (Lahore: Ferozsns, c. 1960), 25–26.
2. Ahmed Shalaby, *History of Muslim Education* (Beirut: Dar al-Kashshaf, 1954), 31.
3. A. S. Tritton, *Muslim Education in the Middle Ages* (London: Luzac, 1957), 36.
4. Cyril Elgood, *A Medical History of Persia* (Cambridge, U.K.: Cambridge University Press, 1951), 234–35.
5. F. E. Peters, *Aristotle and the Arabs* (New York: New York University Press, 1968), 23.
6. Shalaby, *History of Muslim Education,* 32–42.
7. Ibid., 26–27; Mehdi Nakosteen, *History of Islamic Origins of Western Education* (Boulder: University of Colorado Press, 1964), 47–48.
8. Nakosteen, *Islamic Origins,* 73.
9. Shalaby, *History of Muslim Education,* 75.
10. E. G. Browne, *A Literary History of Persia,* vol. 1: *From the Earliest Times until Firdawsi* (Cambridge, U.K.: Cambridge University Press, 1908), 384.

11. Ibid.

12. Nakosteen, *Islamic Origins*, 69–71.

13. S. Khuda Bukhsh, "The Renaissance of Islam," *Islamic Culture* 4 (1930):295–97; Nakosteen, *Islamic Origins*, 67.

14. Nakosteen, *Islamic Origins*, 82.

15. Ibid., 73ff.

16. Ibid., 66.

17. Shalaby, *History of Muslim Education*, 96–97.

18. Edward T. Withington, *Medical History* (London: Holland Press, 1964), 168.

19. James Thompson, *The Medieval Library* (New York: Hafner Publishing, 1957), 342–43.

20. Seyyed Hossein Nasr, *Science and Civilization in Islam* (New York: New American Library, 1968), 80–88.

21. Michael J. Sinclair, *A History of Islamic Medicine* (London: Cylinder Press, 1978), 14.

22. Withington, *Medical History,* 164.

23. Hamdani, *Notable Muslim Names*, 114.

24. Ibid., 115.

25. C. E. Bosworth, *Medieval Arabic Culture and Administration* (London: Variorum Reprints, 1982), 98.

26. Franz Rosenthal, *Knowledge Triumphant* (Leiden: E. J. Brill, 1970), 240–77.

27. Ibid., 252.

28. Bosworth, *Medieval Arabic Culture,* 98.

29. See "'A Pioneer Arabic Encyclopaedia of the Sciences: Al-Khwarazmi's 'Keys of the Sciences,' " in ibid., 97–111.

30. Ibid., 100.

31. Ibid., 110.

6

Transmission of the Higher Learning to Medieval Europe

Be courteous when you argue with the People of the Book, except with those among them who do evil. Say: We believe in that which is revealed to us and which was revealed to you. Our God and your God is one.

The Quran 29:45

Intellectual activity in classical Islam attained its zenith during the eleventh and twelfth centuries with the brilliant efforts of Ibn-Sina, al-Ghazzali, and Ibn-Rushd. As the scholarly tide in Islamic provinces began to ebb, a reverse flow commenced in Christian Europe. Many events indicated a quickening of intellectual life in the Latin West commencing in the eleventh century. Europe's awakening from a long dormant period, characterized by a decaying Roman world, surfaced in all arenas: politics, economics, religion, and culture. Indications of a resurgence of interest in learning and the creation of a new society emerged throughout Western Christianity.

With the introduction of trade and manufacturing, a middle class began to take form. Residing in the towns and cities, they expressed a rising interest in secular, materialistic matters. An increase in economic activity with the concomitant emergence of a wealthier middle class also enriched the resources of the Roman Catholic Church. It, too, prospered under the centralization of power in the kings, the construction of better transportation and communication systems, and a more productive economy. Greater monies accrued to it for the pursuit of its various missionary activities—one of the most important of these being education.

The church stood almost alone as the patron of scholarship and learning in Medieval Europe. Such schools that did exist were founded under its auspices and received support through its revenues. The church provided a place for the literate—a group not particularly valued in feudal society. While manuscript collections existed in monasteries and chapter houses, the church's main concern in education focused narrowly on the preparation of clerics and priests in monasteries and cathedral schools. It was the latter institution—the cathedral school—that eventually gave rise to the medieval university. Cathedral schools offered a curriculum in which the remnants of classical knowledge gleaned from the wreckage of a decaying Roman culture were taught.[1] Although expurgated of much of its richness and rewritten to conform to Christian theology, the Seven Liberal Arts—the name given to that course of studies by Capella in the fifth century—provided the only classical education available at the time. This consisted of the trivium and the quadrivium: the former being grammar, rhetoric, and logic; the latter arithmetic, geometry, astronomy, and music. It was an impoverished curriculum, however, having incorporated little basic information since the fourth and fifth centuries. The trivium focused on reading, writing, composition, and Aristotle's basic work on logic, *The Categories and Interpretations*—which had been translated by Boethius (d. 524) into Latin (a language of the church, but not of the people). Although given less emphasis in the curriculum, the quadrivium—the sciences—introduced the student to basic arithmetical computation, the propositions of Euclid (without the proofs), and the rudiments of geography, astronomy (mostly astrology), and music in its mathematical form. The sciences in the Seven Liberal Arts had their foundation in the etymologies of Isidor of Seville (d. 636), Boethius, and the Venerable Bede (d. 735)—who based their texts on a myriad of classical Roman works that offered little accurate information about the natural world, and much of that derived from myth.

The abysmal level of knowledge in eleventh-century Christian Europe is captured in a quote from Paul Tannery: "This is not a chapter in the history of science; it is a study in ignorance."[2] Even so-called learned men knew scarcely anything of the sciences, while medical practices relied mostly on herbalogy and magic incantations. Astronomy was primarily superstition based on folklore from the Germanic tribes. Arithmetic in a rudimentary form calculated in cumbersome Roman numerals or letters representing numbers. Geometry had not gone beyond that of Pythagoras of ancient Greece, and alchemy consisted of basic metallurgy and the methods of dying cloth.

Those who sought an education beyond the elementary level went to church-sponsored institutions—whether or not they were motivated by a vocation to the religious life. The curriculum in such schools included the Latin Bible and the writings of the early Fathers of the Church—particularly Augustine, who more than anyone defined the theology of the early medieval period. Although John Scotus Erigena (ca. 815–877) prepared some tracts on a more advanced theological level, these remained practically unknown until the twelfth century. His treatises heralded the beginning of Christian Scholasticism.

Erigena initiated a method of inquiry that would be embraced by Jean Roscelin (ca. 1050–1120), who restated the ancient Greek problem of universals in a Christian context—incurring condemnation from the church. Roscelin's work would initiate the basic debate within theological circles on the existence and objectivity of universals. His adversary Anselm (1033–1109) championed the Neoplatonic position of the church. Later, William of Champeaux (1070–1121) carried the debate further. Using a dialectical method at the Cathedral School of Notre Dame in Paris, William greatly influenced one of the most controversial of early schoolmen, Peter Abelard (1079–1142). Abelard—primarily in his work *Sic et Non*—readily embraced the new learning that was introducing a form of dialectical inquiry into European scholarship. Abelard and his form of instruction stimulated the growth of a community of scholars in Paris, which would become the most noted center for the study of philosophy and theology in Medieval Europe.

The Translation of Islamic Scholarship into Latin

The emergence of institutions of higher learning in twelfth-century Europe occurred simultaneously with the translation of Islamic intellectual and scientific works into Latin and their dissemination into the French and Italian states. The ferment in intellectual centers of Europe surrounding the cathedral schools provided a ripe environment for the acceptance of the intellectual heritage of Islam. Abelard had encountered only a limited amount of classical Greek philosophy—the most important being the *Logic* of Aristotle, translated centuries before by Boethius. In addition he may have been familiar with Plato's *Timaeus*, the "Isagoge" of Porphyry—which placed Aristotelian ideas in neoplatonic form—and also the *Categories* of Aristotle as adopted by Porphyry and later translated by Boethius. The importance of Aristotle's logic becomes apparent in the methodology and format of Abelard; and certainly, the scholastic debate of universals is presented in both the "Isagoge" and the *Categories*. But one can only wonder what Abelard would have done had he access to the remainder of the Aristotelian corpus and the commentaries on it by such intellectual giants as Ibn-Sina, al-Ghazzali, and Ibn-Rushd. It remained for Abelard's intellectual successors to incorporate that vast body of knowledge into their own philosophical framework. This occurred in the twelfth and thirteenth centuries during the time that the vast treasure of Islamic scholarship was arriving in Europe and finding a hospitable atmosphere for intellectual activity in the evolving medieval universities.[3]

While some infusion of Islamic scholarship into Western Europe had taken place prior to the year 1100, a veritable flood ensued in the twelfth century, ebbing again early in the thirteenth century. This was a time of philosophical retrenchment in Islam—particularly in the Middle East—with dominance of the higher learning by traditional religious forces and the last flowering of Islamic intellectualism occurring in Andalusia with the achievements of Ibn-Rushd, whose writings on Peripatetic philosophy were condemned and mostly ignored by scholars in other Islamic countries.

For the Mediterranean basin, this marked a period of conflict in the political arena as well, with the northern Christian kingdoms of León and Aragon pushing further south against the dominions of the Moors. The Normans, as well, desired to expand their sovereignty over Islamic Sicily and parts of southern Italy. The Crusades commenced in 1095 and continued for two centuries, bringing European armies into conflict with those of Islam in the Middle East and—somewhat paradoxically— with Byzantium as well. The Crusades achieved little success—the armies of Christian Europe having "liberated" very little of the Holy Land by the mid-thirteenth century. The Crusaders seemed interested less in scholarship than in salvation, glory, and plunder. The armed conflict, however, did stimulate trade and an opening of economic doors around the Mediterranean Sea, fostering the increase of trade in northern Europe as well. On the other hand, the Crusades seem not to have facilitated the dissemination of Arabic manuscripts on scientific and philosophical subjects into Europe.

A subsequent conflict between Christian armies and Islamic forces, however, did activate the process through which the legacy of Greek scholarship finally arrived in European hands. With the continuing advance of the Turkish Ottoman Empire and its absorption of Byzantium and the eventual conquest of Constantinople, Greek scholars and manuscripts arrived in the West—primarily in the Italian states—stimulating a resurgence of interest in Greek classical literature in the thirteenth and fourteenth centuries. But this ensued after the great influx of Latin translations of Arabic works on Greek science and philosophy that occurred during the twelfth century.

Prior to that century, some isolated instances did introduce a few aspects of Islamic information into the Christian West. Perhaps the most noted of these highlight the circumstances surrounding the sojourn of Gerbert of Aurillac—later Pope Sylvester II—in Christian Spain and of Constantine Africanus (d. 1087), who defected from his Islamic homeland in North Africa to seek refuge in the seaport of Salerno.

Gerbert, who died in 1003 after a short papacy, studied for several years in Christian Spain and became acquainted with Arabic literature. It is not known, however, whether he knew Arabic or read directly from Arabic sources.[4] Most likely, he learned about Arabic numbers and the abacus from Latin transcriptions of Arabic manuscripts. After a short stay in northern Spain, he returned to his homeland and—with the support of Hugh Capet—rose through the church hierarchy to the papacy. In addition to an interest in mathematics, he also introduced to Europe a model of the universe based on an Islamic astrolabe. Gerbert stimulated curiosity about the special knowledge known only to Islamic scholars, despite the fact that no translations were available at the time and although he seemingly made no attempt to foster the translation of Arabic manuscripts into Latin. Gerbert's fascination for astronomy and mathematics brought him under suspicion, especially by critics who accused him of dealing with magical powers and went so far as to say that he had sold his soul to the devil in exchange for information about numbers and stars.

Constantine Africanus, who died in 1087, also appeared before the mainstream of translation. We know of him from a somewhat suspect biography written by a monk in Monte Cassino, where Constantine Africanus had retired.[5] The biography suggests that he traveled widely through North Africa and the Middle East, in the tradition of an Islamic polymath. For whatever reasons, he became persona non grata in his native Carthage and sought asylum in the Italian port of Salerno, which had trade connections with North Africa. He is noted for transcribing the medical editions of al-Abbas and the treatises of Hunain and his son Ishaq. Constantine passed these on as his own, however, and gave no credit for his sources. Later translators criticized his liberal interpretation of the manuscripts. Stephen of Antioch corrected his translations around the year 1127.[6] Stephen typified a new breed of translators who prided themselves on the scholarly efforts they employed in converting Arabic treatises into contextual Latin and citing proper sources when necessary. The quality and usefulness of his works greatly exceeded that of Constantine.

The transference of lands from Moslem to Christian hands in Sicily and southern Italy—but especially the Iberian peninsula—sparked the greatest translation activity of Arabic manuscripts into Latin and their dissemination throughout Europe. One might argue that this vast wealth of knowledge would eventually have found its way into Europe in translations from Greek manuscripts maintained in Byzantium. A few historians argue that Latin scholars would have benefited from more precise translations of the Greek volumes, had this been the case. The fact remains, however, that the Arabic translations came first and thus had a monumental impact on the nascent intellectualism of Medieval Europe, fostering the rise of centers of higher learning close to a century before they might have come into existence if Europe had waited for Greek manuscripts from Byzantium.

The aforementioned view also discounts the achievement and progress attained by Islamic scholars in all the areas of knowledge that they inherited from the Greeks. As reviewed earlier, especially in Chapters 3 and 4, the contribution of the Classical Age of Islam to philosophy and science cannot be discounted. Europe would have been the poorer, had it not received such a great influx of original interpretations and commentary on Greek philosophy and science through Arabic volumes translated into Latin. Byzantine scholars added little to advance an understanding of Greek accomplishments in science and philosophy during that same period—choosing to preserve the ancient learning as an intellectual treasure, rather than to advance it. Scholastic philosophy in its Arabic form was far superior to the philosophy of the Byzantine scholars. Medieval Christian philosophers and theologians owed a great debt to the insights of al-Farabi, Ibn-Sina, and Ibn-Rushd; this they acknowledged in their own writing. Whether they agreed with the statements of those individuals or not, they recognized the impact of Islamic scholarship on their own analysis of the nature of God and the material universe.

In science particularly, the advances of the Islamic polymaths went far beyond those of Hellenistic scholars and offered a level of sophistication unsurpassed for many centuries, even in Medieval Europe.

The advantage of that century's timing cannot be denied. Had the Greek texts—rather than the Arabic commentaries—been translated into Latin and had that taken place a century later than it did, a generation of scholars including Grosseteste, Roger Bacon, Peter Lombard, Albertus Magnus, and their successors would have missed the opportunity to assimilate and critique the writings of the great Islamic scholars.

As a result of its conquest by the Normans beginning in 1060 under Roger II (1101–1154), Sicily became a center for the transference of Arabic treatises into Latin.[7] Roger combined the kingdoms of Sicily and his lands in southern Italy, establishing his court at Palermo. Under Muslim rule, Sicily had become an advanced and sophisticated kingdom, far superior to its European neighbors in modes of governance and cultural activities. Roger patterned his administration after many Islamic principles and institutions he encountered there—allowing religious freedom and promoting education and scholarship. His biographer, the Muslim Idrisi, describes at length the prosperity of the Two Sicilies under Roger's enlightened administration.[8] Idrisi also—with the support of Roger—wrote a major book on geography that became the standard text in Europe.

Frederick II (1194–1250), the successor of Roger II through maternal lines, was also the son of Henry VI, emperor of Germany. Under Frederick, the Kingdom of the Two Sicilies became a major bridge between Islamic North Africa and Christian Europe. He devoted his political life to joining his lands in southern Europe with those of Germany in a continuation of the Holy Roman Empire. He was crowned Holy Roman Emperor and established his court at Foggia in southern Italy. Like his predecessor, Frederick admired greatly the Islamic heritage of his southern kingdom and established at his court a palace school patterned on those found at Islamic courts, as well as a center for advanced studies at Naples. He founded the University of Naples in 1224, structuring it on the model of similar institutions established by royal patronage in Moorish Spain—rather than through the aegis of the church, as was the normal manner with European universities. To his palace school he drew scholars—Muslim, Jewish, and Christian—to engage in the translation of Arabic works into Latin. In 1227 he attracted to his court one of the most noted polymaths of the day, Michael the Scot, who had traveled from his native Scotland to Spain to learn Arabic. While at Foggia, Michael presided over a translation center similar to the Bait al-Hikmah of the Caliph al-Mamun of a previous century. Frederick II—from his rich and powerful position—secured manuscripts from the Middle East and North Africa and provided the resources for scholars to devote their time in translation.

Within Frederick's southern kingdom, Salerno particularly became a site noted for its transcription of medical texts, which were made available to physicians in the medical school there and—in later years—to those in southern France and northern Italy. In addition to the works of Constantine Africanus and Stephen of Antioch, another resident of Salerno—Nicholas Praepositus—compiled a large medical work called *The Antidotariam,* based almost completely on Arabic sources.[9] That text became one of the staples of the medical curriculum in universities in Europe for several centuries.

The most fertile ground for translation, however, lay in the Iberian peninsula—a land shared between the Moorish kingdoms in the south and the Christian kingdoms of the north. Following the disintegration of the caliphate of Cordova in 1027, Moorish lands in southern Spain came under the power of nobles who established separate kingdoms. This diffusion of Islamic political power in the south occurred at a time when the northern Christian kingdoms were combining their resources and experiencing an era of consolidation. The conquests most important in hastening the transference of Islamic learning to the Latin West are attributed to those of the kings of Castile in their push through central Andalusia to the border of the Kingdom of Granada. Decisive to the declining fortunes of Islamic culture in Spain was the defeat of the Almohad army at Las Navas de Tolosa in 1212.

Scholarship benefited greatly from the patronage of kings and bishops during the twelfth-century *reconquista.* The intermingling of Islamic, Jewish, and Christian scholars brought forth the largest portion of the translation harvest. The most noted source of translation appeared directly after the conquest of Toledo in 1130 when the newly named bishop, Raymond, founded a translation center in his court.[10] Initially, the center drew on the resources of native and indigenous scholars—primarily Jews, such as Ibn-Daud, a convert to Christianity. Later, Toledo attracted luminaries in the field such as Robert of Chester, Adelard of Bath, Gerard of Cremona, Herman from Corinthia, and—for a time—Michael the Scot. Alfonso X, "the Wise" (1252–1284)—a scholar himself—ignored criticism and threats by supporters at his court in Seville by establishing a palace school and center for translation. In doing so, he drew heavily on the Jewish scholarly community for its personnel.

In addition to the Jews who stayed in Spanish centers of translation and cooperated with Christian and Islamic scholars, Jewish scholars also contributed to the infusion of Islamic science and medicine into Europe in another mode—through migration from Spain into southern France. Carrying with them Arabic manuscripts with which they were conversant, they first translated the texts into Hebrew so that they could be passed along in the Jewish community as it resettled throughout Europe. Later the Jews used these Hebrew manuscripts—translated into Latin for much wider dissemination—as they were courted by the nobility and invited to become part of the intellectual communities of southern France and the Italian peninsula. We have records of several translations of Euclid's *Elements,* Ibn-Sina's *Canon,* and al-Razi's *Antidotarium,* and parts of Ibn-Rushd's philosophical treatise as coming in this manner into common usage in Latin Europe during the twelfth and thirteenth centuries.[11]

The Jews—often expelled from lands when political forces changed—became the cosmopolites of the Mediterranean basin, traveling from Islamic domains into Christian lands and returning to Moorish protection as the Christians took over the Iberian peninsula and expelled them. As merchants and scholars, they spoke both Arabic and Latin and whatever vernacular was required to survive in the locality where they resided. Jews became the natural intermediaries between the Islamic south and the Christian north, and—when they were not being persecuted—acted as translators and ambassadors between these two dominant cultures.

The method of translation proceeded with difficulties akin to those experienced by the early Christian and Arab translators of ninth-century Mesopotamia.[12] The earliest known lexicon of Arabic and Latin words appeared in the eleventh century, but it was evidently little known and little used by the early translators. Ironically, many of the early translators did not know Arabic at all or had only a rudimentary acquaintance with it.[13] They relied on intermediaries—Jews and native speakers familiar with both Arabic and the vernacular, but not Latin—as their assistants. As in Mesopotamia in earlier times, an intermediating language was transposed between the two main language roots. In Spain particularly, Arabic manuscripts were translated into the vernacular or into Hebrew initially by assistants and then converted from those languages into Latin by the so-called translators. Latin at this time lacked—as Arabic had earlier—a sophisticated vocabulary. Often, therefore, Arabic and Hebrew words came over directly rather than through an invented word in Latin.

The first translations were literal—the Latin word being written directly over the Hebrew, vernacular, or Arabic word. Such literal translations lacked the proper grammatical sequence of words and often lost the original meaning. Later scholars would reconstruct these works, placing them into a more understandable and contextual Latin. But this did not occur immediately; and in many instances, the least accurate translations remained the most popular ones throughout the early Middle Ages. Roger Bacon particularly criticized the earlier translations of which he was aware.[14] Eventually, the Arabic manuscripts from Hellenistic sources were compared with the Greek books arriving from Byzantium, and a more accurate Latin version was then rendered. However, original Arabic works were often misunderstood until much later when scholars became more expert in the Arabic language and in the contextual meaning of words and were able to correct the original translations.

The transmission of theories and information from Arabic manuscripts occurred in two formats: digests and epitomes with little or no reference to Arabic sources; and literal translations attributed to the original authors in both Greek and Arabic. Adelard of Bath provides an example of the former in an epitome of science entitled *Quaestiones,* using the form of dialogue with a "nephew" to explain a great many scientific assumptions and facts.[15] Much of *Quaestiones* is misinformed and based on mythical or magical interpretations of natural phenomena. Nonetheless, Adelard declares in it that the Arabs are indeed his mentors in this subject matter, and applauds them for their scientific acumen. This did the Islamic polymaths little service, for in later years when many of the assumptions in *Quaestiones* were found to be false, Islamic scholarship was criticized for its inaccuracies. To his credit, however, Adelard also provided accurate translations of Euclid's *Elements* and al-Khwarazmi's mathematical works in trigonometry.

Constantine Africanus might be considered within this group of compilers and borrowers since his medical works were an amalgam of several Arabic sources, freely organized and translated—and replete with many inaccuracies.[16] Herman of Corinthia also edited a great metaphysical work, *Dissentiis,* which was based mostly on the theological writings of Islamic scholars. It again suffered from misinterpretation and inaccuracies.[17]

Among the most prolific translators and perhaps the most lauded in Western culture is Gerard of Cremona (1114–1187). A scholar of some repute, he was drawn to Toledo—it is written by his biographers— because of his love for Ptolemy's *Almagest,* which was not then available in Latin translation.[18] Although Ptolemy may have been his first love, Gerard—when confronted with the great number of Arabic manuscripts available in Toledo—soon took on a lifetime's work of translating a vast number of these into Latin. In a short biography about him, Gerard's pupils listed some 71 major works translated by their mentor; 16 others have been found since that time—a prodigious effort for a single individual. He became learned in Arabic but still was assisted by Spanish Christians and Jews in his rendering of Arabic books into Latin. The long list of titles attributed to Gerard as translator includes a great corpus of Aristotle and pseudo-Aristotelian writings including the *Posterior Analytics, On the Heavens and the Earth, On Generation and Corruption, On Meteorology,* and five Aristotelian commentaries by Alexander of Aphrodisius.[19] Gerard's other philosophical transcriptions include al-Kindi (three works), al-Farabi's *On the Syllogism,* and two manuscripts of al-Israeli. His medical translations included Ibn-Sina's *Canon,* al-Razi's four major works, 11 volumes of Galen, and a treatise of al-Kindi. In science he was responsible for the availability in the West of Euclid's *Elements* and *Data,* the *Measurement of Circles* by Archimedes, and *Conics* by Apollonius of Perga, 14 other works on Muslim mathematics and astronomy, three sets of astronomical tables, and numerous works on geometry and alchemy.[20]

The wandering Michael the Scot (1175–1234) ranks second to Gerard of Cremona, although Michael was not nearly so prolific as his predecessor. In addition to directing the translation center at Foggia, his travels took him to Bologna in 1220 and later to Rome, where he resided for several years. To Michael, we are indebted for a critique of Ptolemy entitled *Spherics,* written by al-Biruni; and for Aristotle's *The History of Animals* with commentaries by Ibn-Rushd, including "On the Parts of Animals" and "On the Generation of Animals"; as well as Aristotle's *Metaphysics,* the *Physics, On the Soul, On the Heavens,* and also perhaps the *Ethics.* Both Albertus Magnus and Roger Bacon attribute their interest in science to the translations of such works by Michael the Scot.[21]

A host of other translators persisted during this time in bringing forth many volumes of Arabic works into Latin. Their cognomens depict the land of their birth and represent a geographic landscape of Europe, but their efforts were focused primarily in the Spanish towns of Toledo and Seville. To Hugh of Santillia we are indebted for the works of al-Biruni and the *Emerald Table* on alchemy; Herman the German transcribed the philosophic and medical works of Ibn-Rushd and also al-Farabi's *Rhetoric;* John of Seville, a Jewish Christian, brought forward a major tome on alchemy, as well as Ibn-Sina's *al-Shifa*.

Many different versions of the same texts appeared in southern Europe during these early years of translation because of the number of individuals who were involved in the translation process. Some manuscripts were more accurate than others, but these were not always the most widely read or accepted. With such duplication it sometimes took several centuries to uncover misinterpretations and rewrite texts in a more accurate manner that truly represented Islamic intellectualism. The volumes came over in no ordered fashion; sometimes the shortest Arabic treatises were translated first. Early Christian scholars could not trace the evolution of philosophic ideas or the progression of scientific laws or theorems.

The impact of such a large volume of translated material on Christian Europe was dramatic, in large part because of the rapidity of the translation process and the availability of so many works in such a short period of time. Most historians agree that the arrival of the Islamic intellectual inheritance caused a revolution in learning in Europe, arriving at a time when European scholars were striving to acquire a method for engaging in intellectual debate. The introduction of Islamic works and of Greek science and philosophy rekindled the light of learning in Europe. It reawakened scholarship, stimulated the search for a new process of inquiry, and whetted the appetite for new information and ideas. It fostered intellectual debate, which in turn gave rise to universities as well as literary salons, libraries, and observatories. The curriculum previously relegated to the Seven Liberal Arts and the writings of the early Fathers of the Church (primarily Augustine) greatly expanded as it incorporated new ideas. Initially, the transformation seemingly corresponded to geographic proximity: medicine and law in southern Europe, which had such close geographic ties to Islamdom and the Muslim schools in al-Andalus and Sicily; philosophy in Paris, the center of theological debate and in close proximity to the Andalusian bridge from Islam to Christianity; science appeared in many places, although it seems to have found a more hospitable environment in Oxford and central Italy in the thirteenth century and Paris of the fourteenth century.

Let us examine more concretely the impact of the translated Arabic works on various areas of the curriculum, and the acknowledged importance of the new learning to some noted medieval scholars and their ideas. It must be noted that medieval schoolmen viewed knowledge as a whole, in much the same way as their Islamic counterparts.

All objects of knowledge appeared to them interrelated; they thought it inconceivable to pursue any specialized area of knowledge without the circumscribing and core tenets of Christianity. The disciplines as we know them today did not exist in the minds of Christian schoolmen any more than they had in the minds of Islamic teachers. The medieval university, however, did commence a process of organizing knowledge into more recognizable units based on the philosophical categories of the Neoplatonists. These included theology and the various philosophies of Aristotle—natural, mental, and moral.

Islamic contributions to the areas of theology and philosophy were monumental.[22] To the teachings of Augustine—which dominated the field until the twelfth century—were added a great volume of translated works from Islam, primarily through Spain. While there is no way of knowing definitely, it is unlikely that Peter Abelard had the benefit of the thoughts of Ibn-Sina and Ibn-Rushd, even though his methodology as depicted in *Sic et Non* resembled closely Kalam—Islamic speculative philosophy—particularly in the instructional methods of the law colleges. The scholars who followed Abelard drew heavily on Arabic versions of Aristotle and the accompanying commentaries by Ibn-Sina and Ibn-Rushd. The Europeans' acceptance or rejection of the philosophies of these Arabic scholars provided the fomenting milieu out of which emerged Scholastic philosophy in its Latin Christian version. Thomas Aquinas cited Arabic scholars at will in his writings, particularly in the *Summa Theologica*. Indeed, much of his academic life was spent in an attempt to refute a number of their basic philosophical tenets. The recovery of Aristotle is considered by most historians as the greatest treasure from the classical Greek tradition. In addition to nearly all of Aristotle, there appeared the *Meno* and *Phaedo* of Plato as translated primarily by Gerard and Michael, but also by many others including John of Seville. In addition, Scholastic philosophers benefited greatly from the Arabic treatises of the original writings of al-Kindi, al-Farabi, Ibn-Sina, al-Ghazzali, and Ibn-Rushd.

Ibn-Rushd's presentation of Aristotelian philosophy as interpreted by Latin translators initially brought condemnation from church officials, particularly at the University of Paris, for its materialism and its preference for using reason rather than faith in the pursuit of truth.[23] The Parisian interpretation of Ibn-Rushd's philosophy—called "Averroism"—constituted one of the three major schools of philosophy extant during the thirteenth and fourteenth centuries. Siger of Brabant (1235–1281), the avowed champion of Averroist thought, professed at the University of Paris and quoted quite liberally from the writings of

Ibn-Sina and Ibn-Rushd in an opus on metaphysics. In that single work, there are 135 citations to Aristotle, but also 99 to Ibn-Rushd and 39 to Ibn-Sina.[24] Siger's propositions and statements on Aristotle as derived from Ibn-Rushd were condemned in 1277. Albertus Magnus, the mentor of Thomas Aquinas, had at his disposal the Aristotelian corpus and scholarly interpreted them in Christian terms. In his treatises Albertus acknowledged the Arabic versions of Aristotle and other Islamic philosophers as providing the major sources for his analysis. Thomas Aquinas's *Summa Theologica* stands in many ways as a Christian Aristotelian response to Averroism and the teachings of Siger of Brabant. Theologians and philosophers are quick to point out the great similarities between Aquinas's work and that of Ibn-Sina and Ibn-Rushd. All three assumed the monumental task of trying to rationalize faith and reason, and all three depended on the philosophy of Aristotle as their basic source. In large part they appear not greatly divergent in their views and seem much more in accord than in dissension on many basic principles of Aristotelian metaphysics.

According to Daniel,

> Neither Aquinas nor Albert needed to deviate from the main line of European thought, in order to cite ibn Sina or al-Ghazzali in matters where Islam and Christianity agree. . . . In the course of the 13th century the Arab sources were finally absorbed. They took their place as part of the inheritance from the "Gentiles" of all ages and nations.[25]

As the Middle Ages dissolved into the Renaissance, the most noted Islamic philosophers and scientists had assumed their places in a long line of thinkers on whom Western intellectual ideas were based. The texts transcribed and recopied on many occasions constituted a major portion of the curriculum in the universities of Europe. The interpretation of Aristotle that provided the basis for both theological and philosophical debate during this age emanated from the Arabic version of Aristotle coming through Ibn-Sina and Ibn-Rushd.

At the beginning of the eleventh century, mathematics as known in Europe was so rudimentary that it had no direction to go but up in some way. Adelard of Bath, John of Seville, and Robert of Chester all undertook translations of al-Khwarazmi's work on algebra; and through their translations, the study of that subject was introduced into the curriculum. These transcriptions would remain the major texts for teaching algebra until the seventeenth and eighteenth centuries. Euclidean geometry was translated by numerous individuals during the twelfth century—most notably Adelard of Bath—and it, too, remained the basic text on that subject for a lengthy period. In its basic format, the elements of geometry as transcribed from the Arabic into Latin would continue in schoolrooms throughout Europe and the Americas into the twentieth century. Along with algebra, trigonometry was unknown in Europe until the translation of al-Khwarazmi's works by Adelard of Bath and Gerard of Cremona. The tables of trigonometric functions were known in Europe as the Toledian tables of Gerard, but many other translations of trigonometric functions and the tables derived from Arabic studies became available during this period.

In astronomy, Gerard's gift to Europe was his translation of Ptolemy's *Almagest,* his self-stated first love. During this century, several other volumes on astronomy made their appearance—introduced primarily by John of Seville and Plato of Tivoli. Numerous astronomical tables became well known because of their efforts, sparking an interest in observation of celestial phenomena and the construction of observatories.

New texts for the study of biology and zoology relied heavily on Aristotle's *History of Animals,* as translated primarily by Michael and later Gerard. In addition to Aristotelian sources, other Arabic natural histories were translated during this period and found their way into the various texts on natural philosophy that appeared in schools throughout Europe.

Al-Haitham's theory and investigation of optics stimulated scientific inquiry in the thirteenth century.[26] Robert Grosseteste of Oxford and his student Roger Bacon began their experimentation with lenses based on the original theories and observations of al-Haitham. More than his work's initiating influence on optics, however, it was al-Haitham's methodology of science that had a lasting impact on European scientific endeavors through the thirteenth and fourteenth centuries. It provided an alternative to the Aristotelian pronouncements on natural science that were accepted as authoritative by most of the scholastics. Al-Haitham's influence on scientific methodology bore fruit in the centuries following the Middle Ages when a renaissance of learning occurred, initially in the Italian peninsula and later in regions beyond the Alps.

Chemistry emerged as a new area for study in Europe after the translation of manuscripts on alchemy by Robert of Chester and the *Emerald Tables* by Hugh of Seville. Also available to curious minds was Gerard's rendering of al-Razi's *Salts and Alums,* which provided a basic source book on chemical processes heretofore unknown to the

European schoolmen. Roger Bacon also credits an Arabic source—in this case, al-Razi—for stimulating his own interest in alchemy and the beginnings of chemistry.[27] Bacon drew heavily on the many laboratory methods invented by Islamic scholars. His text divided the study of alchemy into two main categories: its speculative and its practical aspects. The latter designated those areas of alchemy that had utilitarian purposes.

Although music had comprised one of the Seven Liberal Arts of the standard curriculum for some centuries, its study in this capacity was primarily theoretical—that is, an emphasis on the mathematical relationships of tones. The translation of the musical treatises of al-Farabi, al-Kindi, and Ibn-Sina by Adelard of Bath provided the study of music with an influx of new ideas and much-needed stimulation. In addition to introducing a method of symbolizing tones and noting time and rhythm in compositions, these translations introduced Arabic instruments to Europe. Most notably, the lute, the tambour, and the guitar have been consistently of great importance to Western musical performances since that time.

We end this catalog with medicine, which—like philosophy—benefited from the translation into Latin of a great number of Arabic volumes, representing the work of both Hellenistic and Islamic physicians. These transcriptions made vast amounts of medical knowledge accessible to Europe. Brought into common usage in Latin were 11 works of Galen, most of the works of Hippocrates, and the Arabic treatises of al-Razi, Ibn-Sina, and Ibn-Rushd. Ibn-Sina's *Canon* on medicine became the most widely accepted text in medicine during the medieval period, with editions continuing in use until the seventeenth century. Despite the availability of texts describing the clinical practices of Islamic physicians, their Christian counterparts tended to ignore much of the valuable information emphasized in them. The importance of hygiene and sanitation, for instance, seems not to have been known; and they were little employed in the healing process. Bleeding, purging, and magic potions persisted for many centuries as the main staples of the European physician's approach to his practice.

Arabic compilations of pharmacology also made their way into Europe in Latin translation during the twelfth century. These, too, endured as the major sources of that subject down to recent history, providing information about thousands of herbs and plants and their value in healing. Surgical procedures discovered and recorded by Abulcassis also became available in the medical schools and hospitals just emerging in Medieval Europe. Until the works of Vesalius (1514–

1564) in Padua, surgical procedures developed by Islamic physicians offered the best directions in such matters available to European physicians.

Through all of this absorption process, Europeans remained grossly ignorant of Islam and the life of Mohammed and the basic tenets of the Muslim religion. Understanding of Islamic theological thought and the tenets of its religion were not a priority in the reemergence of intellectualism in Europe.[28] In 1142, Robert of Ketton transcribed a paraphrase of the Quran into Latin at the request of Peter the Venerable, abbot of Cluny.[29] Widely distributed throughout Europe until the seventeenth century, this version—with its many ellipses—did much mischief in that its portrayal of Islam veered greatly from the text of the original Quran and led to great misunderstanding of the basic beliefs and rituals of Muslims. As a result, Europeans tended to confuse greatly the role of Mohammed and saw him as a rival to Jesus Christ. They generally believed that "Mohammedans" worshipped their founder in much the same way as Christians worship Jesus Christ. Ironically, they charged that the Muslims engaged in idolatry, despite the strong commandment prohibiting it that the Quran contains. The Christians by tradition were less tolerant of other religions than Muslims were in recognizing the beliefs of other sects. Christianity had no parallel for the Quranic mandate demanding tolerance of adherents of other faiths. The Crusaders' brutal treatment of the Saracens hardened the attitude toward Christians of many Muslims, however, and lessened their tolerance. After the Crusades, Islamic civil leaders did persecute Christians to a greater extent than had occurred in prior times. For their part, church leaders suspected that those elements of Islam that honored Jesus as a prophet and Mary as his mother disguised a deceitful motive for encouraging conversion to Islam. The Christians basically dismissed the notion that Islam could honestly admire the important figures of another religion, because Christians could not accord similar honor to Mohammed or any of his followers. The actual persecution of Muslims as heretics, however, happened only rarely until the sixteenth century.[30] Followers of Mohammed living in reconquered Spain did face the choice of conversion or deportation; and from time to time, discriminating legislation prevented their participation in pilgrimages and required them to wear specific dress for identification purposes.

Like the Arab inheritors of Greek science and philosophy of the ninth century, Christian scholars in the twelfth century drew what was interesting and useful to them from Arabic manuscripts, and also only that knowledge they found to be consistent with basic Christian tenets.

They—like the earlier Arabs—were selective borrowers of the culture presented to them in new translations, and chose not to deal with primarily theological and literary themes as they appeared in Arabic literature. In philosophy, they could accept the methods of resolving differences between reason and faith by Ibn-Sina and the pietism of al-Ghazzali. Despite their fear of Averroism, they accepted Ibn-Rushd's comments on Aristotle and found themselves much in agreement with his basic premises. Islamic science and medicine came over intact and were absorbed into the European intellectual stream. European school-men—while rejecting Islam as a religion, and the theological treatises of Islamic scholars—separated theology from the philosophic and scientific writings of those same authors. Aquinas goes so far as to categorize Muslims as a cultural linguistic group, and not on the basis of their religion.[31] European scholars viewed Arab culture through blinders. They chose not to see the aspects that would raise barriers between themselves and their Islamic colleagues. Whatever they may have thought about Mohammed and his successors and their religious life and beliefs, Europe's scholars of the day did not allow it to interfere with their acceptance of genuine scholarship as manifested in Islam's philosophical and scientific treatises. Where Islamic polymaths had demonstrated a mastery and depth in knowledge beyond that known in European academic circles, their intellectual achievements were welcomed and absorbed by Christian schoolmen without prejudice. The more purely parochial and religious writings of those same Islamic scholars tended to be ignored or dismissed by their European counterparts.

Islamic Contributions to the Medieval University

The West has long recognized the importance of the transference of knowledge from Islamic lands during the Middle Ages and its stimulation of scholarship. The knowledge thus infused emanated from informal and private structures of higher learning as they appeared in Islamic society—through independent scholars working in study circles, libraries, hospitals, and observatories. Western scholars, however, have not perceived the formal structures of higher learning in Islam—the mosque-colleges and the madrassahs—as being sources of any chracteristics of the higher educational institutions of learning in the Christian West. Nevertheless, those two religiously oriented institutions dominated higher education throughout Islamdom as a structured and prolific school system that served as alma mater to the vast majority of Arabic-speaking students and faculty. What impact did these schools have on higher education as it emerged in the Christian West? Their effect appears less dramatic than that of the translated corpus of Arabic manuscripts. Yet Western Christianity could not have ignored such institutions and the instructional methodology they employed. Information of them would have come not only through the translated manuscripts themselves, but also through acquaintance with the translators and other Christian and Jewish scholars familiar with life in the madrassahs and mosque-colleges of Spain and Sicily. Seemingly, the introduction of the more formalized aspects of Islamic higher education into the West has a missing link, but recent investigations suggest that such a nexus does indeed exist.[32]

One cannot ignore the parallels in instructional methodology in both systems. Nor can one discount the fact that Islamic models of higher education predate those in Medieval Europe by as much as two centuries, and that ample opportunities existed to allow for exchange of ideas and the flow of information about Islamic higher education to the West through Spain, Sicily, and Byzantium. Further, one recalls that both Islam and the Latin West shared a classical Greek heritage. The intellectual roots of both cultures lay in Neoplatonic idealism and Aristotelian logic. Byzantium—the direct heir to Hellenistic culture—shared a long frontier with the Islamic Empire; manuscripts and scholars moved freely between the two great states. Byzantium also bordered the Christian West, and—similarly—written works and teachers traversed national lines throughout the Mediterranean basin.

Of the possible influence of Islam on Latin instructional methodology and academic structure, the case for the first stands on much firmer ground. The Arabic and Latin academic communities evinced a parallel structure of scholastic methodology, which existed almost identically in both higher educational systems—not only as a method of analysis, but also as a medium for presenting intellectual concepts. Peripatetic philosophy faded in the tenth and eleventh centuries as a formal part of higher education in Islamic schools. But the methodology of philosophy as derived from the Greeks and advanced by Islamic scholars did exist in Kalam, and through it entered the premier institutions of higher learning in Islam: the law colleges.

For both Islamic and Christian scholars, scholastic methodology emerged from the tension that existed between faith and reason. Each culture sought a means to rationalize the faith revealed to them—in one instance through the Quran, and in the other through the Bible—

with the reality of ordinary experience. Each pursued a methodology that relied on logic and Greek philosophy to bring harmony to the discordance of their intellectual lives. In both societies, learned men accepted the challenge to harmonize religious authority—which permeated the civil order—and the intellectual fruits of their own reasoning. For each, the approach in rationalizing the world around them became more structured and formal through the passage of time.

In both Islam and Christianity, basic philosophical assumptions derived from revelation. Yet learned men in each denomination embraced the deductive method, engaging logic to validate interpretations of religious dogma and to inform the conscience on moral behavior while defining right action in a practical world. For both cultures, the bases of revelation remained unquestioned, and the basic tenets of religious faith were presented always as unassailable truth. In Islam, where advanced religious study resided primarily in the study of jurisprudence, Scholasticism found its home in mosque-colleges and madrassahs dedicated to the study of religious law. There it clothed itself in a formalized style with elements parallel to those found in Latin Christian Scholasticism embedded in the medieval university.

Although in later years Scholasticism was most associated with philosophy and theology, it can be argued that its origination in the West occurred first in the study of law—much as it did in Islam. Grabmann demonstrates that Scholasticism appeared first in the study of canon law around the year 1100 in the writings of Bernold of Constance (d. 1100), who used the form of disputed questions to defend the religious pronouncements of Pope Gregory VII.[33] While setting opposing statements on religious issues side by side, he provided a set of rules by which an individual could resolve the contrary views. Evo of Chartres (1116) also used this method, which was sometimes called *sic et non,* prior to Abelard.[34] In his work the *Decretum,* Evo cites rules for reconciling contradictory texts. Those influenced by the work of Evo included Alger of Liege and Hugh of St. Victor, along with Peter Abelard. Canon law received its greatest impetus at this time in the teaching and writing of Gratian of Bologna (ca. 1250), who—borrowing heavily from Evo and Alger—wrote a great tome, *Concordia Discordantium Canonum,* in which he presents some 4,000 disputed statements and also states rules for reconciling them.[35]

For the Christian West, however, Abelard's celebrated *Sic et Non* endures as the nascent opus of scholastic methodology in the study of philosophy and theology. Further evidence of the use of scholastic methodology in the study of law in the West comes from the studies of Kantorowicz, who also investigated the glossators of canon law in the twelfth and thirteenth centuries.[36] He analyzed the works of many teachers of the law—particularly those of Bulgarus (d. ca. 1166), whom Kantorowicz cites as having originated the methodology of disputed questions. Kantorowicz also substantiates the use of the *reportatio* in legal studies at about the same time.

The purpose of recognizing that scholastic methodology appeared first in legal scholarship and then later in theological scholarship is to establish a stronger bond between the study of the law as it appeared in Islamic higher education and the study of both canon and civil law as it emerged in the twelfth-century medieval universities. Makdisi presents evidence that points to the transference of scholastic methodology from Islam to Europe in the form of the legal disputation, thus indicating a tie between the study and practice of law as it occurred in both cultures—with Islamic colleges of law predating by more than a century those that arose in Europe.[37]

Grabmann presents a correlated cause for the evolution of scholastic methodology in the West—not linked directly but, rather, indirectly to an Arabic source.[38] The advance of the disputation as it became known in the West relied heavily on the availability in the early Middle Ages of the remainder of Aristotle's *Organon* (not previously known in Europe) and also his *Prior and Posterior Analytics*—both available in Europe as the result of Arabic manuscripts translated into Latin. These works particularly emphasized dialectic—the basis of scholastic methodology in both its Eastern and Western format. Grabmann argues that the more stylized form of Scholasticism as evident in Thomas Aquinas's *Summa Theologica* could not have followed directly from Abelard's *Sic et Non*, but required the infusion of Aristotle's later works for its final statement. By the middle of the twelfth and certainly by the thirteenth century, scholastic methodology was well formed and stood at the core of the instructional methodology in all faculties of the medieval university.

It is now appropriate to examine more carefully those elements of scholastic methodology that existed in both Islamic lands and the Latin West. These methods appeared in Muslim institutions of higher learning more than a century prior to their identification with the medieval universities of Paris and Bologna.

The Arabic form of *sic et non—khilaf*, defines the process of resolving disputed questions. It came into existence because Islam had no priesthood or ecclesiastical hierarchy to make decisions with regard to faith and morals. Where no clear statement could be found in the Quran or hadith, Islam placed its faith in the Quranic passage that declares that God will not allow His people knowingly to err in matters of faith and morals. Thus, consensus of the community guides the faithful in such circumstances. Two methods existed for deciding if the community of the faithful had reached consensus on a specific issue. The first involved agreement among recognized jurisconsults—with the approval of the caliph—that a certain statement was authoritative. The second came from silence. If no one came forth with arguments against a specific stand, the community could assume that consensus had been reached. The scholastic approach of khilaf—that is, disputed questions—provided the means by which legal scholars underscored that differing views on specific questions existed and that consensus could not be assumed at the particular point in time. Legal scholars established rules for resolving these kinds of disputed questions as an academic exercise; but, often, no direct conclusion was ever proclaimed and promulgated by the ulama—the arbiters of religious law in Islam.

Khilaf constituted an important instructional tool, as well. As they studied with a master, students would compile a great syllabus—the taliqa—that provided them with their own resource material for decision making and instruction. The format employed was that of disputed questions. Students duly noted all known arguments for and against a specific issue and, in the margin, added their own interpretation of the relative value of each.

Christian schoolmen used the same technique of *sic et non* in the study of law, as well as philosophy and theology.[39] In the area of philosophy and theology, the method initially could even be a help in avoiding the charges of heresy that might be proffered by authorities when an individual scholar took a stand that deviated from the prevailing theology of the time. As in its Islamic counterpart, the Latin form of *sic et non* included rules by which a scholar could analyze two contrary statements.

Dialectic—the methodology advocating a specific position on a disputed point—was called *jadal* in Arabic. In both Islamic and Christian intellectual circles, its purpose was to convince an opponent of the validity of a position and, through logic, to discredit the argument presented by the adversary. This procedure drew heavily on the rules of oratory and rhetoric that were formulated in the Greek and Roman worlds and were transferred first into Islamdom and later the Christian West. Several noted Arabic textbooks on the process of dialectic from the Classical Age still exist and continue to be used. Two forms of dialectic arose in the Christian West: one as applied to legal matters, and the other in the more speculative studies of philosophy and theology.[40]

Dialectic appeared in a more formalized structure through the disputation—in Arabic, *munazara*. The disputation—a formal, stylized presentation—could be rendered in either oral or written media. The arrangement of the argument appeared in much the same way in both Arabic and Latin literature. Basically it encompassed the following elements: (1) thesis and counterthesis; (2) arguments for the thesis; (3) objections to the arguments; (4) replies to the objections; (5) pseudo-arguments for the counterthesis; and (6) replies to and refutation of these pseudo-arguments.[41] In both European and Islamic lands, the process of disputation also clarified the provinces of reasoning—distinguishing between what could be argued from revelation, and what from logic and experience. Dialectics as it appeared in the disputation affirmed faith, while rationalizing knowledge gained from the senses with that faith. Two models of the formal disputation come down to us. In Arabic, the *Wadih* of ibn Aqil stands out as the premier statement of the disputation; in Latin, the *Summa Theologica* of Thomas Aquinas is considered the most authoritative model of scholastic methodology. In both, reason and faith are harmonized and revelation is justified.

Disputation occurred as an instructional and teaching device in both the Arabic and the Latin school systems. It provided a means of examining the competence of students in the knowledge base from which they worked and also their skill in presenting a logical argument in defense of a thesis. A student who could not dispute in both written and oral forms at an acceptable level as judged by his mentors could not be incepted into the masters' guild, nor receive a license to teach.

As it occurred in the medieval university, the inception of a student into the guild of masters took the form of a public event, followed by a public celebration. A similar observance did occur in Islamic educational circles, as well. There it was known as *dars iftitahi*. Inception into the *universitas magistrorum* bestowed on the recipient all the rights and privileges of a teacher in the medieval university. It also meant that the chancellor of the diocese would present him with a formal license, attesting to the scholar's new status. A great banquet then took place, during which the recipient provided food and drink for his fellow students and his new colleagues—the masters. This could be a rather expensive celebration for the new master; and there were occasions when a scholar delayed his inception until he could afford the celebrations that accompanied it.

In Islamic higher education, the dars iftitahi took on a more subdued tone. It portrayed acceptance by the brotherhood of scholars in a kind of abstract, generic manner. No formal ceremony marked the event, nor was a major celebration for the student and his colleagues obligatory. The dars iftitahi recognized the acceptance of a student as a peer by the other shaikhs in his region or city. It might also be accompanied by the awarding of a writ of his ability to teach a certain manuscript— a document called the *ijaza*.

While some form of licensing did thus exist in both cultures, they evidenced some distinguishing characteristics. As noted in Chapter 2, the ijaza took the form of a personal letter from a mentor attesting to the fact that the student had completed a course of study under the mentor's direction and could now teach from his own taliqa a certain scholarly opus. In this regard, it was a restricted license. The ijaza did not have official recognition from any formal structure within Islamic society.

The *licentia docendi* in Europe was a document presented to the candidate by the chancellor of the diocese, declaring that the recipient had the academic experience and qualifications to instruct in broad areas of subject matter in any of the church institutions within the diocese. Later, when some of the universities had received a papal charter, the authorization was expanded to allow the candidate to teach in any institution throughout Christendom—*ius ubique docendi*. For a number of years, the granting of the licentia triggered a struggle for power between the masters' guild and the chancellor of the archdiocese over control of higher education. At first—as in Islamic lands— the faculty itself granted permission to teach, upon the student's completion of the disputation. Later, the chancellor of the archdiocese insisted that he alone was empowered to grant such certification. Having more political control within the church structure, the chancellor prevailed. But the masters did not give up so easily, and eventually were able to secure from the chancellor the authority to recommend students for the licentia. Implied in this was the notion that the chancellor would not give the writ to any person not approved by the faculty. Still, the faculty won the right to have their recommendation always honored: That is, the chancellor could not deny a licentia to someone who had been recommended by the faculty.

Despite these basic differences, a number of similarities existed as well. The licentia and the ijaza incorporated the same criterion: demonstrated competence in subject matter and in the skills of instruction. In both cultures, society recognized the grantors' authority to award the degree to deserving students. In each milieu, the degree constituted an authorization to teach or to pursue a professional career in the governmental or religious bureaucracy. Finally, each culture recognized a religious responsibility in licensing. In Europe, the church granted the license directly. In Islamic lands, the ijaza was written by a religious person—the shaikh—attesting to the orthodoxy of the student in the subject matter studied.

As a result of the preoccupation of the higher learning with scholastic methodology, humanistic studies suffered a decline in both Islam and the Christian West. In both cultures, liberal studies gave way to the more specialized professional studies of the religious sciences, law, and medicine. Both educational systems consigned the arts (in Europe, the Seven Liberal Arts) to preparatory status—prior to undertaking the more advanced studies of law, medicine, and theology. Not pursued for their own sake, the humanities suffered from the neglect of scholarly work. In many instances, the arts did not lend themselves to the prevailing intellectual methodology of the time—Scholasticism—and thus languished. Paetow gives five causes for the neglect of the humanistic studies in medieval universities—the first four apply equally well to studies in the madrassahs and mosque-colleges of Islam—(1) strict clerical feeling against profane literature; (2) renewed interest in science; (3) rise of the lucrative studies of medicine and law; (4) increased popularity of logic, which led to Scholastic philosophy and theology; and (5)—which applies only to Western institutions—popularity in the schools of good medieval Latin literature.[42] In any event, humanistic studies tended to decline with the rise of Scholasticism in both Islam and the Christian West. In the West, such studies would be revitalized in the fourteenth and fifteenth centuries, during the Renaissance.

The methods of instruction—although formalized in scholastic processes—closely resembled each other in Europe and Islamdom. They fostered a system of discipleship, and a close relationship existed between the mentor and his students. Those deemed worthy by the master would be accorded status as assistants to him and would receive special attention. Basically, students of both cultures would have felt very much at home in either Paris or Baghdad.

A few distinctions, however, are noteworthy. In the West—particularly in northern universities, patterned after the Parisian model—all students and masters had taken religious vows, holding either major or minor orders in the Catholic Church. As such, they stood apart from other individuals in society and were subject to canon law, rather than civil law. This special status had both advantages and disadvantages: Quite often, the protection afforded to students and masters by the church angered townspeople and those civic authorities who wished to extend their influence over the behavior of all residents. Town–gown conflict in Europe sometimes erupted into violence, such as the St. Scholastica Day riots at Oxford in 1355 during which an estimated 50 students and villagers were killed.

In Islamic society, students and scholars tended to blend in more with the general citizenry—not distinguished by any special status from their neighbors. Since Islam has no clergy or hierarchical structure, students and scholars performed both religious and civic duties in the same manner as any other person. They enjoyed no special exemption from the dictates of the theocracy that governed Islamic society.

If we cannot trace in any direct fashion the transference of Scholasticism in its Islamic form of the ninth and tenth centuries to the rise of medieval Christian universities in the eleventh and twelfth centuries, how might such a transaction between the two cultures possibly have occurred? Bridges between the two cultures existed in a variety of places around the Mediterranean Sea—in Spain, Sicily, southern Italy, and Byzantium. What part might each of these areas have played in the transference of scholastic methodology from Islam to the Christian West? Spain—as the center of translation activity, where most of the Arabic texts first appeared in Latin—emerges as one possibility. It is difficult to comprehend that the transmitters who embraced the value of texts on philosophy, theology, medicine, and science would ignore the methodology by which these areas were sustained and nourished in Islam. Medical texts provide a case in point. Medicine as practiced in Islam employed the methodology of Scholasticism. Is it possible that Latin physicians would accept the knowledge therein and reject the process of its derivation? Sicily and the Italian states, where a rebirth in legal studies first appeared in the Christian West, enjoyed close proximity to Islamic schools of jurisprudence. Again, it seems probable that the study of law as transposed into its Latin form carried with it scholastic methods including disputed questions, the disputation, and the great syllabus.

Perhaps the weightiest evidence points to Byzantium as the most prominent bridge between Islamic Scholasticism and that in the medieval universities of the West. It is known that Photius, who later became the patriarch of Constantinople, served as an ambassador at the court of the Caliph al-Mutawakkil in about 855. During his stay at the court, he would have had ample opportunity to observe Islamic scholars engaged in rational arguments and would have been exposed to texts that demonstrated both the method of disputed questions and the disputation. After returning to Constantinople, Photius wrote a major work in which he presented disputed questions on biblical, dogmatic, philosophical, grammatical, and historical issues in a format similar to what he must have observed in the capitol of the Abbasid caliphate.[43] The easy access between Byzantine and Islamic lands would have encouraged scholars to experience Arabic scholastic methods, either through direct contact during sojourns across the border or through translated texts available in the major libraries. Due to a series of iconoclastic quarrels in Eastern Christian Orthodoxy, Greek priests and monks had fled to parts of southern Italy, establishing a fertile ground for the receipt of Byzantine scholarship. The proximate ties between Orthodox Christianity and Roman Catholicism, coupled with increased trade between Italian ports and those of the eastern Mediterranean, would have facilitated the migration of scholarly works in their Greek form into the Italian peninsula.

Although a solid route cannot be traced, the recent writings of Orientalists argue compellingly that the rise and evolution of Scholasticism in Christian Europe owes a considerable debt to Islamic sources and certainly to Arabic literature as transcribed into Latin. As in so many theories, there does seem to be a missing link in this particular explanation for the flow of knowledge. More investigation is needed. With the ever greater availability of Arabic manuscripts, a clearer picture should emerge as to how the transference actually occurred.

If propositions that establish a causal relationship between the instructional methodology of Islamic educational institutions and that arising a century later in the Christian West seem strained, the direct link between formal structures of higher education in Islamic lands and the universities that emerged in Europe appear even more tenuous. Despite similarities in structure and function and the presence of formal institutions of higher learning in Islamdom that predate the medieval university, one could contend that the establishment of such institutions arose out of similar circumstances in both societies, and that they evolved in a pattern common to both in meeting the needs of their particular and separate situations.

Both Islamic communities and Western Christianity founded institutions of higher learning through the aegis of an endowment. Endowment as used in Europe to further higher education differed somewhat from the system of waqf in Islamic law. Wealthy patrons in Europe donated assets to religious communities to provide room and board for their masters and students. Such structures bore the name "colleges"; and, while they housed students and faculty, they did not constitute a formal part of the university. A gift to a religious community was a gift to the church, and the donor lost all control over the given assets. Further, colleges initially did not control the instructional program of the university, so the endowing of a college could have no impact on the teaching and learning functions of higher education. Thus, an endowment was freely given with no hope of controlling the organization or educational programs of the university, which remained tightly in the hands of the masters' guild. In the Christian West, a donor could not enact a contract to dictate any future control of his grant.

Such was not the case under Islamic law, as we have seen. Waqf offered an opportunity to support education and yet preserve an individual's assets, while retaining control over its use. Through an endowment in Islam, the donor could dictate the qualifications for the instructor in the college he proposed to found and also the approach taken to the religious sciences studied. The donor in Islam could also provide for the continuance of the institution through a method of determining the trustees after his death, who could include members of his own family.

The basic motive underlying the system of endowment both in Islamic lands and in Europe appear similar: the desire to perform charitable works and earn salvation. But the manner in which the dictates of the endowment were implemented created an important distinction in the two structures as they later evolved.

Though institutions of higher learning in both regions created a living-learning environment for students in the form of colleges, some important distinctions between the two forms again shed light on the ultimate destinies of the institutions. In Islamic society, the college endured as a self-contained structure. It sustained only one shaikh, who controlled the curriculum and the academic lives of his students and those who assisted him. The mosque-college and madrassah were distinguished by a dedication and loyalty of the students to the one master and his approach to the subject matter.

In Medieval Europe, the college—while constituting a resident hall— supported several masters and a number of students who were bound together not so much by the familial relationship between the two groups, but by a mutually shared dedication to a religious rule. Colleges in Europe took their model from the monastic system as it had evolved in the earlier centuries of Christianity and continued into the medieval period. Initially, no instruction took place in European colleges; students and masters performed their teaching and learning functions in the context of the university guild and its structure. Only later did colleges offer instruction within their confines. The religious orders that founded colleges differed from their monastic colleagues in that they depended on donations from the public for their survival. Unlike traditional religious groups, they did not own lands that provided their sustenance. Thus a close link emerged between the founding of the mendicant orders—such as the Dominicans and the Franciscans—and the appearance of colleges. Donations to these new religious communities supported their educational mission. In the Christian West, colleges drew support not from a single patron, but from many donors. The administration of the endowed funds was a collegial function of the religious order involved.

While some historians label the large madrassahs and mosque-colleges of the eleventh and twelfth centuries as universities, such structures were not comparable to the medieval university. Essentially, Islamic society never developed a university structure grounded in a community of scholars banded together in a formal way, dedicated to both instruction and scholarship. The tightly bound guilds of both masters and scholars that emerged in Medieval Europe—giving rise to universities—evolved because citizenship in European countries tended to be a parochial matter. Persons traveling from one city to study in another were considered foreigners and were not equally protected by the laws of the city in which they now resided. In order to insure themselves from physical and economic repression, foreign students and masters committed themselves to societies for mutual protection—called "guilds." Through the strength of numbers and the threat of economic boycott, the academic guilds became powerful political forces within the city structure. As a collective, the guilds made decisions with regard to the curriculum, the method of instruction, and the criteria for examination and inception of new members. As an incorporated body, guilds were granted privileges from the papacy and rights from civil government. They accrued the right to govern themselves, except in the cases of serious crime.

Islamic law did not recognize the juridical status of a collection of individuals. This prevented scholars from coming together to seek particular rights and privileges. Thus, Islamic scholars acted independently and did not bind themselves into a group with a corporate mission. Throughout the Islamic world, every Muslim held the rights of citizenship, and was protected by Islamic law no matter where he resided. Therefore, no need arose for either students or masters to unite for protection or further their professional roles. These were already secure. Although Islamic scholars considered themselves part of a religious brotherhood, they were not bound together by a charter of incorporation nor were they governed by specific rules and regulations agreed to by a majority of the membership.

In European cities, the model of a religious community with a ruling superior and those pledging loyalty to him defined the status and role of both students and faculty. This provided a means for disciplining the membership and for assuring that certain functions undertaken by members of the guild would be accomplished. To alleviate repression and the excessive use of power, individual members elected the leaders of the guilds and thus were empowered to displace and change leadership as needed. Ordinarily, rectors of the various universities did not serve for more than a few years.

Medieval universities still exist in one modern form or another, after all these centuries. The means to change both structure and function existed within the collegial and university systems of the Christian West, but did not take root in institutions of higher learning in Islamic cultures. Although medieval universities resisted change at times and for centuries refused to incorporate the fruits of the Renaissance— particularly in the areas of science and classical literature—they eventually succumbed to the pressure of outside forces and reformed themselves from within by altering both the curriculum and the instructional methodology.

In Islamic educational circles, undying loyalty between the master and students was assumed; and because the master had attained his position through the system of waqf or by civil appointment, he could not be replaced except under extraordinary circumstances—usually a charge of heresy proffered by the ruling religious leaders, the ulama.

Despite common roots for both Islamic and European education in Greek classicism and the methodology of Scholasticism, Islamic institutions of higher learning have altered little since the twelfth century, choosing to continue in their dedication to the religious sciences— mainly jurisprudence—and excluding the advanced knowledge in the sciences and social sciences that has blossomed through the efforts of scholars in Western Europe and the Americas.

Notes

1. For a recent history of the development of the curriculum of the Middle Ages in Europe, see Bruce A. Kimball, *Orators and Philosophers: A History of the Idea of Liberal Education* (New York: Teachers College Press, 1986), 13–73; Frederick B. Artz, *The Mind of the Middle Ages* (Chicago: University of Chicago Press, 1980), 180–83.

2. Norman Daniel, *The Arabs and Medieval Europe* (London: Longman, 1975), 263.

3. For detailed accounts of the impact of Islam on medieval Latin Europe, see ibid., 263–98; W. M. Watt, *The Influence of Islam on Medieval Europe* (Edinburgh: Edinburgh University Press, 1972); Joseph Schacht and C. E. Bosworth, *The Legacy of Islam*, 2nd ed. (Oxford: Clarendon Press, 1974); Archibald Lewis, ed., *The Islamic World and the West* (New York: John Wiley and Sons, 1920).

4. Artz, *Mind*, 199–200.

5. Daniel, *Arabs and Europe*, 143–44; Philip K. Hitti, *History of the Arabs* (London: Macmillan, 1956), 579.

6. Daniel, *Arabs and Europe*, 264.

7. Will Durant, *The Age of Faith*, The Story of Civilization Series, no. 4. (New York: Simon and Schuster, 1950), 703; Hitti, *History of Arabs*, 612.

8. Durant, *Age of Faith*, 705.

9. Donald Campbell, *Arabic Medicine* (London: Kegan, Trench, 1926), 127.

10. Charles H. Haskins, "The Renaissance of the Twelfth Century," in Lewis, *Islamic World and West*, 79–86.

11. J. Windrow Sweetman, *Islam and Christian Theology* (London: Butterworth Press, 1955), 52.

12. Artz, *Mind*, 239–40.

13. Sweetman, *Islam and Christian*, 50–51.

14. Durant, *Age of Faith*, 912.

15. Daniel, *Arabs and Europe*, 265.

16. Campbell, *Arabic Medicine*, 122–23.

17. Daniel, *Arabs and Europe*, 271.

18. Sweetman, *Islam and Christian*, 81.

19. Mehdi Nakosteen, *History of Islamic Origins of Western Education* (Boulder: University of Colorado Press, 1964), 184, 278, and 280.

20. Durant, *Age of Faith*, 911.

21. Ibid., 912.

22. See Daniel, *Arabs and Europe*, 230–62; Sweetman, *Islam and Christian*, 38–57; and Haskins, "Renaissance," 79–85.

23. Daniel, *Arabs and Europe*, 277–78; Artz, *Mind*, 262.

24. Daniel, *Arabs and Europe*, 277.

25. Ibid., 238.

26. Artz, *Mind*, 245–47; Nasr, *Science and Civilization in Islam*, 50; H. J. J. Winter, *Eastern Science* (London: John Murray, 1952), 72.

27. Artz, *Mind*, 241; Hitti, *History of Arabs*, 366.

28. See Daniel, *Arabs and Europe*, 230–48; Schacht and Bosworth, *Legacy*, 9–32.

29. Daniel, *Arabs and Europe*, 237–38.

30. Ibid., 254.

31. Ibid., 279.

32. George Makdisi, *The Rise of Colleges* (Edinburgh: Edinburgh University Press, 1981), 224–81.

33. M. Grabmann, *Die Geschichte der Scholastischen Methode*, vol. 1 (Berlin: Academia Verlag, 1956), 253.

34. Ibid., 242.

35. Ibid., 217.

36. H. Kantorowicz, "Quaestiones Disputatae of the Glossators," *Revue d'Histoire du Droit* 16 (1938): 1–67.

37. Makdisi, *The Rise*, 262–63.

38. Grabmann, *Geschichte*, 219–20.

39. Makdisi, *The Rise*, 255.

40. L. Paetow, "The Arts Course at Medieval Universities with Special Reference to Grammar and Rhetoric," *University Studies*, University of Illinois, 3 (1910): 20.

41. Makdisi, *The Rise*, 255.

42. Paetow, "Arts Course," 20.

43. Makdisi, *The Rise*, 259.

7

The Higher Learning in Classical Islam: Final Thoughts

Lord, bestow on me wisdom and let me dwell among the righteous. Give me renown among posterity and place me amongst the heirs of the Blissful Garden.

The Quran 26:83–85

How is one to judge and place into perspective Islam's classical period in the long history of the higher learning? The previous chapters have highlighted the brilliant contributions of both institutions and men to the intellectual heritage of world civilization. Following the classical period, both East and West tended to ignore many of their achievements. Neither culture drew from the great richness that it offered. Christian scholars drank heavily from the well of philosophy replenished by the Islamic hakims yet ignored the men, religion, and environment that generated it. Later academicians would forget the nourishment given by Islam in the pursuit of knowledge—particularly science—and honor its foundations primarily in European sources. Islam itself failed to draw continuously from its own creative genius in philosophy and science; exploration of both would wane and almost disappear as the higher learning became increasingly absorbed with religious and legal issues. This work, however, has emphasized the role of Islam during its early centuries in the preservation and expansion of the intellectual heritage of the Greek world before transmitting

177

it to Christian Europe, which was awakening at last from its intellectual dormancy.

Islamic society continued those activities from earlier times that our world associates with the advance of civilization. It anchored itself in a book and a tradition for guiding human behavior through the principles of justice and respect for personhood. It became a state governed by laws that protected both individual and societal rights. Additionally, the spirit of Islam in the classical era strove to improve the human condition through knowledge. It abandoned its Arab roots in animism and superstition in favor of a personal God who created an ordered universe that reflected His own perfect goodness. For the scholar, the pursuit of knowledge lay in unveiling the secrets of that cosmos in both its supernatural and material forms—the true path to understanding the nature of God.

As in most accounts of early historical periods, what we know about the higher learning in classical Islam is confined to the high points— the peaks, and not the valleys. We know about the rich, the powerful, the influential, and the gifted. Yet each of these groups represented a mere fraction of the citizenry of this age. Of the total population, the number who could read or write is unknown. Considering how few can perform these feats even in today's society—particularly in undeveloped countries—we can only assume that throughout the Islamic lands many remained illiterate. The important consideration here, however, is the effort made by early Muslims to expand literacy and encourage understanding of the Quran. The mandate that believers read the Word of God spawned elementary schools—kuttabs—in cities and villages throughout Islam's vast dominion. Most children did have access to learning; to what extent parents took advantage of that situation is unknown.

On one matter, however, we have certainty. Basically, schools for children did not admit girls. Although Tritton notes several exceptions to the rule, they were rare indeed; nor is there any assurance that these special young women received their education in formal settings, rather than at home.[1] The basic injunction in this regard was the admonition: "Do not teach your daughters to read nor let them learn poetry; teach them the Koran, the chapter Light."[2] Applying our modern standards we might fault Islam for its sexism, but women's education throughout history provides a dismal lesson in male chauvinism, with the consequent loss of a great resource of vitality and creativity. The practice of not educating women still persists in many Islamic countries, although in recent decades some loosening of that proscription has occurred. Even in "enlightened" countries throughout the world, equalization of educational opportunity still faces major barriers from gender bias.

Learning for boys was relegated primarily to the rudiments of reading, writing, and counting. The curriculum focused on memorizing passages from the Quran and simple arithmetic functions. There seemed no sense of progression from grade to grade nor of striving for a higher order of cognitive skills. Elementary instruction strove to educate as many as possible in basic skills and not to indulge the higher intellectual abilities of the few. Thus, elementary schools were not the road to higher education. A large gulf separated the two educational systems. Certainly, some masters might encourage brighter pupils to pursue studies at a higher level, but no channel existed through which a pupil could advance with ease into higher studies. One who desired learning beyond the most elemental level in adab, the religious studies, jurisprudence, or philosophy and science sought his own way, and asked individually if he could join the halqa of a shaikh. The availability of such opportunities was much more limited than the basic instruction in literacy offered in the villages. Since the leader of a study circle acted independently in selecting his disciples, a young man had no assurance that he would be chosen even if he had the necessary educational background and ability. Other factors might determine that decision—including ability to pay, present level of enrollment, adequacy of facilities, and personality differences.

Institutions of higher learning—in their various forms—emerged not to provide a continuation of course work beyond elementary studies, but to meet two distinct needs in society derived from Islam's encounter with the intellectually more advanced cultures rooted in Greek philosophy and science. The first was to clarify the meaning of the Quran and to adapt its principles to an ever-changing environment. The faithful—particularly the newly converted—required guidance in how to conduct their daily lives in harmony with the revelation of God transmitted through the Prophet Mohammed. The second need was to reconcile that revelation with intellectual and scientific experience.

To meet the first need, formal structures of higher learning were established that focused on religious studies and legal interpretation. Although interconnected, the curriculums of each were offered in separate institutions. Religious studies became located in the study circles of mosques, while jurisprudence found a home in mosque-colleges and madrassahs. However, the vitality that early on stimulated discourse and creativity in these schools gave way over time to formalism and orthodoxy.

Innovation in the religious sciences ended when the study of Greek philosophy was discontinued and replaced by Islamic Scholasticism. Al-Ghazzali had championed the limited use of dialectic and logic, fearing that its unbridled use in all areas of intellectual thought would lead to a loss of faith. His compromise between rationalism and simple faith ushered in a period of harmony, pietism, and conformity in religious studies. Theology could not be challenged, but only explained and applied to daily living. The formal schools of higher education continued in this path down to the present, teaching in the same manner from a curriculum developed during the classical period.

According to Makdisi, the law schools began to stagnate when the civil authorities provided a paid *mufti* to provide fatwas—legal opinions—for the public.[3] This had the effect of taking that function with its remunerative aspect away from scholars of the law. Makdisi argues that, without the stimulation of deriving legal opinions on a continuing basis, legal scholars lost their incentive and motivation to pursue scholarship in jurisprudence. Accompanying this, the reduction of the various personal law schools to only four orthodox schools, which endure to the present time, had a deteriorating impact on scholarship. *Ijtihad*—the process of personally interpreting a legal opinion—seems to have disappeared in the thirteenth century, again depriving scholarship of a methodology that had been stimulating individual thought and investigation by the instructors in the law colleges.

Exclusion of the foreign sciences and the subordination of humanistic studies to the religious sciences and jurisprudence, had a deleterious effect on the continuation of scholarship and the life of institutions of higher learning in Islam. The system of waqf accompanied by the patronage of madrassahs and mosque-colleges by royal and noble patronage served as a conservative bridle on higher education. Through endowments and state support, law colleges tended to serve the status quo and to maintain the orthodoxy of the ruling class.

The natural sciences and social sciences were pursued by individuals in private circumstances and did not enter the mainstream of Islamic higher education—either in the curriculum, its structures, or in the instructional methodology undertaken by them. The eleventh century witnessed the triumph of traditionalism in Islam, beginning with the fundamentalist approach of ibn Hanbal and his school of law, later affirmed by al-Ghazzali in his philosophical argumentation against the abuse of rationalistic processes to question faith, and then politically institutionalized by Nizam al-Mulk—the vizier to the Seljuk sultans—who assured the traditional position of Islam by founding madrassahs of a conservative nature throughout the Middle East.

Despite brilliant contributions in philosophy and science from the leaders of spontaneous study circles, this strain of the higher learning also succumbed to the forces of piety and the limited use of rationalism fostered by al-Ghazzali and Asharism. A fear prevailed that the continued use of philosophy might lead to a denial of God's power over the universe, and the development of heresy. No legitimate way emerged for scholars in Islamic higher learning to undertake investigation and experimentation, so necessary for the advancement of the natural and social sciences. The Islamic faith in its accepted form discouraged any method of analysis that fostered the raising of hypotheses because it did not conceive of any benefit in establishing a relationship between cause and effect arising from natural phenomena. With control of the institutions of higher learning in the hands of the traditionalists, natural science and social science could not progress. Science and technology were suspect and considered unnecessary for leading a full life within Islamic culture. Without the invigoration of continued study in natural and social phenomena, the higher learning in Islam lost the stimulus for intellectual inquiry and the impetus to seek out new knowledge. The fruits of the brilliant philosophers and scientists of Islam would pass to Medieval Europe and kindle the search for knowledge that had been extinguished with the decay of the Roman Empire and the advance of barbarian tribes from the north and east.

In addition to the loss of a scholarly mission to pursue knowledge in all intellectual and scientific areas, institutions of higher learning also suffered from structural characteristics that abetted their intellectual inertia. Madrassahs and mosque-colleges lacked an organizational device for continuing self-examination and reform of their structure and function over a long period of time. They never did develop the guild as a corporate entity that could raise the necessary money for their continuance and provide a method for assuring the perpetuity of the corporate structure. While professionals, artisans, and tradesmen in Islamic lands did establish guilds—niqabat being the term for such a group—to protect interests and provide camaraderie for their members, these institutions did not develop the binding organizational ties that defined the guilds of Medieval Europe. The niqabat promoted professionalism, setting standards of scholarship and morality for teachers.[4] It was more fraternal than corporate, and lacked the organizational structure and legal standing to act in solidarity vis-à-vis the government or other institutions. The guilds reinforced the independent nature of scholarship and instruction for teachers and saw their mission as embracing all those who considered themselves as teachers. The individual niqabat was not coterminous with a distinct institution of higher learning.

In Europe, the resources of the college and the university lay in the hands of a collective—the masters' guild—that nourished a professional commitment to meeting societal needs, serving knowledge, and perpetuating itself as a defined organization associated with a specific educational structure. One obligation of the guild in Christian lands was continually to seek out and acquire new financial resources to support its educational mission. In Islam, waqf as a source of funding mosque-colleges and madrassahs did not provide for perpetuity beyond the limited means provided in the original document, which was often a self-serving contract to protect the interests of a particular family or sect. No means emerged to replenish or increase the financial resources of a school or to employ personnel with new ideas and approaches to instruction. The destiny of such institutions resided in the hands of the benefactor as dictated in his writ of waqf and with the shaikh who took the responsibility alone for continuance of the institution.

The absence of a strongly organized community of scholars worked against the continuation of institutions of higher learning in Islamdom in another—and perhaps more crucial—way. Since Islamic scholars worked independently, they did not come together as a community of scholars for intellectual stimulation, questioning each other and raising hypotheses for further investigation. They lacked a collaborative approach to major issues within the community and did not build on each other's knowledge and experience as readily as they could have, had they organized themselves into a scholarly community. In his isolation, the shaikh of a mosque-college of madrassah simply was not challenged by his colleagues to pursue scholarship in any different direction than he had learned from his own mentor.

Sufism also played a role in altering the course of intellectual inquiry among many learned men. Far from being just a Muslim sect, Sufism traces its roots deep into human history. It knows no cultural or religious bounds, but has been manifested in the lives of men searching for mystical unity with the cosmos wherever and whenever they lived. Sufism calls an individual to a simple life of meditation and piety in the inward journey toward harmony with the created universe. The Sufi considers his path to be a solitary adventure; the skills of transcending from the mundane world to an ethereal plane—an altered state of consciousness beyond the normal range—can be learned through individual efforts, sometimes with the support of a master, but cannot be taught. The most noted hakims who adopted Sufism were Jabir ibn-Hayyan (Geber), the alchemist; al-Ghazzali, the religious leader; and Umar al-Khayyam, poet and mathematician. The principles of Sufism greatly affected their lives as scholars, and their example prompted many others to adopt Sufism, as well. Umar al-Khayyam's hierarchy of scholars exemplified the Sufi view that transcendent knowledge was of far greater value than that of a more practical, mundane order. The inner life of the soul that provided the source for al-Ghazzali's religious and intellectual views derived from his conversion to Sufism after he had steeped himself in Greek philosophy. Speaking of Ibn al-Arabi— whom he calls "the greatest sheikh"—Idries Shah states, "Instead of making use of these abilities to carve a place in scholasticism, he claimed, like many another Sufi, that when one has a powerful intellect, its ultimate function is to show that intellectuality is merely a prelude to something else."[5] Those shaikhs who followed the path of Sufism strove for inner peace, rather than exploring the world through observation and rationalism. Further, Sufism called them to a life of solitude; and while many shaikhs who accepted it did welcome disciples who studied with them in a halqa, they did not join with other intellectuals in a community of scholars—thus forgoing the stimulation and challenge that discourse with others might have provided.

Nor can one discount the societal forces outside the institutions of higher learning that contributed to their loss of vitality—if not their outright destruction. The dimming of the light of intellectual inquiry was accompanied by the destructive forces of invading armies from the Orient, which had no tradition in learning and no respect for intellectual endeavors. The period of nomadic conquests from the Orient during the eleventh through thirteenth centuries dealt Islamic culture a devastating blow from which it did not recuperate for many more centuries. While the Seljuk Turks in their conquests of Mesopotamia and Persia were not so destructive of institutions as later invading armies, they did act as repressors of intellectual activity. Converted to the Islamic faith, they tended to adopt a fundamentalist approach to religious matters. They desired to preserve the status quo and to defend their own usurpation of civil authority. While leaving the caliph as a figurehead and as a religious leader, the Seljuks assumed the reins over society and championed the traditionalist point of view. The attitude of Nizam al-Mulk and his founding of madrassahs anchored this position throughout the Middle East. The consolidation of power in petty nobles in Egypt and al-Andalus hastened the decline of learning as well. Their interests were served better by restraint and religious orthodoxy than by intellectual freedom, and they chose not to support institutions of higher learning and libraries. With the end of the caliphates in Baghdad (1258) and al-Andalus (1248) came the disappearance of centralized support for the libraries and literary salons, as well as the support of individual scholars.

The Mongols arrived like a rampaging mob out of the East, destroying everything in their path. In later years they converted to Islam—finding it more accommodating to their lifestyle than Christianity, which they encountered during their invasion of Europe. Prior to their conversion, however, they had destroyed the vestiges of the higher learning in their first sweep through the eastern provinces of Islam to the Mediterranean coast (in 1260). That paragon of learning and the high culture of Islam—Baghdad—fell victim to pillage and fire; thousands lost their lives. The wholesale destruction of manuscripts and the killing of teachers and students cannot be calculated. Similar devastation occurred throughout all the cities of eastern Islam during the Mongol invasions. Only the reputation of al-Tusi as a great astronomer salvaged some remnant of Islamic intellectualism. He convinced Hulagu—Jenghiz Khan's grandson— to build the observatory at Maraghah and support studies in astronomy and mathematics.

In al-Andalus, which provided the final burst of Islamic intellectualism—particularly in philosophy, medicine, and the sciences—the reconquista destroyed or caused to be abandoned the mosque-colleges and madrassahs of its major cities, while preserving many of the texts in libraries. These later entered Christian lands in their Latin translations and were widely disseminated throughout Europe during the twelfth century. The invading armies of Christian monarchs uprooted the Muslim community and its culture, replacing it with a less advanced civilization lacking in scientific knowledge and initially lacking an interest in intellectual enterprises. Christian universities in Spanish lands took centuries to attain the level of intellectual sophistication reached by Islamic madrassahs and mosque-colleges at a much earlier period.

Political events of the twelfth and thirteenth centuries disrupted and retarded Islamic culture. The demise of the caliphates and the dismemberment of much of the empire into smaller provinces under the leadership of local leaders ended the Pax Islamica that had reigned for several centuries during which the settlements of Islam had escaped invasion and destructive civil war. The rise of nationalism spawned the emergence of many competing states within Islamdom and rival claimants for positions of sovereignty. The resources of Islamic states went less for intellectual and scientific advancement and more for arms. The fabric of Islam as a coherent faith with loyalty to a single authority in the caliph was rent apart, never to be rewoven. Dissension, distrust, and hostility have plagued Islamic peoples and their nations since the twelfth and thirteenth centuries. The continual upheaval and the entrenchment of reactionary forces—including the Ottoman Empire, which ruled over much of this land for a number of centuries—kept Islamic higher education culturally and geographically confined, and outside the mainstream of the technology and science advancing in Western society. The disruption of trade routes and the establishment of smaller nations created barriers between the flow of both information and scholars. No longer did shaikhs migrate from city to city establishing circles of learning, and the dissemination of new works on Islamic culture and jurisprudence was hindered as the frontiers between the various nations were secured.

In many provinces, Arabic gave way to vernaculars that had not entirely disappeared through years of dominance by Arab culture. Despite the fact that Arabic remained primarily the written language of Islamic peoples, various dialects reasserted themselves within Islamdom—creating language barriers. Communication among the various national groups grew more difficult, and Arabic no longer reigned as the universal language of intellectualism and science among Islamic scholars. These combined circumstances hastened the dormancy of the higher learning in Islamic society. While the outside events draw the most attention from historians, one can argue—after carefully weighing the evidence—that the decline of Islamic higher education resulted as much from internal rigidity as from loss of interest in the scientific method. Islamic society folded into itself, drawing a curtain not penetrated by foreign scholars for many centuries.

This book has attempted to unveil a part of that hidden past by celebrating the Classical Age of Islam—a brilliant chapter in the intellectual history of the human race. It has introduced the main actors in that drama and their distinguished contributions in our understanding the human condition and the physical world—men and achievements long unrecognized in Western experience. It has been argued here that much of the instructional methodology developed by Islamic schoolmen sparked the rise of medieval universities, from which we in the West trace our academic genealogy. For the most part, educators in the West have only a dim view of the advances made by Islamic scholars to their various fields of interest; these pages have been intended to emphasize that Islam served as more than a bridge to the roots of our intellectual heritage in ancient Greece. It also molded and increased that knowledge before its transference to a new generation of scholars in another culture. We stand now—as did the Scholastics of Paris and Bologna—the intellectual heirs of al-Khwarazmi, al-Razi, Ibn-Sina, al-Haitham, and Ibn-Rushd. As a society we can repay our debt to them only by honoring their memory and the faith that inspired their search for knowledge, and resolving to live by the humanitarian and intellectual values of openness, tolerance, and integrity so valued by them and the other hakims who gave shape to the higher learning in Islam during the classical period.

Notes

1. A. S. Tritton, *Muslim Education in the Middle Ages* (London: Luzac, 1957), 2, 7, 140–43.

2. Ibid., 2.

3. George Makdisi, *The Rise of Colleges* (Edinburgh: Edinburgh University Press, 1981), 291.

4. Mehdi Nakosteen, *History of Islamic Origins of Western Education* (Boulder: University of Colorado Press, 1964), 57; Ahmad Shalaby, *History of Muslim Education* (Beirut: Dar al-Kashshaf, 1954), 155–56.

5. Idries Shah, *The Sufis* (Garden City: Anchor Books, 1971), 162.

Chapter Guide to the Readings

1 ISLAM AND ARABIC: THE FOUNDATIONS OF THE HIGHER LEARNING

General works on Islamic civilization that the reader would find useful, and that provided resources for this chapter, include A. J. Arberry, *Aspects of Islamic Civilization* (Ann Arbor: University of Michigan Press, 1983); Philip K. Hitti, *History of the Arabs* (London: Macmillan, 1956); Mehdi Nakosteen, *History of Islamic Origins of Western Education* (Boulder: University of Colorado Press, 1964); Marshall G. S. Hodgson, *The Venture of Islam,* 2 vols. (Chicago: University of Chicago Press, 1974); and *The Encyclopaedia of Islam* (Leiden: E. J. Brill, 1960–1965).

Specific works on Islamic education are difficult to find in most libraries, but the reader will find A. S. Tritton, *Muslim Education in the Middle Ages* (London: Luzac, 1957), most helpful. Ahmad Shalaby's doctoral dissertation, *History of Muslim Education* (Beirut: Dar al-Kashshaf, 1954), provided a plethora of specific details on many aspects of education in the classical era.

2 FORMAL INSTITUTIONS OF HIGHER EDUCATION

A more elaborate account of the structures and concepts introduced in this chapter can be found in the following volumes: For insights into Islamic law, the short work by Noel J. Coulson, *A History of Islamic Law* (Edinburgh: Edinburgh University Press, 1964), provides an excellent source. Joseph Schacht's *An Introduction to Islamic Law*

(Oxford, U.K.: Clarendon Press, 1964) provides a longer, more detailed alternative on the same subject. George Makdisi's articles and books introduce the structures of Islamic higher education of the eleventh century to the English-speaking reader. Of particular value is George Makdisi's *The Rise of Colleges* (Edinburgh: Edinburgh University Press, 1981) with its meticulous scholarship. Of more general interest would be the previously noted books by Tritton and Shalaby.

3 HELLENISTIC INFLUENCE ON THE HIGHER LEARNING

The impact of Greek philosophy on the Arab world is explored in great detail by F. E. Peters, *Aristotle and the Arabs* (New York: New York University Press, 1968); Richard Waltzer, *Greek into Arabic* (Oxford: Bruno Cassirer, 1962); and Franz Rosenthal, *The Classical Heritage of Islam* (Berkeley: University of California Press, 1965). The Islamic perspective on science and learning is presented at some length in two volumes by Seyyed Hossein Nasr: *Islamic Science,* World of Islam Festival Publishing (Westerham, Kent: Westerham Press, 1976); and *Science and Civilization in Islam* (New York: New American Library, 1968). For more information about the specific philosophers, the reader should consult S. H. Nasr, *Three Muslim Scholars* (Cambridge, Mass.: Harvard University Press, 1964); *The Life of Ibn Sina,* a critical edition and annotated translation by William E. Gohlman (Albany: SUNY Press, 1974); al-Ghazzali, "Deliverance from Error," translated by W. M. Watt in *The Faith and Practice of Al-Ghazali* (London: George Allen and Unwin, 1953); Al-Farabi, *The Philosophy of Plato and Aristotle,* translated and introduction by Muhsin Mahdi (New York: Free Press of Glencoe, 1962), and *On the Perfect State,* translated and commentary by Richard Waltzer (Oxford: Clarendon Press, 1985); A. M. Goichons, *The Philosophy of Avicenna and Its Influence on Medieval Europe,* translated by M. S. Khan (Delhi: Motilal Banarsidass, 1969); Henry Corbin, *Avicenna and the Visionary Recital,* translated by Willare R. Trask (New York: Pantheon Books, 1960); Al-Ghazzali, *The Alchemy of Happiness,* translated from the Hindustani by Claud Field (London: Octagon Press, 1980); and Mohammed Ahmed Sharif, *Ghazali's Theory of Virtue* (Albany: SUNY Press, 1975).

4 THE FLOWERING OF ISLAMIC SCIENCE

The most readable and informative sources in this area are two books by Seyyed Hossein Nasr: *Islamic Science,* World of Islam

Festival Publishing (Westerham, Kent: Westerham Press, 1976); and *Science and Civilization in Islam* (New York: New American Library, 1968). Other important works are H. J. J. Winter, *Eastern Science* (London: John Murray, 1952), and the classic study by George Sarton, *Introduction to the History of Science,* vol. 1 (Baltimore: Wilkins and Wilkens, 1927).

For medicine and pharmacology, the following volumes are recommended to the interested reader: Donald Campbell, *Arabic Medicine* (London: Kegan, Trench, 1926); E. G. Browne, *Arabian Medicine* (Cambridge, U.K.: Cambridge University Press, 1962); Fielding H. Garrison, *An Introduction to the History of Medicine,* 3rd ed. (Philadelphia: W. B. Saunders, 1924); Edward T. Withington, *Medical History* (London: Holland Press, 1964); and Martin Levey, *Early Arabic Pharmacology* (Leiden: E. J. Brill, 1973). The Islamic perspective is presented in the two volumes on science by S. H. Nasr, as well as in S. A. R. Hamdani's *Notable Muslim Names in Medical Science* (Lahore: Ferozsns, ca. 1960).

5 SPONTANEOUS CENTERS OF THE HIGHER LEARNING

The reader desiring to learn more about informal structures of the higher learning in Islamdom during the Classical Age should read those sections in books listed above as references for formal structures of higher education during that same period: Shalaby, Tritton, and Makdisi. For additional information on Khwarazmi's *Keys of the Sciences,* the reader should see C. E. Bosworth, *Medieval Arabic Culture and Administration* (London: Variorum Reprints, 1982).

6 TRANSMISSION OF THE HIGHER LEARNING TO MEDIEVAL EUROPE

For reference material dealing with the transmission of Islamic scholarship to the Latin West, the reader should consult Norman Daniel, *The Arabs and Medieval Europe* (London: Longman, 1975); Archibald Lewis, ed., *The Islamic World and the West* (New York: John Wiley and Sons, 1920); and—for a concise, very readable treatment—W. M. Watt, *The Influence of Islam on Medieval Europe* (Edinburgh: Edinburgh University Press, 1972). Sections by Will Durant, *The Age of Faith,* The Story of Civilization Series, no. 4 (New

York: Simon and Schuster, 1950), and Frederick B. Artz, *The Mind of the Middle Ages* (Chicago: University of Chicago Press, 1980), offer information on the translation of Arabic texts into Latin and their impact on European scholars.

An excellent resource on the medieval university is the one volume work of Charles Haskins, *The Rise of Universities* (Ithaca: Cornell University Press, 1957). The monumental three-volume work of Hastings Rashdall, *The Universities of Europe in the Middle Ages* (Oxford University Press, 1936), remains the definitive treatment of those institutions and is highly recommended. For the most complete description of institutions of higher learning in classical Islam, the reader should consult George Makdisi, *The Rise of Colleges* (Edinburgh: Edinburgh University Press, 1981).

Bibliography

Books

Ahmad, Aziz. *A History of Islamic Sicily*. Edinburgh: Edinburgh University Press, 1975.

al-Daffa, Ali Abdullah. *The Muslim Contribution to Mathematics*. London: Croom Helm, 1978.

Al-Farabi. *On the Perfect State*. Translated and commentary by Richard Waltzer. Oxford, U.K.: Clarendon Press, 1985.

————. *The Philosophy of Plato and Aristotle*. Translated and introduction by Muhsin Mahdi. New York: Free Press of Glencoe, 1962.

Al-Ghazzali. *The Alchemy of Happiness*. Translated from the Hindustani by Claud Field. London: Octagon Press, 1980.

Al-Nadim. *Al-Fihrist*. Leipzig, GDR: Flügel, 1872.

Arberry, A. J. *Aspects of Islamic Civilization*. Ann Arbor: University of Michigan Press, 1983.

————. *Chester Beatty's Library: A Handlist of the Arabic Manuscripts*. 8 vols. Dublin: Hodges, Figgis, 1958–59.

Arnold, Thomas and Alfred Guillaume. *The Legacy of Islam*. Oxford, U.K.: Clarendon Press, 1931.

Artz, Frederick B. *The Mind of the Middle Ages*. Chicago: University of Chicago Press, 1980.

Avicenna. *A Treatise on the Canon of Medicine of Avicenna Incorporating a Translation of the First Book*. Translated by O. C. Gruner. London: Luzac, 1930.

Az-Zarnuji. *Instruction of the Student: The Method of Learning*. Translated by G. E. von Grunebaum and Theodora M. Abel. New York: Kings Crown Press, 1947.

Boorstin, Daniel J. *The Discoverers.* New York: Random House, 1983.

Bosworth, C. E. *Medieval Arabic Culture and Administration.* London: Variorum Reprints, 1982.

Boyle, J. A., ed. *The Cambridge History of Iran.* Cambridge, U.K.: Cambridge University Press, 1968.

Browne, E. G. *Arabian Medicine.* Cambridge, U.K.: Cambridge University Press, 1962.

———. *A Literary History of Persia.* 4 vols. Cambridge, U.K.: Cambridge University Press, 1902–24.

Campbell, Donald. *Arabic Medicine.* London: Kegan, Trench, 1926.

Corbin, Henry. *Avicenna and the Visionary Recital.* Translated by Willare R. Trask. New York: Pantheon Books, 1960.

Coulson, Noel J. *A History of Islamic Law.* Edinburgh: Edinburgh University Press, 1964.

Daniel, Norman. *The Arabs and Medieval Europe.* London: Longman, 1975.

———. *Islam, Europe, and Empire.* Edinburgh: Edinburgh University Press, 1966.

———. *Islam and the West: The Making of an Image.* Edinburgh: Edinburgh University Press, 1960.

Dermenghem, Emile. *Muhammad and the Islamic Tradition.* Translated by J. H. Watt. New York: Harper and Brothers, 1958.

Deyer, John L. E. *A History of Astronomy from Thales to Kepler.* 2nd ed. New York: Dover Publication, 1953.

Dodge, Bayard. *Al-Azhar: A Millennium of Muslim Learning.* Washington, D.C.: American International Printing, 1961.

———, ed. and trans. *The Fihrist of al-Nadim.* 2 vols. New York: Columbia University Press, 1970.

———. *History of Education in the Arab World.* New York: Arab Information Center, 1963.

Donner, Fred McGraw. *The Early Islamic Conquests.* Princeton, N.J.: Princeton University Press, 1981.

Durant, Will. *The Age of Faith.* The Story of Civilization Series, No. 4. New York: Simon and Schuster, 1950.

Elgood, Cyril. *A Medical History of Persia.* Cambridge, U.K.: Cambridge University Press, 1951.

The Encyclopaedia of Islam. Leiden, Netherlands: E. J. Brill, 1960–65.

Garrison, Fielding H. *An Introduction to the History of Medicine.* 3rd ed. Philadelphia: W. B. Saunders, 1924.

Gibb, Hamilton A. R. *Mohammadanism.* London: Oxford University Press, 1949.

——. *Studies on the Civilization of Islam.* Boston: Beacon Press, 1962.

Goichons, A. M. *The Philosophy of Avicenna and Its Influence on Medieval Europe.* Translated by M. S. Khan. Delhi: Motilal Banarsidass, 1969.

Goldziher, Ignaz. *Mohammed and Islam.* New Haven, Conn.: Yale University Press, 1917.

Grabmann, M. *Die Geschichte der Scholastischen Methode.* Berlin: Academia Verlag, 1956.

Graziani, Joseph S. *Arabic Medicine in the Eleventh Century.* Karachi, Pakistan: Hamdard Foundation, 1980.

Guillaume, Alfred. *Islam.* New York: Penguin Books, 1956.

Hamdani, S. A. R. *Notable Muslim Names in Medical Science.* Lahore, Pakistan: Ferozsns, ca. 1960.

Haskins, Charles. *The Rise of Universities.* Ithaca, N.Y.: Cornell University Press, 1957.

Hawting, Gerald R. *The First Dynasty of Islam.* Carbondale and Edwardsville: Southern Illinois University Press, 1987.

Hayes, J. R., ed. *The Genius of Arab Civilization.* Cambridge, Mass.: MIT Press, 1983.

Hitti, Philip K. *Capitol Cities of Arab Islam.* Minneapolis: University of Minnesota Press, 1973.

——. *History of the Arabs.* London: Macmillan, 1956.

Hodgson, Marshall G. S. *The Venture of Islam.* 2 vols. Chicago: University of Chicago Press, 1974.

Hourani, George F., ed. *Essays on Islamic Philosophy and Science.* Albany: SUNY Press, 1975.

Iqbal, Afzal. *The Culture of Islam.* Lahore, Pakistan: Institute of Islamic Culture, 1967.

Iqbal, Muhammad. *The Development of Metaphysics in Persia: A Contribution to the History of Muslim Philosophy.* London: Luzac, 1908.

Islam: Philosophy and Science. Paris: UNESCO Press, 1981. *Islamic Philosophical Theology.* Albany: SUNY Press, 1979.

Karpinski, Louis C. *Robert of Chester's Latin Translation of the Algebra of Al-Khowarizmi.* New York: Macmillan, 1915.

Kimball, Bruce A. *Orators and Philosophers: A History of the Idea of Liberal Education.* New York: Teachers College Press, 1986.

Khadduri, M. and J. J. Liebesny, eds. *Law in the Middle East,* Vol 1. Washington, D.C.: Middle East Institute, 1955.

The Koran. Translated by N. J. Dawood. New York: Penguin Books, 1956.

Lapidus, Ira M. *Muslim Cities in the Later Middle Ages.* Cambridge, Mass.: Harvard University Press, 1967.

Levey, Martin. *Early Arabic Pharmacology.* Leiden, Netherlands: E. J. Brill, 1973.

Lewis, Archibald, ed. *The Islamic World and the West.* New York: John Wiley and Sons, 1920.

Lewis, Bernard. *The Arabs in History.* 3rd ed. London: Hutchinson's University Library, 1956.

The Liberal Arts and the Future of Higher Education in the Middle East. Beirut: American University, 1979.

The Life of Ibn Sina. A Critical Edition and Annotated Translation by W. E. Gohlman. Albany: SUNY Press, 1974.

Little, A. G., ed. *Roger Bacon Essays.* Oxford, U.K.: Clarendon Press, 1914.

Little, A. G. and F. Pelster. *Theology and Theologians.* Oxford, U.K.: Clarendon Press, 1932.

Lloyd, G. E. R. *Greek Science after Aristotle.* New York: W. W. Norton, 1973.

Macdonald, Duncan J. *Development of Muslim Theology, Jurisprudence, and Constitutional Theory.* New York: Charles Scribner's Sons, 1903.

Makdisi, George, ed. *Arabic and Islamic Studies in Honor of Hamilton A. R. Gibb.* Leiden, Netherlands: E. J. Brill, 1961.

―――. *The Rise of Colleges.* Edinburgh: Edinburgh University Press, 1981.

Mez, A. *Islam.* Translated by S. Khuda Bukhsh and D. S. Margoliouth. London: Luzac, 1937.

Mohmassani, S. *The Philosophy of Jurisprudence in Islam.* Leiden, Netherlands: E. J. Brill, 1961.

Nakosteen, Mehdi. *History of Islamic Origins of Western Education.* Boulder: University of Colorado Press, 1964.

Nasr, Seyyed Hossein. *Ideals and Realities of Islam.* London: Allen and Unwin, 1966.

―――. *An Introduction to Islamic Cosmological Doctrines.* Cambridge, Mass.: Harvard University Press, 1964.

―――. *Islamic Science.* World of Islam Festival Publishing. Westerham, Kent, U.K.: Westerham Press, 1976.

―――. *Science and Civilization in Islam.* New York: New American Library, 1968.

———. *Three Muslim Scholars*. Cambridge, Mass.: Harvard University Press, 1964.

Neugebauer, Otto. *The Exact Sciences in Antiquity*. Princeton, N.J.: Princeton University Press, 1952.

Noldke, Theodore. *Sketches from Eastern History*. London: Adam and Charles Black, 1892.

O'Leary, DeLacy. *How Greek Science Passed to the Arabs*. London: Routledge and Kegan Paul, 1949.

Peters, F. E. *Aristotle and the Arabs*. New York: New York University Press, 1968.

The Quran. Translated by Richard Bell. Edinburgh: T. & T. Clark, 1937.

Rahman, Fazlur. *Islam and Modernity: Transformation of an Intellectual Tradition*. Chicago: University of Chicago Press, 1982.

Rashdall, Hastings. *Medieval Universities*. Oxford, U.K.: Clarendon Press, 1936.

———. *The Universities of Europe in the Middle Ages*. 3 vols. Oxford, U.K.: Clarendon Press, 1936.

Riche, Pierre. *Education and Culture in the Barbarian West*. Translated by John J. Contreni. Columbia: University of South Carolina Press, 1978.

Rosenthal, Franz. *The Classical Heritage of Islam*. Berkeley: University of California Press, 1965.

———. *A History of Muslim Historiography*. Leiden, Netherlands: E. J. Brill, 1952.

———. *Knowledge Triumphant*. Leiden, Netherlands: E. J. Brill, 1970.

Sarton, George. *Introduction to the History of Science*. Vol. 1. Baltimore: Wilkins and Wilkens, 1927.

Saunders, J. J. *A History of Medieval Islam*. New York: Barnes and Noble, 1965.

Sayili, A. M. *The Observatory in Islam*. Ankara, Turkey: Turk Tarih Kurumu Basimevi, 1960.

Schacht, Joseph. *An Introduction to Islamic Law*. Oxford, U.K.: Clarendon Press, 1964.

Schacht, Joseph and C. E. Bosworth. *The Legacy of Islam*. 2nd ed. Oxford, U.K.: Clarendon Press, 1974.

Seale, Morris S. *Muslim Theology*. London: Luzac, 1964.

Semaan, Khalil I., ed. *Islam and the Medieval West*. Albany: SUNY Press, 1980.

Shah, Idries. *The Sufis*. Garden City, N.Y.: Anchor Books, 1971.

Shalaby, Ahmad. *History of Muslim Education*. Beirut: Dar al-Kashshaf, 1954.

Sharif, Miyan. *A History of Muslim Philosophy*. 2 vols. Wiesbaden, FRG: O. Harrassowitz, 1963.

Sharif, Mohammed Ahmed. *Ghazali's Theory of Virtue*. Albany: SUNY Press, 1975.

Shustery, A. Mahomed Abbas. *Outlines of Islamic Culture*. 2 vols. Bangalore, India: Bangalore Press, 1938.

Siddiqi, Amir Hassan. *The Origins and Development of Islam Institutions*. Karachi, Pakistan: Jamiyat Ulfalah Publications, 1962.

Sinclair, Michael J. *A History of Islamic Medicine*. London: Cylinder Press, 1978.

Singer, Charles. *A Short History of Scientific Ideas*. Oxford, U.K.: Clarendon Press, 1959.

Sourdel, Dominique. *Medieval Islam*. Translated by J. M. Watt. London: Routledge and Kegan Paul, 1983.

Suyuti, Jalaluddin As. *History of the Caliphs*. Translated by H. S. Jarrett. Calcutta: Asiatic Society, 1881; reprint ed., Karachi, Pakistan: Karimsons, 1977.

Sweetman, J. Windrow. *Islam and Christian Theology*. London: Butterworth Press, 1955.

Tannery, Paul. *Mémoires Scientifiques*. Vol. 5. Paris: Edouard Privat, 1922.

Thompson, James. *The Medieval Library*. New York: Hafner Publishing, 1957.

Thorndike, Lynn. *University Records and Life in the Middle Ages*. New York: Columbia University Press, 1944.

Tritton, A. S. *Materials on Muslim Education in the Middle Ages*. London: Luzac, 1957.

————. *Muslim Education in the Middle Ages*. London: Luzac, 1957.

Ullman, Manfred. *Islamic Medicine*. Islamic Surveys, Vol. 11. Edinburgh: Edinburgh University Press, 1978.

von Grunebaum, G. E. *Essays in the Nature and Growth of a Cultural Tradition*. London: Routledge and Kegan Paul, 1955.

————. *A Study in Cultural Orientation*. 2nd ed. University of Chicago Press, 1953.

————., ed. *Theology and Law in Islam*. Wiesbaden, FRG: Harrassowitz, 1971.

Waltzer, Richard. *Greek into Arabic*. Oxford, U.K.: Bruno Cassirer, 1962.

Watkin, J. *The Function of Documents in Islamic Law*. Albany: SUNY Press, 1972.

Watt, William M. *The Faith and Practice of Al-Ghazali*. London: George Allen and Unwin, 1953.

———. *The Influence of Islam on Medieval Europe.* Edinburgh: Edinburgh University Press, 1972.

———. *Islamic Philosophy and Theology.* Edinburgh: Edinburgh University Press, 1962.

———. *Islamic Political Thought.* Edinburgh: Edinburgh University Press, 1968.

———. *Muhammad at Mecca.* Oxford U.K.: Clarendon Press, 1953.

———. *Muhammad at Medina.* Oxford, U.K.: Clarendon Press, 1956.

Welch, A. T. and Pierre Cachia, eds. *Islam: Past Influence and Present Challenge.* Albany: SUNY Press, 1979.

Winter, H. J. J. *Eastern Science.* London: John Murray, 1952.

Withington, Edward T. *Medical History.* London: Holland Press, 1964.

Articles

Arasteh, A. "Islamic Contributions to Educational Methods." *Educational Theory* 7 (January 1957): 28–37.

Bukhsh, S. Khuda. "The Renaissance of Islam." *Islamic Culture* 4 (1930) 295–97.

Kantorowicz, H. "Quaestiones Disputatae of the Glossators." *Revue d'Histoire du Droit* 16 (1938): 1–67.

Kennedy, E. S. and Jovad Hamadanizadeh. "Applied Mathematics in Eleventh Century Iran." *Math Teacher* 48 (1965):441–46.

Makdisi, George. "Ashari and Asharites in Islamic Religious History." *Studia Islamica* 17 (1962): 37–80; 18 (1963): 19–39.

———. "Madrasa and University in the Middle Ages." *Studia Islamica* 25 (1970): 126–37.

———. "Muslim Institutions of Learning in Eleventh-century Baghdad." *Bulletin of the School of Oriental and African Studies* 24 (1961): 1–55.

———. "The Scholastic Method in Medieval Education: An Inquiry into Its Origins in Law and Theology." *Speculum* 49 (October 1974): 640–61.

Moody, Ernest A. "Galileo and Avenpace: The Dynamics of the Leaning Tower Experiment." *Journal of the History of Ideas* 7, 2 (April 1951): 375–422 and 3 (June 1951): 163–93.

Paetow, L. "The Arts Course at Medieval Universities with Special Reference to Grammar and Rhetoric." *University Studies,* University of Illinois, 3 (1910): 20.

Sayili, Aydin Mehmed. "Islam and the Rise of the Seventeenth Century Science." Ankara, Turkey, *Bulletin* 22, 87 (July 1958): 353–68.

Shahjahan, Muhammad. "An Introduction to the Ethics of al-Farabi." *Islamic Culture* 59, 1 (January 1985): 45–52.

Index

199

About the Author

CHARLES MICHAEL STANTON, a native of Wyoming, attended Stanford University from which he received three degrees. He taught and served as an administrator at Colgate University and Boston College before joining the faculty of Saint Louis University. He has devoted his teaching and research efforts to the study of higher education and curriculum theory—areas in which he has published numerous articles and papers.